Enduring Innocence

Enduring Innocence

Global Architecture and Its Political Masquerades

Keller Easterling

The MIT Press Cambridge, Massachusetts London, England

MIT Press books may be purchased at special quantity discounts for business or sales promotional use. For information, please email special_sales@mitpress.mit.edu or write to Special Sales Department, The MIT Press, 55 Hayward Street, Cambridge, MA 02142.

This book was set in Adobe Garamond and Rotis Sans Serif by Graphic Composition, Inc., and was printed and bound in the United States of America.

Library of Congress Cataloging-in-Publication Data

Easterling, Keller, 1959–
Enduring innocence : global architecture and its political masquerades / Keller Easterling.
p. cm.
Includes bibliographical references and index.
ISBN 0-262-05079-X (permanent paper)
1. Architecture—Sociological aspects. 2. Architecture and globalization. 3. Architecture—Political aspects. I. Title.

NA2543.S6E18 2005
720'.1'03—dc22

2005040877

10 9 8 7 6 5 4 3 2 1

Contents

Acknowledgments

Many people deserve thanks for their help or advice in preparing this book.

The book has received funding from The Graham Foundation, Yale University's Griswold Fund, and Yale University's Frederick Hilles Publication Fund.

The journals *Grey Room, Harvard Design Magazine, Praxis, Perspecta, Pasajes de Arquitectura y Critica, Metalocus,* and *Cabinet* have published versions of this research in recent years. Comments from the following editors improved and amplified the text. *Grey Room* (Branden Joseph, Reinhold Martin, and Felicity Scott), *Harvard Design Magazine* (William Saunders), *Praxis* (Ashley Schafer, Amanda Reeser, Megan Miller), *Perspecta* (Noah K. Biklen, Ameet N. Hiremath, Hannah H. Purdy), *Pasajes de Arquitectura y Critica* (José Ballesteros), *Metalocus* (J. J. Barba), *Log* (R. E. Somol and Sarah Whiting), and *Cabinet* (Sina Najafi).

Several books or catalogs included material from this book as an article or chapter: *Cybercities Reader* (Stephen Graham), *After the World Trade Center: Rethinking New York City* (Michael Sorkin and Sharon Zukin), the catalog for the National Building Museum's *Up, Down, Across: Elevators, Escalators and Moving Sidewalks* (Alisa Goetz), and *The Frontiers of Utopia and Other Facts on the Ground* (Anselm Franke and Eyal Weizman).

Research assistants Chinnie Ding and Todd Reisz have contributed enormously.

Several schools of architecture have allowed rehearsals of this material in school lectures. Among these are Princeton University (Dean Stan Allen), Yale University (Dean Robert A. M. Stern), Columbia University (Dean Mark Wigley), University of Pennsylvania (Chair Detlef Mertins), and Southern California Institute of Architecture.

For each of the sites discussed in this book, a number of people have provided tours, local information, research materials, or images.

For DPRK: Jaehuck Choi, Igor Siddiqui, Andrew Benner, and Seyong Jang.

For El Ejido: Penny Herscovitch, Michael Kokora, Roberta Cook, Luiz Castillo Villegas, Miguel Barahona Garcia, Miri Ben-Haim, Albert Recio, Ramon de Torres, Ángel Soler and Plataforma Solar de Almería/Ciemat, Mujeres Progressistas, Shane Curnyn.

For Franchise: Jon Lipman and Susan Lauer (Maharishi Global Construction), Kevin Benedict (Palmer Design), Peyton Taylor (World Golf Village), Jordan Crandall, Yale's Digital Media Center for the Arts and the Wildcards project (researchers: Melanie Kiin, Ann Marie Brennan, and Andrew Mazor).

For Park: Nina Rappaport, Robbert Lohmann, and Carel C. van Helsdingen (FROG), Wim Reuvers (ECT Terminals), David Pelletier (Hillwood), John Dimmit (JC Penney).

For Shining: Colonel V. J. Kumar (STPI), Jodi Katz (Intelsat), Vyjayanthi Rao, Satya Pemmaraju, Kanu Agrawal.

For Subtraction: Stacey Loizeaux (CDI).

The "Enclave" conference sponsored in Spring 2004 by Yale University's Center for the Study of Globalization, Yale University's Center for Cities and Globalization (Arjun Appadurai, Carol Breckenridge, and Vyjayanthi Rao), and Yale University's School of Architecture contributed to a discourse that surrounds and supports this book. The conference, co-organized with Vyjayanthi Rao, included contributions from Allan Sekula, David Joselit, Stephen Graham, Xiangming Chen, Rahul Mehrotra, Pankaj Joshi, Leslie Lu, Stefano Boeri, Ingo Gunther, Peter Lamborn Wilson, AbdouMaliq Simone, and Arjun Appadurai.

Students at Yale and Columbia have been special interlocutors in seminars and studios that focus on the sites collected here. They have been very generous with their thoughts and enthusiasms.

Thanks also go to my friends Peggy Deamer, Catherine Ingraham, Laurie Hawkinson, and Sanford Kwinter, and for their help and advice.

Roger Conover at the MIT Press was extremely helpful in refining the voice and content of this book. Lisa Reeve, Gillian Beaumont, Matthew Abbate, and Jean Wilcox, also for the MIT Press, were helpful in preparing the book for publication.

This book was written with love for Detlef Mertins.

Enduring Innocence

Introduction

This book tells the stories of *spatial products* in difficult political situations around the world. These products—resorts, information technology campuses, retail chains, golf courses, ports, and other enclave formations—are familiar commercial formulas that index the world by marketing or scheduling protocols, thus presumably avoiding the political inconveniences of location. They are generally considered to be the Teflon formats of neoliberal enterprises. Architects often treat them as banal or unresponsive to recognized systems of architectural language, and indeed, architecture is, for these formats, often only a by-product of data and logistics. Yet, when adopted by rogue nations, cults, diplomats, and other impresarios, even the most perfunctory spatial products are imbued with myths, desires, and symbolic capital. They may gain entry into any situation. Freighted with desires, sporting their global currency and their duty-free legalities, they can slither through jurisdictional shallows. They can become political pawns, as objects of desire and contention in negotiations between warring countries, messy democracies, and violent distended conflict. Effective as a solvent of differences, the hilarious and dangerous masquerades of retail, business, or trade often mix quite easily with the cunning of political platforms. Moreover, their recipes for organization are also recipes for political constitution, and the disposition of that organization embodies a capacity for collusion, persuasion, and aggression.

Architecture presumably has more to learn than to teach in the study of global politics. As the warm pools for new urban contagions, however, these real estate cocktails are also critical materializations of digital capitalism. A special kind of architectural research may contribute to global studies some vivid evidence of another set of mechanisms, perhaps as telling as financial and political indicators in characterizing the market's weakness, resilience, or violence.

This book collects six stories of spatial products and their political misadventures. For instance, one of its segments visits tourism in North Korea, while another visits high-tech agricultural formations in Spain that have reignited labor wars and piracy in the Mediterranean. A third segment compares fantastic forms of sovereignty in commercial and spiritual organizations, and a fourth looks at automated global ports. The shape of microwave urbanism in IT enclaves in South Asia and the Middle East, and the global industry of subtracting buildings, are two more subjects.

Spatial Products

Different from the deliberately authored building envelope, spatial products substitute spin, logistics, and management styles for considerations of location, geometry, or enclosure. The architect and salesman of such things as golf resorts or container ports is a new orgman.[1] He designs the software for new games of spatial production to be played the same way whether in Texas or Taiwan. The coordinates of this software are measured not in latitude and longitude but in the orgman argot of acronyms and stats—in annual days of sunshine, ocean temperatures, flight distances, runway noise restrictions, the time needed for a round of golf, time needed for a shopping spree, TEUs, layovers, numbers of passengers, bandwidth, time zones, and labor costs.[2] Data streams are the levers of spatial manipulation, and the orgman has a frontier enthusiasm for this abstract territory. He derives a pioneering sense of creation from matching a labor cost, a time zone, and a desire to generate distinct forms of urban space, even distinct species of global city.

Logistical spatial products make vivid the fact that architecture is a theater of activity, as that word is used in the military to express the consequential sequencing of organizations, activities, claims, and exchanges. Manuel Castells claimed that the "culture that matters for the constitution and development of a given economic system is the one that materializes in organizational logics"—what Félix Guattari might have called the "techno-scientific semiotics" that are stored in the operational strata of organization and practice.[3] Architecture is a technology—the medium of an open platform storing both structure and content. The information it stores, as both data and persuasion, is literally a product, property, or currency.

Yet global familiars such as resorts, enclaves, and repetitive commercial formats are made no less hyperbolic, volatile, and extravagant by abstraction. Elaborate costumes and stylistic affectations are often treated as the window dressing for a product that supposedly achieves neutrality by operating as a revenue envelope. Fiction and myth are, in this case, especially slippery, disposable, and comedic for the very reason that absolute meaning may finally be measured only in revenues or the techniques of "market science." Charged with no responsibility for historical or political reconciliation, the product's ersatz myths may be even more extreme. However familiar these spaces may be, the mixology between cocktails and cultural attributes may create territory that is at once strange and intimate, exposed and in disguise, real and fictional.

As lubricating agents of a market, spatial products are usually presumed to be innocent of involvement in the extreme spaces of war. Yet even the most banal space has been a military target, acting as an apparatus or a provocation of aggression. Moreover, the architecture of warfare evident in detention camps, military bases, and border crossings is eerily similar to our own familiar offshore real estate cocktails, with their devices for security and territorial conquest. Like any camp or zone of conflict, the next free trade zone, data haven, tax shelter, or residential golf development seeks immunity as an exceptional condition, a legal lacuna or island entitled to special sovereignty and exemption from law. Giorgio Agamben's argument that the camp is a place of legal exception or lawlessness becomes all the more compelling when he also argues that this condition can be naturalized or stabilized as a political paradigm that reappears in the "*zones d'attentes* of our airports and certain outskirts of our cities."[4]

A strange political content harbors in the world's familiar cyberpoles, technopoles, and agripoles—air-conditioned Dubais and Jebel Alis of the architectural soul. The classic indicators of political contention may not be effective in exposing their disguises. They ideally exist in a self-reflexive political quarantine. Yet attempts to secure political exemption may, paradoxically, land an organization in the crosshairs of the conflict they thought they had banished.

Worlds

Spatial products aspire to establish worlds or global regimes—domains of logic that are given franchise to expand their territory with nonnational sovereignty. Marc Augé writes about "contemporaneous worlds" as the "tightly woven, complex fabric of contemporaneity"—a global cultural current, expertise, or habit such as the fashion world or the sports world. The "worlds" we create, as Augé writes, are constantly "recomposed," expressing "all at once the singularity that constitutes them and the universality that relativizes them." Arjun Appadurai writes about "imagined worlds" as "the multiple worlds that are constituted by the historically situated imaginations of persons and groups spread around the globe." The mixtures of worlds, as Appadurai describes them, create variegated "scapes," such as "mediascapes" and "ethnoscapes."[5] Naturalizing the migration and negotiation of traveling cultural forms allows these thinkers to avoid impossible constructs about an authentic locality. The stories in this book build on such intelligence to discuss, among other things, the worlds of tourism, high-tech agriculture, shipping, or retail, but they offer a less genial view of these regimes, focusing not on their blending but on their fierce segregation.

The orgmen viceroys of individual worlds conquer both ephemeral and stable territories on land, on the ocean, and in the air, with classic intentions to accumulate wealth. For instance, the spatial products of tourism territorialize a belt of median air and water temperatures. Those of high-tech agriculture occupy a sea of photosynthesis, annexing locations with abundant sunshine and wind direction. Pools of satellite microwaves or resources including water, oil, and natural gas are also coveted or embattled territories. These belts of special conditions constitute volatile, nonnational spaces that move around the world like weather fronts on airborne, landed, or maritime currents. In a sense, each world sails its own sea. Its boundaries are taut and strong, but also elastic and fluid to facilitate the quiet acquisition of yet more territory.

[see *Seas*]

World is a plural condition. There is no one world—only many worlds. Worlds share no single logic, but proliferate as multiple monotheisms of retail or trade in a totemic market.[6] They maintain their logics, fictions, and boundaries by limiting and excluding information—remaining righteous and pure. Worlds aspire to be perfect utopias, singular domains attempting to coerce compliance and compatibility from anything foreign to them. With either evangelism or subterfuge, the orgman must expand into new territory by reformatting its bytes, containers, ships, and infrastructures for compatibility. The boundaries expand and exclude, extend and tighten, allowing the world to increase in size but not necessarily in diversity or intelligence.

Whatever the claims of globalizing connectivity, these stories find more traction in the territory where multiple worlds collide. This is the space of mobile stretchy firewalls and insulation—the space of uneven developments, fences, and stratification, or the space of friction and logical fallout between segregated regimes.[7]

Believers and Cheaters

Regimes or worlds of righteous belief are easy to find. Righteousness is a form of violence that most people cultivate. In marriages, families, professions, nations, and other consortiums of power, we are often in the process of recoding worrisome contradictory information to conform to our own story, our theoretical beliefs, the operational lore of our profession. The Bill Gates of our own milieu, we require all other things to be compatible to our format. We respin a little fragment of gossip, secrete or limit information to make ourselves whole. Regimes and domains on all scales decide what will constitute information and what contradictions will simply be eliminated. They change the law that protects someone's dwelling or put a population in a microwave shadow. Bristling with security systems and intelligence-gathering devices, the regime is hungry for information, but it prefers to recognize only compatible information that reinforces its innocence and righteousness. In this solipsistic lockdown, information-rich becomes information-poor. To desire a state of monism and purity: this is the violence of remaining intact.

Nevertheless, the more righteous and innocent the regime, the more necessary it is to cheat. Although it is trying to maintain only its own information, its own traditions, and its own security, the organization often needs additional help. A world requires both an evil enemy to make it appear just, and an unacknowledged "extra" to keep it alive. Husbands and wives feel entitled to an extra wife or husband. The European Union needs younger people to counter its aging population. Banks need another, more pliable currency than the regulated one they have. Corporations need an offshore shelter for their money. And everyone needs cheap labor.

The righteousness of the believer, the confidence games of the cheater, or any oscillation between the two are all successful strategies. All can elude their day of reckoning. For the believer there is only the tautology of belief—a fairy tale, uncluttered by details. The believer fights only "just" and righteous wars. For the cheater, there are so many lies that the reckoning can find no place to begin. Ironically, the continual proliferation of masquerades and fictions is essential to the life and refreshment of the originally attractive myth. Of course, the cheater's repertoire of masquerades and shifting stories often includes several versions of the believer himself. The stone-cold bluff of the liar and the sunny elegiac aphorism of the believer are both more successful than measure or reason—for as long as they can fill the air and use political consensus or decree to evade consequences.

Disposition

In the entrenched wars between righteous worlds, the submission of one world to another, or the aggression of lawlessness and cheating, constitute an agency that is reflected in organizational structure. Market data and organizational protocol attend not just functionalist endeavors and economic imperatives, but also behaviors or postures. Just as one might evaluate the reactivity or volatility of a chemical mixture, one might evaluate the disposition embedded in an organization's arrangement.

The spatial cocktails in these stories mix, in peculiar and sometimes effortless ways, with political protocols and politicized economic agendas, as what Pierre Bourdieu has called "symbolic capital."[8] Bourdieu identified cultural practices in which special gestures or disguises were used to enhance the value or status of exchanges and rituals in culture. Similarly, Scott Lash's distinction between the "lighter symbols" of semiotics and the "heavy symbols" embedded in practices identifies heavy symbols as components of an elaborate cultural language that exists in an active condition.[9] Spatial products act not only as glyph or monument to an overt political text, but as heavy information that becomes a nuanced, unexpressed subtext of action or practice. Just as an expression in dialogue is a trace of an action, and nothing like the sentence one would find in prose, so the heavy symbol has the cultural responsibilities of language in another register. It is not *langue* but *parole,* or, following Giorgio Agamben, we might understand it as "face"—word on the threshold of action. It communicates not as noun but as verb, as gesture or glyph of action.[10] It is about—taking Gilbert Ryle's distinction—"knowing how rather than knowing that."[11] Spatial products perhaps resist semiotics but offer other precise expressions of value and exchange stored in arrangement and presence.

The *organization* of these spaces also possesses disposition. One test of organizational disposition is a willingness to accept error or contradictory information. The stories in this book speculate about organizations that are more robust and resilient when they are information-rich and more weak, rigid, or explosive when they are information-poor. They borrow some additional terms from Gregory Bateson to make further distinctions. Bateson often used the terms symmetrical, complementary, and reciprocal to characterize organization, and to link organizational architecture and behavior. For Bateson, a symmetrical relationship described an escalating rivalry and mimicry between two parties: twins fighting for supremacy. A complementary relationship described submission and recognition of hierarchies between parties: a beta dog kneeling before an alpha dog. Both symmetrical and complementary relationships could generate a fragile stability, but both also excluded information to maintain their order, and so could also sponsor rivalry, insurgency, or violence. A reciprocal relationship, on the other hand, neutralized an escalating symmetry or a hierarchical submission by surrendering interest in the fight, multiplying both enemies and friends, and entering into a more complex web of cooperative engagements.[12] Reciprocal relations could counter symmetrical entrenchment with cooperative structures, avoiding warfare that would arrest a vital flow of exchanges. In Bateson's terms, the believer would assume a symmetrical entrenchment, and the cheater would often oscillate between symmetrical and reciprocal dispositions.

If organization, as reflected in architecture and urbanism, possesses disposition, the means to aggress or collude, it may also be an adversary or a competitor. It may be brittle or stretchy. Its software or hardware is capable of political manipulation or violence, and also capable of storing or unleashing this agency in its inception, planning, and building as well as its occupation.

As it mixes with overt or covert lawlessness, architecture possesses the means to war.

Resistance

Given the sweetness and sentimentality that often accompany power, whether that of the believer or the cheater, the stories that comprise this book assume that motives, however different, may use similar devices and disguises, and that effective activism will now rarely look like classic resistance. Rather resistance may come cloaked in its opposite, just as capital can be cloaked in the costumes of resistance. Within the intractable logics of tautological worlds and the games they play to extend their currency, the masquerades of market, state, and resistance alternately blur and resolve into crisp masks. Capital's contradictions are not the ultimate details that initiate a new utopia. Rather, they are the ingredients that make capital more robust or more lithe by providing either new information or fresh masquerades. Similarly, the various masquerades of resistance need not correspond to those of a tragic counterculture with its principled self-valorizations—righteous dispositions they share with war. Instead, resistance may find another set of switches and toggles with the potential for political manipulation.

A consideration of segregated worlds resists the monism lurking in many theories of global politics, those of the radical as well as those of the neoliberal. The totalizing theories of Marx seem to induce mimicry—epic world system organums portraying a monolithic spectacle, market, or empire. Hardt and Negri's *Empire* is only one, recent text that demonstrates this philosophical habit of mind, suggesting, at times, the possibility of something approaching univocal, although not classically Marxist, political upheaval. The Debordian spectacle is taken to its logical ultimate. Yet however nourishing these critiques of the pervasive market spectacle may be, the stories in this book do not focus on the market's monolithic holism. Nor do they portray a resistance that can heroically match the purity of modernism. They explore instead the backstage networks that Bruno Latour has called "the unconscious of the moderns"—the space of mediation rather than the space of the singular or pure.[13] They join Arjun Appadurai in finding world system epics to be "inadequately quirky" theories of global development.[14] They

Only the Many

The stories collected here resist several forms of monism that have attracted architecture culture. Monism certainly attends the search for the one transcendent God-given idea or, in the absence of God, the attempt to reason toward the unifying theory or the true mechanics of nature. Yet a secret desire for the one and only may also appear in the competition between immanent ideas. In the fabled profile of the avant-garde, for instance, intelligence must be successive rather than coexistent. Identifying the tendency to purification that attends transcendent modernism, Bruno Latour describes those avant-garde campaigns which are "obsessed with the construction of one immanence or the destruction of another."[15] Each manifesto must kill the previous manifesto, project the new utopia, and pose for a group photo. It must be the one.

Architects perhaps secretly long for monism, for the chance to gather the world onto a single sheet of paper and control it with geometry, be that geometry epigenetic or Euclidean. Architecture has often adopted those cybernetic scripts that focus on recursivity and predictability in complexity, as well as those Deleuzian scripts that, drained of their politics, reinforce the preexisting attraction to geometry. As it deploys digital tools, the discipline has often not focused on the active network of which these digital tools are a part—a network that has embedded itself into our bodies and markets, and all the other places in the world where people are dying, fighting, and making money. These territories would never provide demonstrations of connectedness and synergistic feedback. Rather, the discipline has focused on the imaging that appears on the screen. The screen dramatizes our geometric manipulations and software domains. In a sense, the discipline has privileged the front of the computer rather than the back of the computer—the screen rather than the network.

The stories collected here investigate the backstage of digital capital that materializes on the network side of the computer. They look at the germs, errors, pirates, and exceptions that make holisms, homologies, and universals impossible. Belief in their existence or nonexistence is irrelevant to a potentially productive focus, not on purification and refinement but on translation and multiplication. This focus favors the partial and incremental, exceeding the strictly formal or semiotic to enter the organizational and political strata of space-making. The stories and contemplations are about the many—not the one, or the one and the many, but only the many. They multiply worlds. Multiply logics. No Empire, but empires. No global village, but global villages. No one world, but many segregated worlds.

present no singular logic, but rather the evidence of rich contradictions and multiple logics. Spatial products provide evidence of what Lash and Urry have called "disorganized capitalism": capitalism disaggregated or disorganized from its modernist or anticipated alignments.[16] The stories are curious about another degree of deviance, duplicity, or cheating present in the mix.

Attracted, as they are, to things epic, architectural discourses on globalization have also remained inadequately quirky, embracing the dream of "one world" of globally legible boutique hotels and entertainments. Too often, the discussion still circles around questions of center and periphery, looking for evidence of a domineering modernism or postmodernism pushing its ecumenical sign on an authentic locality that must be preserved. Equally conservative is the portrayal of a *soft* world of connectivity that constantly, but only gently, learns and adjusts, providing the illusion of differentiation in recursivity, naturalizing the market with a redemptive overlay of complexity. In this portrayal, architecture is often only a servant to worlds where catastrophes, errors, or negations are in the family of the whole, where corporate contrition kills with a masquerade of kindness, and where we are all drops of water in globalization's many maritime metaphors.

The material collected here should, then, nourish a special kind of political imagination and ingenuity. Political practices often gravitate to one of several well-rehearsed roles: the earnest public servant, the political theorist, or the strident activist. Given the failures of some of these principled political stances to engage with more disorganized or elusive forms of political subterfuge, this book describes not only the classic political stance that declares its name in a democratic process, but also other politics that rely on fiction or corruption. Relinquishing the architect's monologue of sincerity and innocence, it studies the ethical masquerades of the double agent or nonbeliever who uses multiple personae to engage the market's confidence games and patterns of cheating.

The orgman's territorial parameters reinforce a belief in the possibility of optimization and error elimination. Spatial products that attempt to avoid political entanglements also attempt to avoid error. Yet that belief often results in a much more massive failure or error. This space of naturally occurring errors and loopholes is political territory. Error is mined in the areas of intolerance, logical exception, and organizational fallout that result from the collisions of worlds. In this discussion, the word "error" refers specifically to the naturally occurring extrinsic information. Error is the germ that adds additional material to the pool, or mutates an existing sequence of instructions. It provides the additional information, the learning that extends the intelligence of the organization. As extrinsic information, error might be a means of penetration or resistance—the means of altering an organization by remote or ricochet. [see *Error*]

Piracy is a useful construct here—one that yields a continuum of characters from the privateer and military entrepreneur to the terrorist and murderer: enough variations on the confidence game to provide reflections of diplomats, viceroys, orgmen, and elected officials. This book proffers a productive piracy in which an additional set of regulators, wild cards, and fictions, loaded with unorthodox powers, become tools for practitioners sensitive to the political composition of an urban landscape. Architecture articulates these complex mixtures of latent political postures and economic agendas. Finally, carte blanche relies on a collection of guises or masquerades, any one of which can be used to suit an episode in the confidence game. The multiplication of fiction that manages to mask or neutralize a sense of consequences may also identify a condition that is susceptible to comedy and mischief, or penetrable to another masquerade. [see *Pirate*]

Stories

Hoping to model its premise in its own organization, this book avoids the structure of a litigious, corrective proof, an exercise in academic ventriloquy, or a three-part Presbyterian sermon on the logics of a political theology. The journalistic travelogue or the encyclopedic compendium of discoveries are not appropriate templates either.[17] The six stories collected here offer not a totalizing theory about world systems but, rather, critical evidence arranged with the help of storytelling techniques. Emphasizing the political instrumentality of fiction, spin, and error in culture, this "footnoted fiction," or "faction," persuades and theorizes by sequencing facts and orchestrating voices so that supposition meets its contradiction, gravity and frivolity share space, and piety appears next to a broad gaffe.

Piratical Architecture

Architecture—the discipline often assumes—is innocent, and therefore not an activity like that of all the other pirates of both Empire and counter-Empire. Yet it is typically considered to be a conservative profession, involved in fortifying the very worlds under discussion here. It even seeks the same political immunity. Architects are not trained to pirate, except in the service of their own careers. Multiple voices, tactics, and political craft are deployed in self-promotion. When typecast in its customary tragicomic roles, the discipline often reinforces the boundaries of its own world—its own autonomy as an art form within which to write monologues that preserve its integrity.

Architecture has well-developed techniques for parsing the lighter glyphs of architectural semiotics cast in geometry and idiom. The discipline is, however, less accustomed to parsing the "heavy symbols" of activity and disposition. With what seems like self-parody, an architect might even work to reify the datastreams of the orgman with geometric constructions that make it possible to represent these landscapes with an enclosure. Beyond the light language of appearance is a heavy language stored in the operational strata of the assembly. The discipline not only employs information technology, it *is* information technology with political affect independent of enclosure. Relinquishing the guise of sincerity or applying the duplicitous craft of careerism to the actual business of making space requires an expertise that insists on never knowing enough. Responsibility for Empire's often grisly atrocities may not necessarily be an act of righteousness, but only another seduction. This book considers architects to be seafaring, satellite-faring, data-faring organizers of territory who might be at least as effective as orgmen in manipulating the comedies and fictions of the marketplace. A piratical architecture does not evaluate the integrity of expression or the regrettable urge to reform. It intervenes in the patterns of believers and cheaters, evaluating the ability of masquerades to leverage change.

In addition to the stories, three contemplations, titled *Seas, Error,* and *Pirate*, provide a more speculative substrate for the spatial and political phenomena encountered in the stories. While they are interspersed with the stories, they may be read in any order, alone or in an alternating sequence with the stories. Each examines agency and mechanism in organization, and each is in some way another side of the other—with similar but ramifying philosophical intersections. Just as organizations share compatibilities, such as the dimensions of a container, an annual temperature, or a labor cost, so these stories are cross-referenced, often by means of a stray detail. For these indexed moments, the material resists the micro-regime of the narrative, and may continue into another story or contemplation with an echo or a repetition. Each story, each tale of a political island, also has its own island, its own offshore subplot that appears as a parallel text.

The evidence comes not from texts that track the project of architecture for and within the discipline, but rather from more unusual, often ephemeral sources. Internal debate within any discipline—whether in architecture, cultural studies, or politics—can nurture new theories and terms. Yet these terms can also hibernate there, unchallenged by the extremes of the ordinary, by worlds far more hyperbolic than any of the ordained fictions of logical thinking. Not the literature of our own society but a wire service for the *Korea Times*, statistical tallies for port organizations, global TV, or the orgman's office jokes and market-tracking softwares are the architectural texts for millions of acres of buildings and infrastructures around the world. The stories look at the anatomy of organizations, their self-promotion, global web chatter, and collision with political events. However contemporary the material, it is usually an echo of common, sometimes ancient, swindles and fantasies. The accounts provide emotional and hilarious evidence of architectural aspirations that only eventually involve the discipline. Space is undoubtedly a pawn in this fragile divide between war and piracy. The stories suggest that architecture may find its opportunity, its gravity, and even its seduction not in the style pages, but in the runaway fictions of the news wires and international pages. Architecture may have no choice but to find its politics—to counter innocence with ingenuity.

The camp as dislocating localization is the hidden matrix of the politics in which we are still living, and it is this structure of the camp that we must learn to recognize in all its metamorphoses into the zones d'attentes *of our airports and certain outskirts of our cities.*

—Giorgio Agamben[18]

If you turn round suddenly, as in the children's game "Mother, may I?," they will freeze, looking innocent, as if they hadn't budged; here, on the left, are things themselves; there, on the right, is the free society of speaking, thinking subjects, values and of signs. Everything happens in the middle, everything passes between the two, everything happens by way of mediation, translation and networks, but this space does not exist, it has no place. It is the unthinkable, the unconscious of the moderns.

—Bruno Latour[19]

DPRK

On board the love boat, Western tourists in high-tech hiking apparel are entertained by exotic dancers in high-heeled boots and thongs.

On the shores of puritan North Korea, security guards patrol the port in dark gray suits with lapel pins featuring the nation's founder, Kim Il Sung, and taciturn park guides stand watch in blue slippers and 1950s hairstyles.[1]

The impresarios of tourism index the globe with flight times from major cities, beachside water temperature, days of sunlight, quality of sand, and length of stay. Tourism maintains a Vatican-like state-within-a-state offering political asylum, internal escape, and immunity to all those converts who recognize and endorse its images. Whatever their location, resort formulas will deliver a profit in territories with abundant sunshine, pale sand, and an average temperature of nineteen degrees Celsius. The cruise ship is tourism's paramilitary enforcer. Sailing on a sea of favorable conditions, the fleet of conquest looks for sovereignty over a mobile market share that is much more valuable than solid turf. Spatial products of tourism are designed to freely conquer territory that is unencumbered by the inconveniences of politics. Yet the same fantasies and fictions they deploy possess an ancient political instrumentality. [see *Seas*]

Tourism, arriving late to the world's last remaining Cold War sites, provides a broad cartoon of this political instrumentality. In countries like Vietnam and Cuba, tourism has landed even on the very battle lines of previous conflicts. Perhaps the most extreme of these stories surrounds the *I Love Cruise* and the Kumgang resort in North Korea.

The first reports about the *I Love Cruise* in newspapers and websites in 1998 told a tale both vaguely familiar and hyperbolically fictional, filled with the circumstantial detail and non sequiturs that often become predestined events in fairy stories. According to these reports, Hyundai's cruise ship departed from the South Korean port of Tonghae and traveled through international waters toward the DPRK (Democratic People's Republic of Korea)—the northern half of the peninsula that is black in nighttime satellite photographs, its shape perfectly outlined by the lights of adjacent countries that possess adequate electricity. Sometime before dawn, when the on-board karaoke and Siberian dancing girls shut down for the night, North Korean warships escorted the vessel into the military port of Changjon, just north of the Demilitarized Zone (DMZ). Changjon is the closest port to Mount Kumgang, Korea's spiritual equivalent of Mount Fuji, unseen by South Koreans since 1945.[2]

Passengers, dressed in outdoor gear, then disembarked for four days to consume a package of hiking tours, spa treatments, and shopping in a newly erected resort. From the windows of the tour buses that ferried them around, they could just see over the walls and barbed-wire fences lining the compound to the failing agricultural villages and prefabricated houses beyond. A complex of buildings—including a domed theater where the Pyongyang circus performs, and a shopping center—offered the tourists a new line of North Korean products, including an ant liquor designed to cure impotence. The floating Hotel Haekumgang, moored near the cruise ship, accommodated guests in the evening. To prevent North Koreans from seeing the resort, all of the workers serving the tourists, except for a few guides, were ethnic Koreans from China. Hiking tours in the mountains visited spectacular falls, peaks, and seascapes. Tour guides and military personnel were stationed at two-kilometer intervals along the walls and hiking routes, their hairdos frozen in mid-century.[3]

The *I Love Cruise* was just the first step in an ongoing negotiation of tourism between North and South Korea. Kim Jong Il, "Respected and Beloved General" of North Korea's oxymoronic communist dynasty, and Chung Ju Yung, head of the South's Hyundai *chaebol,* initiated this tourist enterprise in 1998 under the auspices of the South's Sunshine Policy for reunification. (The Tongil Group, a company controlled by the Moonies of the Unification Church, initially wanted to establish a ski resort in the North and was an early competitor with Hyundai.)[4]

More telling details of the fairy tale: In a special proviso of the initial Kumgang deal, Kim Jong Il and his top officials requested from Hyundai thirty thousand 25-inch color television sets, newly branded with a "Kumgansan–

Mt. Kumgang" label, thus disguising their identity as South Korean products.[5] Among the fleet of cruise ships was the original *Island Princess* that appeared in the *Love Boat* television series.[6]

By 2005, ski resorts, golf courses, conference centers, sports facilities, and IT campuses mixed with theme parks, and a Sea World-style aquarium, were to stretch from Mount Kumgang all along the eastern seaboard to Mount Paektu, and were to attract 1,500,000 tourist per year.[7] All of these programs were to be supported by airports, roads, and rail lines. Hyundai's strangely laconic architectural renderings evoked not contemporary Las Vegas-style resorts, but Disneyland or world's fair expositions populated by Cold War Hilton-style hotels and corporate high-rises.

Hyundai was to pay the DPRK $942 million over a period of six years for the exclusive rights to develop the tourist project—money that would become the North's single largest source of income.[8] The money was ostensibly to prop up the depleted economy, but some have speculated that it went to a Hong Kong bank account for a party organization called "Bureau 39," making North Korea's ruling elite the chief beneficiaries.[9]

Like the special economic zone at Rajin-Sonbong north of Mount Paektu near Russia, and the casinos in the capital, Pyongyang, the cruise would be considered a cash cow for the state. Gambling deliriously with enormous losses, Hyundai ran it for three years until finally negotiating a shorter and less expensive overland route through the Demilitarized Zone, a route that finally replaced the cruise. It now projects the same ambitious plans onto a new agreement with the North that establishes Mount Kumgang as a special tourist zone permitting, among other things, casinos.[10]

All along the hiking routes, carved into the mountain and written into the scripts of the tour guides, are the poems of Kim Jong Il and the aphorisms of Juche, North Korea's philosophy of self-reliance. Juche combines the political dictates of Stalinism with Confucian traditions and the general outlines of missionary Christianity. Kim Jong Il's father, Kim Il Sung, received some of his education from missionary Christians, and Juche served as his substitute for Stalinist-Leninist dogma when, as a rebel in the north, he was allied with the Soviets. Juche is the philosophy of an *über*-utopia, an absolute condition, a political tautology. Its perfection inspires both agitated joy and righteousness. While many analysts have characterized Juche as a kind of cult, it may be

1.1 The *Island Princess*, once featured on the *Love Boat* television series, joined Hyundai's fleet of cruise ships for the *I Love Cruise*. Image courtesy of Hyundai-Asan.

something more like an extreme version of familial Confucian loyalty. The tenor of the devotion shared by citizens of the DPRK has been likened to that of fundamentalist Christianity.[11] Containing violent content in a gentle pious cadence, Juche's motivational aphorisms coached the North Koreans through their recent episodes of grinding poverty and famine, encouraging limited rations and even suicide as a means of supporting the military and the ruling elite.[12]

In the years since the tour began, four thousand large plaques commemorating such things as a poem by Kim Jong Il or a Juche aphorism have been installed on the mountain. Hyundai has renovated the old tourist hotel, and the tourist compound now includes Gucci and Prada stores.[13] The Mount Kumgang website used to feature a cruise ship. Now it features images of hip older tourists wearing credentials around their necks, a young woman in resort gear expressing wonder, a shoreline filling with colorful inflatables, and a set of Mount Kumgang scenic bank cards.[14] New additions to the tour include dancing bears in fuzzy costumes, as well as polystyrene tigers placed in the mountains and polystyrene bears that appear to fish in ponds. As a recent group completed their tour, the staff expressed its farewells by singing along to a loudspeaker broadcast of the Everly Brothers song "Bye Bye Love."[15]

Produce one bullet for our guns by sacrificing one chicken.
—Juche aphorism[16]

Self-detonating explosion demands a resolute and pathetic decision. The spirit of suicidal explosion can be cherished only by those who thoroughly resolve to voluntarily choose death for the sake of the party and the leader.
—Juche aphorism[17]

We should be honored by the fact that we adore our greatest leader Kim Il Sung, our greatest leader in 5,000 years.
—Thirty-foot-high slogan carved into a mountain face at Mount Kumgang[18]

[Juche] is the opaque core of North Korean national solipsism.[19]

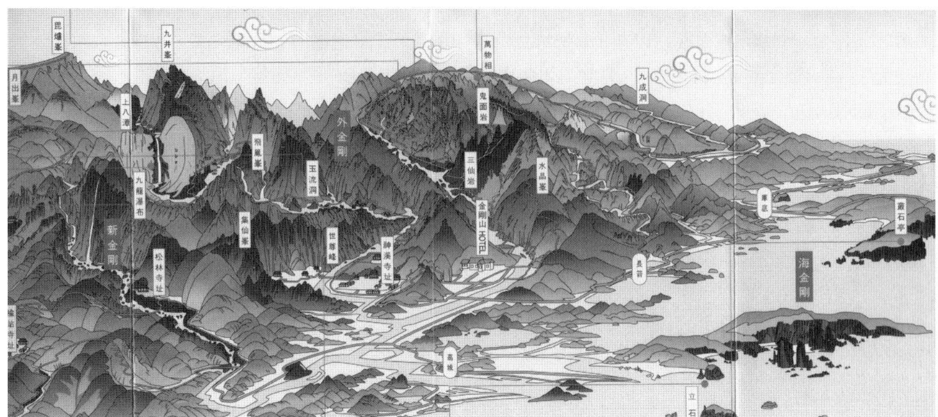

1.2 Mount Kumgang Tour, promotional brochure. Image courtesy Hyundai-Asan.

The *I Love Cruise* and the plans for tourist projects it sponsored are global handshakes synchronizing the disparate logics of shamanism, communism, Confucianism, neo-Christian mythology, Juche, and capitalism. A country in need of food, roads, electricity, telephones, or up-to-date factories has, in this deal, skipped over the great body of free-market practices to a peculiarly comfortable recognition of the most familiar spectacles of global commerce. Bargaining with the extrapolitical territory of the free trade zones, casinos, airports, and cruise ships is now within the repertoire of rogue nations as well as transnational corporations. North Korea now uses not only nuclear weapons as pawns of extortion and brinkmanship but also a special pirate space with its own temporary amnesties from socialist principles. Although they may still dramatize production with the mid-twentieth century heroics of the industrial or agricultural worker, both Koreas have transferred their faith to the tourist, the gambler, and the information specialist. They have discovered the resort and the IT campus as new factories of production.

This comfort with laundered identities and forbidden desires is due not simply to the fact that Kim Jong Il watches a lot of TV and video, although he does. He has a satellite dish that allows him access to Japanese, American, and South Korean TV shows, like MTV or CNN, and cartoons including Donald Duck, Tom and Jerry, and Bugs Bunny. Super Mario Brothers is a favorite video game, and Paul Anka a favorite among many musicians.[20] Yet the phenomenon of the Mount Kumgang tour may have less to do with neoliberal naturalizing of the spectacle and more to do with compatibility, even attraction, between fictions, delusions, and fetishes in the fairy tales of both communism and capitalism—fairy tales in which tourism and landscape are active solvents.

The more I examined my data, the more inescapable became my conclusion that tourist attractions are an unplanned typology of structure that provides direct access to the modern consciousness or "world view," that tourist attractions are precisely analogous to the religious symbolism of primitive peoples.

—Dean MacCannell[21]

Biographical sketches of Kim Jong Il and Chung Ju Yung contribute more fictions to the mix—not only vestigial Cold War legends of competition between capitalist and socialist logics of production, but new mystical content transcending those anachronistic cults of modernity. As if designed for the convenience of this collaboration, the tourist area under consideration in Kongwon Province, and the range of mountains from Mount Kumgang to Mount Paektu in the northernmost part of the country, constitute sacred territory for both Kim Jong Il and Chung Ju Yung. Both rely on persuasive narratives about a larger enveloping nature with the spiritual power to overcome political differences.

Kim Jong Il was chosen "by acclamation" to succeed his father Kim Il Sung, whose birth in 1912 marked the beginning of the "Juche era." There are several versions of the legend, but as one version goes, when Kim Jong Il was born, a swallow appeared to an elderly man to tell him of the birth of a great general, and three stars led the world to a cabin at Mount Paektu, where the infant was discovered.[22] Kim Jong Il was really born in a Soviet camp in the north, where his father was fighting against the Japanese. Kim Il Sung joined forces with other Chinese guerillas and Russian rebels. His bravery and charismatic leadership later prompted the Soviets to name him a leader in Pyonyang. His son, Kim Jong Il, is called a "contemporary God."[23] Yet, for all of the official North Korean reports of his heroic feats and brilliant books, there are also reports of an eccentric reclusive life, often spent in pajamas, playing with his collection of music boxes or attending to the children who live in his house.[24] The Kumgang tour guides, however, typically refer to the beatific presence of their leader, the "Sun of the Twenty-first Century" and successor to the "Eternal President," who is forced to stand alone against countries like the United States and Japan.[25]

The north is also the hallowed birthplace of Hyundai's Chung Ju Yung. Often cast as a Horatio Alger of sorts, he grew up in poverty in northern Korea, and then assumed the role of the quintessential self-made opportunist in postwar Korea. The kinds of industries and organizations that Chung planned for the North reflect both old and new notions of globalization. Like a mid-century capitalist, he developed successful automobile enterprises, but as a new orgman of globalization logistics he also led Hyundai into the twenty-first century with ship-building ventures aimed at a global container trade. When he led five hundred head of cattle across the Demilitarized Zone during the famine, it seemed that his proprietary attitude toward the North mixed philanthropy and statesmanship with capitalist ambitions of colonizing the sister state, and exploiting its resources and cheap labor. A new biographical on-line museum displays two thousand items collected from Chung's frugal life, including several pairs of shoes (with holes) that he wore for fifteen years.[26]

Hyundai has many unrealized plans for infrastructure and manufacturing that will exploit cheap North Korean labor and resources. For instance, part of the initial Kumgang deal would have permitted Hyundai to drill for oil in the North, bottle and sell mineral water from the region, and build a power plant in Pyongyang.[27] Hyundai also proposed another special economic zone in Haeju for eight hundred firms, among them manufacturing firms that would increase North Korea's exports twenty-fold.[28] When Chung died in the spring of 2001, Hyundai was in line to receive infrastructure contracts like an expressway from Taegu to Pusan, and other business deals related to unification.[29] The cruise remained open during Chung's lifetime, in part because of his persistent belief in a capitalist logic that was dramatized by a mixture of autobiography and emblematic imagery at the Kumgang site.

With Dynasty, the black sedan that he [Chung Ju Yung] was in, as the leading vehicle, several tens of trucks full of "Unification Cows" came over the military demarcation line that attracted great response from all people at home and abroad. [30]

See Mount Kumgang and die.[31]

I am fond of going among the people and soldiers and spending time among them. I find my life worth living and feel my best pleasure when I learn how they live and work, and take care of them, talking with them and sharing their feelings.
—Kim Jong Il [32]

All these myths join the stories, habits, and even cults associated with the cruise resort. The name *I Love Cruise* was a calculated reference. When the *Love Boat* television series, associated with Princess cruise lines, began in 1977, it gave the then dormant cruising enterprise an entirely new life. During the next twenty-five years, cruising outpaced any other tourist industry.[33] After *The Love Boat,* cruise ships became floating TV spaces—not only because TV images created and nurtured its market, but also because the ships themselves translated the image on the screen to the physical environment, usually through spaces that signaled formality with abundant luxury appointments. Fresh from schools of hotel management, the orgmen from Princess, Carnival, and Disney also logistically transposed cruising from a luxury to a mass-market spatial product, making it more responsive to economic volatility, and giving it the power to steal a segment of the market from landed resorts.

However ephemeral or abstract the market data may be, these variables are often the determinants of building footprints. The elaborate time-share diagrams of Cancun developers, for instance, chart visitor rotations in a way that makes palpable the mining of time as property. Synchronizing the time it takes the wife to shop with the time it takes the husband to play a round of golf, the resort planner may develop the formula for a new leisure conglomerate with golfing, specialty shopping, spas, and accommodations. Renovations undertaken to the rhythms of time-sharing may require an entirely new, usually much larger, building. The strip of beach in Cancun, like the strip in Las Vegas, develops larger and larger megaresorts to contain the expansive choreography of leisure. Mixed with other cultural scripts, these conglomerates of pleasure and entertainment have great vitality, as they propagate, hybridize, and differentiate faster than we can characterize them as the offspring of Disney, Jerde, or Portman.[34]

On the ship itself, cruising is an elastic assemblage of programs and services styled, scheduled, and accessorized with the signature techniques of a tourist brand. Management can reliably forecast the number of veal parmigianas needed on "Italian Night," and provide a choice of scheduled activities including everything from bingo and exercise class to art auctions and nightclubbing. Like the landed resort, cruising is an enclosure of familiarity. It is a libidinous hyperdomesticity in which the children are safe, and someone else is cooking within a ship that is a dream of cleanliness. The cruise schedules activities in ports of call, but travelers often choose to take a taxi into town and shop with cruise-mates so that the experience of a new space seems more familiar. An amnesty from the politics and responsibilities of domestic life recenters life around the needs and desires of the body: sunning, eating, drinking, spa treatments, and romance. *The Love Boat* and the *I Love Cruise* are accurately named, since part of the allure of cruising is sex. In a poll conducted by *Cosmopolitan* magazine and Royal Caribbean Cruise Line, 80 percent of the vacationers said they "felt more amorous at sea," and 48 percent said they had more sex, most shortly after boarding. The formula seems to work, since most passengers are repeat customers.[35]

Increasingly familiar are several new species of cruise ship that explore cruising's own expanded ambitions of territorial autonomy. Two such ships—the *World of ResidenSea* and the *Freedom Ship*—are essentially kinetic islands with permanent residents that travel slowly and continuously around the world, completing one rotation every three years. Purportedly still in the planning phases, the *Freedom Ship—City at Sea* is to be 4,320 feet by 725 feet by 340 feet high. Commercial and residential lots are available for purchase. The ship's educational system is to provide field trips in locations all around, as well as sponsor a global soccer league. A cartoon of the special sovereignty of non-national commercial territory, the ship fully collapses domestic life with the duty-free desires of cruising.[36]

We've been on forty cruises, one every two months. We're addicted. We have 40,000 miles on Holland America—they gave us a special emblem. We like other ships, too. The Costa Riviera was fun. They had a man with a monkey going around the ship and served pizza all day long. We also love Carnival's Jubilee. It's a beautiful ship.[37]

Envision an ideal place to live or run a business—a friendly, safe and secure community with large areas of open space and extensive entertainment and recreational facilities. Imagine that this community levies no local taxes—no income tax, no real estate tax, no sales tax, no business tax, no import duties. Finally, picture this community continually moving around the world. You are beginning to understand Freedom Ship, a soon to be constructed, massive ocean-going vessel. With a length of 4,320 feet, a width of 725 feet, and a height of 340 feet, Freedom Ship will be one of the wonders of the world—a mobile modern city featuring luxurious living, a major world trade center, and an extensive duty-free international shopping mall.[38]

. . . the society of the spectacle . . . in which language not only constitutes itself as an autonomous sphere, but also no longer reveals anything at all—or better yet, it reveals the nothingness of all things.

—Giorgio Agamben[39]

Tourism's supposed activity and event inevitably sponsors speculation about the laughable goal of authenticity. Dean MacCannell's early, durable argument in *The Tourist* analyzes the impossibility of the search. Still, the question occupies many careful thinkers in parsing tourism's symbolic references and its relevance as a cultural artifact or a commercial product. The repertoire of tourist adventures continually expands to include such things as industrial processes, scripted heritage, explorations of the body, and extreme forms of exertion. Critical commentary also expands beyond the identification of perceived discrepancies in the accurate depiction of historical or contemporary culture. Analysis also dissects the marketing techniques, urban scripts, and elastic programmatic envelopes of tourism. Architecture, even as the featured attraction or most iconic object of desire in the tourist installation, is still only the accessory to a larger active substrate—what Debord might have called "another facet of money."[40]

The mutual attraction between the DPRK and tourism exposes political disposition in both worlds. Fiction, the cheerful friend of politics and tourism, generates symbolic capital not because the comedy of its fake crests, seals, and epaulets actually means something, but precisely because there is a tacit agreement that it means nothing. Absurdist gestures and cultural gibberish are techniques in tourism's sleight of hand, the means by which it floats irreconcilable motives over a revenue stream. Filled with so much elaborate fiction, it provides the perfect opportunity for playacting, for loudly chanting beliefs while looking the other way as they are unenforced. At Mount Kumgang, both sides pretend to be what the other wants just long enough to make the deal.

The totalizing formulas shared by the spectacle of tourism and the utopia of Juche offer a special political instrumentality. Debord's dystopia portrays the pervasive spectacle as an all-encompassing, tragic and righteous story of "lost unity" within which tourism's ephemeral experience-as-revenue would be nothing more than "pseudo-use" value.[41] Stalinism's utopia is the story of an ultimate, permanent revolution. The fundamental confidence game of both totalitarianism and the total spectacle must maintain faith in the transcendent and unknowable whole; the eternal dynastic leader or final critique of capital. Yet utopias or self-reflexive worlds of belief also require shifting stories and multiple masquerades to continually refresh the original myth or brand. Without them, the smokescreen lifts, and faith falls away. Not only do tourism and totalitarianism utilize the same tools of mental vacuity, they become each other's next masquerade. The fact that both masquerades require the obfuscation of meaning is not a tragedy of meaninglessness. Rather, this meaninglessness *is* the meaning as well as the opportunity for political leverage.

The reclusive leaders of the DPRK, with their Kumgansan television sets, are the perfect tourists. The staging of power in the DPRK shares techniques with tourism. At Kumgang, the choreographed activities of tourism merge miraculously with the choreography of a communist state. Mount Kumgang and the DPRK's capital city of Pyongyang are both communist theme parks of sorts. In fact, Pyongyang has often been called a "Stalinist theme park."[42] In Pyongyang, the military and ruling elite go to restaurants, nightclubs, and casinos, even though a few miles outside the city there is widespread and extreme malnutrition.[43] Kim Jong Il treats his cronies to shopping sprees in special stores that sell Western products. Pyongyang is a theater, a Potemkin village, and as many as a thousand people may be called upon to play shoppers and pedestrians when Kim Jong Il stages urbanism for visiting dignitaries. The military particularly appreciate this assignment, since it permits them to wear civilian clothes.[44]

Let's consider the Najin-Sonbong area as a pigsty. Build a fence around it, put in karaoke, and capitalists will invest. We need only to collect earnings from the pigs.[45]

The Kumgangsan Hotel was excellent in the past, but has been spoilt since Hyundai abandoned it soon after renting it.
—DPRK official[46]

Different from the placeless destinations that so neatly organize most touring, the *I Love Cruise* initiated a resort that was less like *The Love Boat* and more like reality TV. The rules were quite strict. No photography, no "inappropriate" conversations with the North Korean guides, no tape recorders, no powerful lenses, no Japanese or American flags, no photography of the nearby villages, no short skirts, tattered jeans, spitting, or smoking.[47] Until they were fined for

1.3 "Biro-bong, the highest peak of Mount Kumgang." Young followers of the Democratic People's Republic of Korea claiming Mount Kumgang for their cause. Image source: Cha-yong Cho, *Diamond Mound/ Zozayong* (Seoul: Emille Museum, 1975).

doing so, tourists threw cartons of milk from the moving tour bus to children in a nearby village. Reports circulated that in one case the military authorities had detained the ship to search passenger luggage for a short skirt and unauthorized photographs. The tour was suspended several times, once to protest the detention of a South Korean tourist accused of attempting to persuade one of the North Korean guards to defect. Immigration officials routinely extracted fines for small inconsistencies or omissions on the forms.[48]

During the early days of the cruise, Hyundai regularly paid an extra $100 to $300 for these infractions over and above the $300 per passenger it was already paying.[49] Hyundai spent hundreds of millions on buildings, docks, and electrical infrastructure. By early 2001, Hyundai estimated its loss at $20 million, and had paid only $342 million of the $942 million promised to the DPRK.[50] In spring 2002, Hyundai was handling approximately four thousand tourists a month, claiming that the project would never be profitable without an overland route, golf course, duty-free shopping, and winter skiing.[51]

Yet the South Korean *chaebols,* with their concentrations of money, power, and state subsidy, are caricatures of hypercapitalism capable of naturalizing fiscal recklessness. Designed as nation-building organizations, the *chaebols* were initially orchestrated to create a competitive selection of exports. Arguably, their hierarchical structure and resistance to labor organization is a reflection not of Confucianism but of the military climate within which the *chaebols* were originally formed.[52] (Hyundai built barracks and roads for the United States military during the Korean War.) Today, however, Hyundai pursues a twenty-first-century script of global exchange. It has developed a ubiquitous presence in an increasingly diversified range of industries, pursuing global territory in order to avoid domestic restrictions. With more favorable interest rates abroad, the *chaebol* can borrow money at outrageous debt-to-equity ratios, sometimes as high as 92 percent.[53] Yet the delusions or irrationalities that sometime accompany symbolic capital also led the South Korean government to bail out Hyundai in 2001. President Kim Dae Jung was even facing an 85 percent disapproval rating in the South in part because of a general impatience with the North's unpredictability. The previous year, however, he had won the Nobel Peace Prize for unification efforts like the Kumgang tour. Saying that tourism could not "be differentiated from politics and the economy," the

South's Korea National Tourism Organization (KNTO) entered into partnership with Hyundai in order to continue the tour.[54]

One of the chilling consequences of these financial deals was the death of Chung Mong Hun in the summer of 2003. He was Chung Ju Yung's fifth son, and the designated liaison to the Kumgang project after his father's death. The administration that succeeded Kim Dae Jung accused the younger Chung of funneling 100 million dollars to the North in 2000, just in time for the historic summit in June of that year. The payments may have ensured the continuation of the negotiations that secured the Peace Prize for Jung, as well as the continuation of the Kumgang project so dear to Chung Ju Yung. Returning from a trip to the North, and preparing to announce a daily bus service between the North and South in September, Chung Mong Hun learned of a tightening investigation and additional allegations against him. He jumped from the twelfth story of the Hyundai-Asan Building, where his office was decorated with pictures commemorating the negotiations in Pyongyang and Kumgang.[55]

While North Korea has sometimes alienated the golden goose with too many restrictions, it has also permitted significant intrusions. Kumgang has hosted May Day celebrations between North and South trade unionists, goodwill sporting events like table tennis and motorcycle or car races, family reunions, and fashion shoots.[56] Reunions are now streamlined with an on-line visa-processing site.[57] Even Japanese tourists were permitted to visit the site, playing out a historical coda of the conqueror returned as tourist.[58] In September 2002, work began on a rail line linking Seoul and Sinuiju, as well as a rail line between Onjong-ri (at the foot of Mount Kumgang) and Chojin. Restaurants and convenience stores have appeared in the resort.[59] In addition to renovating the hotel, Hyundai has been given permission to build temporary tourist bungalows around the newly built spa. The company is also to begin work on two golf courses, a ski lift, and a bungee jump.[60]

[see *Franchise*]

The DPRK claims to favor the entry of technological innovation while filtering out other bad habits of the market, yet it continues to embark on far stranger adventures with capitalism. North Korea's partial economic recovery has given the country some relief from the period of famine they now call the "arduous march." There is still no television or Internet connection with the outside world for most of the country, but the opening of three hundred large markets, forty of which are in Pyongyang, has been widely publicized.[61] The Unification Church, which had originally made a bid for the Kumgang project, has entered into an agreement with Fiat to build an automobile factory in the North, the Peace Motor Company, that will produce a jeep as the first affordable, "middle-class" car. Hyundai is also slated to build sixteen automobile factories in the North, as well as a technology park just north of the Demilitarized Zone for which the proposed name is "Mount Kumgang Valley."[62]

In September 2002, North Korea legislated an additional special economic zone in Sinuiju, 132 square miles on the western border with China and across the Yalu River from Dadong. Like Rajin-Sonbong or the Kaesong Industrial development, the zone would have no visa restrictions, and would operate free from government involvement for fifty years. North Korea granted management of the Zone to a thirty-nine-year-old manufacturing and agricultural entrepreneur, Yang Bin, named by *Forbes* magazine as the second-richest man in China. As if reverse-casting the roles in historical epics of global trade, Yang, although born in Nanjing, acquired Dutch citizenship and returned to the rust belt of Shenyang to build a 220-hectare development called Holland Village. Housing, offices, retail, and recreational space were fashioned in the style of a Dutch architectural confection complete with windmills, a reconstruction of the Amsterdam railway station, and an artificial beach and wave pool. Yang's company, Euro-Asia Agricultural, sold orchids, among other things, and planned to build 100,000 greenhouses in the North Korean Special Economic Zone. The agreement with North Korea was signed on September 23, but by October 4 the Chinese government had already cracked down on Yang for alleged tax evasion and corruption.[63] [see *El Ejido*]

George W. Bush's description of Kim Jong Il: "a pygmy."[64]

A DPRK description of Donald Rumsfeld: "a political pygmy."[65]

We slipped a note kind of under the door into the Pentagon and said, "Look, let us go up there . . . and burn down five of the biggest towns in North Korea—and they're not very big—and that ought to stop it." Well, the answer to that was four or five screams, "You'll kill a lot of non-combatants," and "It's too horrible." Yet over a period of three years or so . . . we burned down every [sic] town in North Korea and South Korea, too. . . . Now, over a period of three years this is palatable, but to kill a few people to stop this from happening—a lot of people can't stomach it.

—General Curtis LeMay describing the use of napalm in the Korean War[66]

The cheerleaders dispense their smiles politically. At Thursday night's opening ceremonies, they halted when the American and Japanese delegations arrived.

—Description of North Korean cheerleaders at the 2003 World University Games[67]

North Korea maintains self-respect by sampling a culture that is more intensely opposed to it—alienating or denigrating that culture even while accepting profits from it. The husband can more easily have an affair with the Other, an interloper or a femme fatale, than with the neighbor's wife. Righteousness needs to cheat, but it also needs a monstrous evil enemy. Perhaps nothing raises the polish of Juche's perfection like the evils of capitalism. Likewise, the capitalist must also choose opportune moments to declare the DPRK evil and itself pure. America's belligerent stance toward North Korea, characterizing it as part of an "axis of evil," galvanizes the DPRK's most violent military programs, and places the two countries back in the Cold War architecture of symmetrical mimicry, fragility, and innocence. This, together with the neoliberal belief in a slow inculcation of capital's superior logics, constitutes a military-market containment of sorts.

Yet beyond these hard-boiled logics are wildcards, secret handshakes, and surprise endings that may also be successful in diverting a political theater. The *I Love Cruise* replaces the homeostasis of a Cold War game theory situation such as "Prisoner's Dilemma" with the unpredictability of the confidence game. As if to serve as a mascot for the maritime metaphors that populate globalization theories, it was a cruise ship, after all, with all of its promiscuity and luxury, that was able to penetrate the North. Able to slip through jurisdictions and political boundaries, this true pirate space was better equipped to gain both access and immunity—the Mata Hari that made a space for political negotiations.

Similarly, change may ride on excess, corruption, and exploitation, and the most elaborate desires may provide resistances or incentives that either leverage this change or exacerbate human rights problems. The more absurd and slippery the market script, the greater likelihood that it can maintain an effective disguise. Connoisseurs of the world's curiosities will pay to sample the North's various forms of sporting exertion or see its sheltered animal species. One inevitability: the North's cheap labor will find its way into the spas, golf courses, factories, and oil wells of the larger coastal development. A political imagination spots details of the bargain that may reasonably possess tactical powers to influence labor, economy, or environment. For instance, if it is designed to do so, a building component produced in large quantities potentially translates to both jobs and domestic industries in the North. The buildings that house reunions and goodwill sports, the only events North Koreans are permitted to attend, will necessarily be used for other programs, and so will introduce new cultural material to the North. Since the terrorist attacks of September 11, 2001, the North, pleading concerns about security, requested that many diplomatic sessions be held at Mount Kumgang. Consequently the resort has become the home base for summits between North and South, as well as the headquarters for the Red Cross and for family reunions.[68]

[see *Error*]
[see *Pirate*]

Occasionally, through some rapprochement between disguises, a sudden loosening of dogma, a sudden amnesia about conflict, appears when everyone is ready to make the deal. While the market runs on logic, it also runs on risks and comedies, ridiculous products and ephemeral desires. In the vacuity and amnesty of tourism's pirate space are powerful political mechanisms. An ethical swindle can enhance an ethical stance. Some sleight of hand with program, market, or materials, some counterpiracy, might add into the mix alternative choices that make many human rights undeniable by unusual means.

Extreme dangers also mingle with these indirect political consequences. A number of incidents, including the bombing of resorts in Bali in October 2002, may have been opening volleys in a war on tourism. Given their association with nature and peaceful cultural exchange or, their lack of overt political text, they may be attractive sites for summits or peace negotiations. Still, tourist installations are not politically neutral, "third-way" revenue streams but, rather, tantalizing signals of an arrogant belief in political immunity and superiority. For the terrorist, the destruction of tourism provides the perfect

1.4 Hyundai's floating Hotel Haekumgang at Mount Kumgang. Image courtesy Hyundai-Asan.

exposé of duplicity in disguise. Declarations of innocence are similar to declarations of war.

In excess of a Marxist historiography is an ancient history of piracy and confidence games that uses whatever it likes as a disguise (perhaps even classic forms of political resistance). Global tourism is rich with both conciliatory and inflammatory signals. Still, since a capacity for masquerade currently protects the fairy tales of communism and capitalism at Mount Kumgang, both sides are gambling on the possibility that capitalism's contradictions and shifting stories will cause it not to perish but to flourish. Indeed, fiction and masquerade have even succeeded in generating political meaning through lack of meaning, thus tripping the lock on an all-pervasive spectacle considered to be capital's ultimate critique.

Offshore

Jeju's utopia, Ieodo, is a mystic, uncharted island of the imagination, its beauty and a tribute passed on from one generation to the next from a time immemorial. Today, that concept well lends itself to the strivings of the islanders to make Jeju the vacation hub of Northeast Asia in the Asia-Pacific era of the twenty-first century.

—Woo, Keun-Min, Governor, Jeju Province[69]

Sammu is the term meaning there's no thief, gate or beggar in Jeju. From the old days, Islanders have made "diligence, thrift, interdependence" their virtue in order to pioneer rough and harsh surroundings. So they didn't steal or beg, which led to the condition of no use for the gate. Also, all the houses were the descendants of Tamna or of scholars who were banished due to their great will to keep their principles. Therefore they all valued their honor highly. They also knew everything about each other, which prohibited them from doing anything bad or dishonorable.[70]

In 2002, a North Korean delegation, gathering information about capitalist business practices in the South, visited Jeju, an island off the southwest coast of the Korean peninsula that calls itself the "Hawaii and Las Vegas of Asia." These are just two of the identities it claims.[71] The island is also currently planning to become the Singapore of Korea, a center of business, tourism, and international trade. Jeju locates itself not solely in relation to the Korean peninsula, but rather, like Cancun, in relation to flight times to major cities on the Eastern rim. It hopes to attract nine million tourists and industries, including information-processing, computer management, fish farming, and tree nurseries. The Korean government intends to contribute $3.6 billion to this effort in the next ten years. The Jeju stadium hosted World Cup Tournament events in 2002 as a debut of the tourist infrastructure it has been building for years. Like Kumgang, it has become a sister tourist space of diplomacy through tourism, sporting events, and summits—one that is also developing new models of eco-tourism and agricultural tourism.[72] Fifty percent of the island's 1,845 square kilometers is forest and another 30 percent is agricultural, with the chief source of income from tangerines.

Mount Halla, at the center of the island, displaces most of the settled areas to the coast.[73]

As the storage places for cultural exceptions and secrets, ocean islands are like the inland island of Mount Kumgang. Not only refugees and criminals but also hidden business practices are exiled to or stored on islands. Islands are the place where the doppelgänger lives, and where extra desires and fantasies flourish. They are the sites of stories, other wives, confidence men, and pirates. Islands are the world's mythomaniacs, not only sidestepping reality with a fabled existence, but also declaring exemptions from the laws that govern behavior on the continent. Islands also harbor the ingredients of culture that fall outside permissible boundaries or between cultural indices. Consequently, they are often penal colonies or, during war, stationary battleships. Jeju has been both. It was a penal colony before modern times, and for a hundred years after that a military headquarters for both the Japanese and the Americans. Many Jeju families also suffered losses in a revolt that the mainland Korean army squelched in 1948. American soldiers, having determined that it was a "Red Island," brought over Korean police and army members who massacred 30,000 people, some of them children.[74]

Islands off the coast of both Koreas remain the storage places of bitter fights that most recently surfaced in the world wars of the twentieth century. The United Nations' new Laws of the Sea (1982) exacerbate this latent conflict. They establish, for any nation, an exclusive economic zone 200 nautical miles off the shore. For archipelagos of the South China Sea, this new law creates not only many overlapping boundary lines, but a rush to lay ancient claim to islands or rocks that extend, for instance, national property rights to fishing or offshore oil.[75]

Yet Jeju has developed a very cagey amnesia for conflict. The island offers offshore exemptions such as casinos, duty-free shops, tax shelters, free-trade zones, visa waivers for 173 countries, and luxury resorts and tourist installations. The island hopes to be a capital of golf, providing a golfer's amnesty in the form of 50 percent reductions in greens fees. It promotes itself as a honeymooners' paradise and is a frequent location for shooting Korean movies.[76]

Jeju is also writing several public-relations scripts based on its ancient traditions. They refer, for instance, to "Jeju's utopia, Ieodo . . . a mystic, uncharted island of the imagination." The Tamna ancestry is rendered equally mystical and heroic.[77] Referencing a history of "overcoming trials with patience and prudence," Jeju projects an image of strength through virtuous behavior. It publishes messages of healing and psychologized care for its own citizens. The island also offers an emotional message about a global family of citizens. While there are a half million citizens living on Jeju, they claim a population of one million by maintaining a relationship with anyone who has ever lived there. Many of these efforts are intended to provide a home for those who fled or were exiled from Jeju during its many conflicts. Not only does the island welcome these citizens, but it treats them as part of an extended source of intelligence for solving problems, a "Think Tank Network of brains from Jeju Island."[78]

As the finale to a conference of the Pacific Asian Tourist Association (PATA), Jeju offered a special tour of Mount Kumgang that quickly sold out. The association issued a homily about tourism's ability to "bring peace, harmony, and prosperity to the people of the Korean Peninsula."[79]

El Ejido

"These are what New Yorkers like," he says. He turns and pulls a plastic covered package of small, green tomatoes from a pile. "Swedes like their tomatoes small, green and packaged in plastic. Whatever they want, I give them. Here, the consumer is king."[1]

How do you stay open to business and closed to people? Easy—first you expand the perimeter, then you lock down.
—Naomi Klein[2]

High-tech agriculture, like tourism, indexes the globe according to selected climatic attributes. It favors territories with large annual amounts of sunshine combined with cooling winds, water, cheap labor, and relaxed trade agreements. The tilted planet reveals luxuriant veins of sunshine bleeding across the Mediterranean and the Southern Hemisphere—a sea of photosynthesis. For the tourist industry, the cruise ship facilitates the conquest of these abstract territories by eliminating some of the necessary attachments and inconveniences of a single culture-laden location, and delivering the selected audience to any of the appropriate climates or attractions in accommodations to which they are accustomed. In the agricultural industry, greenhouses are the equivalent. By regulating and optimizing water, growth medium, temperature, and genetic constitution, greenhouses deliver horticultural necessities as abstracted variables independent of the complexities of the land. [see *Seas*]

The greenhouse is a germ of agricultural urbanism that intensifies not only production but also labor and waste in agripoles the size of a city. No longer used only when land or sunshine is sparse, as a structure within a field, greenhouses themselves are also propagated by the square mile in gigantic fields as a massive three-dimensional construction. An agricultural landscape is typically considered to be a cultivated form of exurban countryside, a self-cleansing counterbalancing organization of overlapping ecologies between animals, atmosphere, and vegetation. A landscape of greenhouses, however, is a continuous field of twelve-to-twenty-foot structures. Since most greenhouse formations cultivate flowers, fruits, and vegetables for export, they are also international formations. Since the 1970s, the substitution of plastic sheeting for glass has made greenhouse construction a less expensive proposition, thus transforming a few horticultural techniques into a boom industry in Spain, Italy, Egypt, Jordan, Morocco, Tunisia, Cyprus, the Canary Islands, New Zealand, Japan, China, and South Korea.[3] Asia has the largest total area of greenhouses, with approximately 1,800 square miles, but the Mediterranean also has approximately 400 square miles. A global network of plasticulture urbanism is gradually conquering areas of peak sunshine around the world.[4]

This new colonization of photosynthesis joins the long-standing imperial practice of importing out-of-season vegetables from the colonies. Yet in the networks of international agripoles, national and private powers crisscross the oceans in a contraseasonal exchange as mobile territories, sometimes seceding from their local conditions. The autonomous world of high-tech agriculture has elastic boundaries that extend and tighten with a flexibility that allows them to continually close around the next optimal condition with the cheapest labor. Plasticulture urbanism encounters climatic and environmental issues, conflicts over labor and immigration, and economic wars over food.

"Thousands and thousands of immigrants work in this zone where, it must not be forgotten, they did not appear by magic but because we needed them from an economic point of view," declared Andalusia's regional president Manuel Chaves. "If they left, El Ejido's economic activity would collapse."[5]

One international agripole that is the Rome or Alexandria of this sea of photosynthesis is the province of Almería in southern Spain. In the 1970s, when greenhouse technology surfaced as a technique for growing more than cut flowers, southern Spain, with its three thousand annual hours of sunshine, average temperature of 67 degrees Fahrenheit, and underground aquifer, became

potential photosynthesis (average in grams per square meter per year)

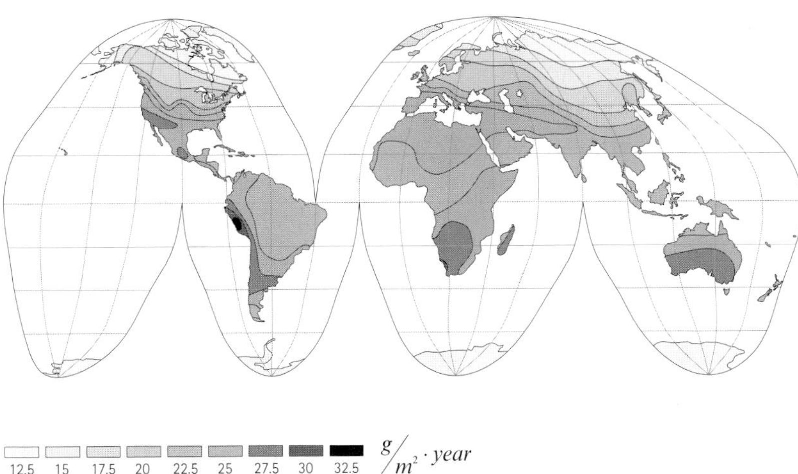

2.1 Global map of average photosynthesis per year. Image prepared by Shane Curnyn for *Praxis* 4, Landscape Issue, 2002.

a laboratory for the technology—a giant horticultural experiment called the "Almerían miracle."[6] The Spanish developed a technique of stretching plastic over structures previously used in vineyards. Landsat images of the area show the entire Almerían region, from the sea to the foothills of the Sierra Nevada Mountains, literally coated white with this type of greenhouse. In 1970, there were only 300 hectares of greenhouses in Spain, near Barcelona.[7] In 1971, there were 7.72 square miles in Almería alone, and by 2001 there were over 177 square miles concentrated there, half the size of all five boroughs of New York City.[8] Farmers recycle only 6,000 of the 20,000 tons of plastic they use per year.[9]

This billion-dollar industry, likened to the discovery of oil, has turned one of the poorest regions of Spain into one of the wealthiest.[10] The small town of El Ejido in the Almerían province is completely engulfed in plastic, a white landscape visible at the end of every street. The population and income of the city exploded in thirty years: from 17,000 people in 1970 to 50,000 in 2000.[11] During a good year, a farmer with just 10 acres can make $500,000.[12] New banks, SUV dealerships, luxury stores, and *unifamiliares,* or single-family subdivisions, appear around the town. There have always been brothels in Almería. The contemporary brothels, however, resemble a compound of self-storage units arranged in a jagged stepped configuration like individual miniature condominiums, with roll-up doors and their own parking place. The women working there migrate from Africa, or are trafficked from Eastern Europe. The golf courses and artificial lakes of the tourist industry that has always flourished on the Costa del Sol continues to expand to serve northern Europeans, intermingling with the greenhouses in a planimetric soup of development patterns. Just a mile from the greenhouse fields, one can dine, not on greenhouse vegetables, but on Wiener schnitzel.

A few miles drive to the northeast, where the greenhouses abruptly end, the landscape presents another anomaly. The soil in Almería is the poorest in the whole of Europe. In fact, the Tabernas area just east of Almería is Europe's only real desert. During the 1960s, the profitable industry was not tomatoes by the millions of tons, but film-making. *Dr. Zhivago, Cleopatra,* and *Lawrence of Arabia* used the landscape for location shooting, and Sergio Leone used it to simulate the deserts of the American west for "spaghetti westerns" like *The Good, the Bad and the Ugly, A Fistful of Dollars,* and *A Few Dollars More* with

2.2 Aerial photograph showing the Almerian Peninsula coated in greenhouses. Source: <https://zulu.ssc.nasa.gov/mrsid/mrsid.pl>.

Clint Eastwood. Mini-Hollywood, a theme park near El Ejido, has a western main street, performances by cowboy cast members, and a zoo for African animals such as zebras, monkeys, and tigers.[13]

Emblazoned on the flag of this sovereign world of photosynthesis, appearing in every feature of its crest is the dearest object of plasticulture desire: the tomato. Nurturing tomatoes in plastic greenhouses is an extremely complex game of cheating the seasons, requiring the manipulation of environmental factors, mechanisms of international finance, and the juridical pacts of international diplomacy. The tomato is the most durable player in this game. In the horticultural nursery cum stock market, the actual growth of a tomato signals growth in profits. Trade bargains, the differentials of labor costs, and the lust for enhanced and stylized vegetables can transform this fruit into a semi-precious nugget and an object of international piracy.

In this laboratory landscape, every possible need or desire of a tomato is completely optimized. Plastics factories standing within the complex of fields manufacture the necessary tons of plastic sheeting. Distribution stations, also within the fields, quickly absorb and deliver the vegetables to Málaga for shipping to the rest of the European Community, or air-freighting to other parts of the world. Growers can, by remote control, inject fluids rich with various chemicals and nutrients into the hydroponic IVs. Many of the roads between the greenhouses are paved to prevent the spread of disease. The pattern of development in this agro-industrial area is oriented in a wavy north-south pattern that permits cross breezes and prevents lingering shadows during the day. A growth medium provides the soil in this desert. It lies atop a layer of clay and sand, both of which are in abundant supply in the area.

A comedy of intense control and endless research accompanies the quest for the perfect tomato. Multinational seed companies are headquartered in the El Ejido–Almería area, on the highway with the plastics factories and other essential ingredients of a greenhouse agripole. These companies continually merge and change names, only occasionally revealing their affiliation with larger biotech or drug companies. They act as private versions of a state or university extension agency, often developing laboratories in areas of greenhouse concentration around the world. In their installations one can see, in miniature, the factors of global competition. They test the performance of competing glass and plastic, arched or flat-roofed greenhouse types. Breeding for a myriad of genetic factors is best controlled by hormonally stressing female plants into a hermaphroditic state within which they can be milked for seeds. In the most high-tech greenhouses the plants grow in linear bags of growth medium punctured with tubes that deliver fluids and nutrients. The entire enclosure is computer-controlled, buzzing, burping, and opening flaps in response to a shift in wind or a moment when the sun temporarily slips behind a cloud. Plastics are even manufactured to block the visible wavelengths of flies and mosquitoes, making it impossible for the blind insects to infect the plants. Seeds that produce over twenty kilos of vegetables per square meter per growing season can even be dated for planting during a specific week of the year.[14]

Plasticulture surrounds itself with the aura of intelligent responsiveness that attends most contemporary high-tech endeavors. Yet flexibility and responsiveness do not necessary describe a disposition of openness. Rather, the responsive organization is often one that is able to simultaneously extend and exclude. Optimizing the cheapest low-tech construction to deliver high-tech results with maximum profits relies on the continual perfection of the formula and the vigilant elimination of failure.

Still, perfectly engineered worlds are also the most susceptible to failures resulting from attempts at complete control. Among industrial managers, a control error is one in which it is hoped that the denial of information will prevail. In blinkered entrenchment, contradictory evidence is banished as false knowledge so that a bloated market can continue to grow or siphon resources from its host site. In the case of El Ejido, the lurking difficulty surrounds the need for labor cheaper than any that can be found in Spain.

El Ejido is one of the most remarkable landscape formations on earth—one that is visible from space. Still, it might have remained invisible, like so many distended or secessionary spaces within which collective democratic demands are overlooked or unenforced. Yet, however perfectly engineered they may be, Spain's greenhouse agripoles need something extra to stay alive. They need to tighten the boundaries of their world while also cheating selectively outside of those boundaries. Labor, as the secret requirement for perfection and control in Almería, eventually exposed a complex ethnoscape in the region. North Africa supplied an inexpensive but illegal labor force, and when Spain covertly accepted that labor, it reignited a centuries-old conflict in this part of the Mediterranean.

[see *Error*]

Last week's attacks were triggered by the stabbing death of a 26-year-old Spanish woman, Encarnacion Lopez, on Saturday February 5, allegedly by a mentally ill Moroccan man who tried to snatch her purse in a flea market. The stabbing came on the heels of the murder of two Spanish farmers by a 22-year-old Moroccan worker, who reportedly slit one man's throat and bludgeoned the other man's skull. The night before Lopez's funeral, some 10,000 people gathered in El Ejido and chanted anti-immigrant slogans. Gangs organized a "punishment mission" and made plans to carry out Ku Klux Klan-style nighttime attacks, but were stopped by authorities before reaching the part of El Ejido inhabited by immigrants. . . . Twenty-five years after the death of the nationalist military leader-Francisco Franco, Spain is facing a resurgence in far-right fascist activity by youths seeking a return to the "racial purity" and "moral order" preached by the Generalissimo. Fascist groups, whose symbol is the old Francista flag, featuring a black eagle in place of the shield on today's Spanish flag, propagate their hatred via rock music and the Internet. (In fact, authorities in El Ejido say the recent violence was organized through a neo-Nazi Internet campaign.)[15]

In the larger cartographic landscape, the two opposing European and African shores mirror each other symmetrically and competitively across the Mediterranean. Like rival twins, they share the same calendar of sunshine. Responding to swings of prosperity and poverty, they have traded alternating rhythms of occupation, resistance, warfare, and expulsion over hundreds of years. Sited in a pivotal location, this theater of the tomato war is a translocal valve of labor, race, and migration problems in Europe.

Yet currently, given the great differential between Spain's relatively successful economy and that of Morocco, for instance, North Africa is expected to remain in a complementary and submissive relationship. The North African immigrants, providing the approximately 20,000 workers required to maintain the greenhouses, work eight hours per day for approximately $25 per day in temperatures of over one hundred degrees Fahrenheit. Since most have open-ended contracts, these can be terminated any time for any complaint or insurgency, even if they are asked to perform extra work. Most of the $300–500 that a picker makes—half what a Spanish worker would expect to be paid—will be sent home, since Spanish wages are five times those in most of North Africa.[16] The $3,000 fine for hiring an illegal worker seems not to be strictly enforced.[17] If workers are given work visas, the employers must then

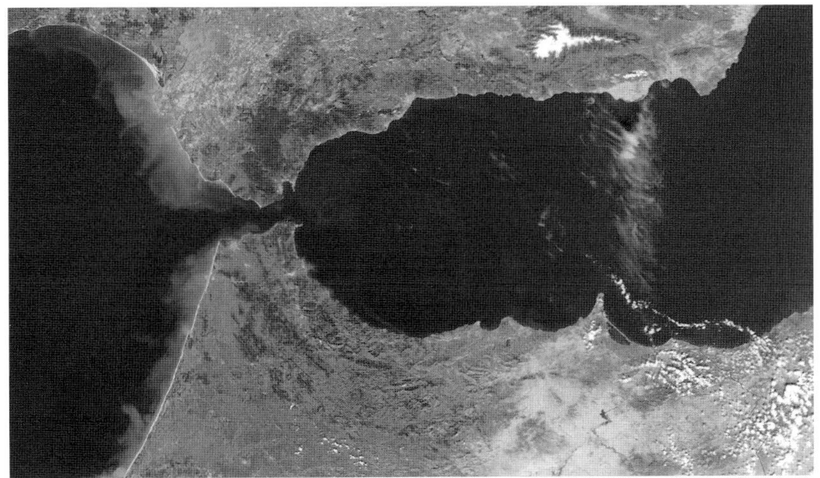

2.3 Aerial photograph of the symmetrical shores of Spain and Morocco. Source: <http://www.mapya.es/sig/pags/sig/intro2.htm>.

pay their social security, a sum of money that, for both parties, seems only to disappear. The Spanish are also concerned that providing papers for these workers will make Almería and El Ejido entry points for immigrants seeking work elsewhere in Spain or Europe.

Typically, the workers do not rent permanent housing, and landlords complain that when they do, too many people share the apartment. They live in *charbolas* or temporary shelters in fields that have become cities of both people and vegetables. El Ejido's *Plan of Rural Hygiene* and *Plan of Rural Regulation* read like a scheme for urban reform. For instance, the plans establish rules of waste removal and ventilation. Yet the citizen subjects of the plans are not the greenhouse workers, the human inhabitants of the agripole, but, rather, the tomatoes themselves. The workers' housing, constructed from the same materials as the greenhouses, draws no law or regulation.[18]

For some time the sons of local landowners have organized in bands that terrorize the Moroccans with Ku Klux Klan-style masked manhunts. In these hunts, routinized to last from Saturday night through the whole of Sunday, as many as fifteen young men may descend on the home of a Moroccan.[19] The most intense violence erupted in early 2000, in the midst of tensions over a new labor law, when a Moroccan worker killed his boss and another man in a fight. Soon after, on Saturday, February 5, 2000, a mentally ill Moroccan man killed a Spanish woman in the market. Throughout Sunday and into Monday, groups of farmers, high school students, and townspeople, some of them galvanized by a neo-Nazi website, set out to avenge the killing by setting fire to the houses of Moroccans, overturning cars, beating with pipes, and stoning.[20] Policemen were not in evidence during the raids on the houses, but did counter [see *Seas*] the Moroccans' organized attempts to fight back.[21]

And it is the dissolution of the subject of grievance which creates a wordless victim, object of an unquenchable hatred. The immigrant is first and foremost a worker who has lost his name, a worker who is no longer perceptible as such. Instead of the worker or proletarian who is the object of an acknowledged wrong and a subject who vents his grievance in struggle and disputation, the immigrant appears as at once the perpetrator of an inexplicable wrong and the cause of a problem calling for the round-table treatment. Alternately problematized and hated, the immigrant is caught in a circle, one might even say a spiral: the spiral of lost political otherness, doomed to the un-

nameable form of hatred that goes hand in hand with the realists' wish to rid problems of 'emotions'.
—Jacques Rancière[22]

Special free trade zones or special economic zones that legally alter the status of an immigrant or labor population are often able to avoid any reckoning with global compacts concerning wages, labor, or citizenship; the record of this extra population exists in a legal and political blackout. Another way to contain an extra labor population is continually to alter its status by oscillating between an acceptance of and blindness to its presence. Seasonal relationships with agricultural labor between Europe and North Africa or Eastern Europe alternate between temporary acceptance and patriotic rejection. During the periods of acceptance, the immigrant is to be invisibly compatible. During the periods when the host country wishes to reassert its national and racial identity, the immigrant is banished.

In El Ejido, some classic tools of resistance would, at first, appear to be instrumental. A concentration of workers in a vast agricultural factory is capable of resisting. Housing has also been a classic means of enfranchising the worker. Principled protest and political activism call for the alteration of laws, and for the adherence to labor and human rights standards. Yet the real situation is in camouflage. The worker is not organized, but organized against. The concentration of workers in the fields is not an empowering gathering but, rather, a kind of containment.

The Almerían peninsula precisely illustrates the space of exception or "dislocating localization" about which Giorgio Agamben writes in *Homo Sacer: Sovereignty, Power and Bare Life*. Like some other border conditions and special economic zones, it exists in a legal shadow. Those trapped within this space of lawlessness, with no recourse to political processes, are reduced to their corporeal presence, its labor, and its market value. Like the thousands of tons of sheet plastic, they are a disposable component of plasticulture urbanism.[23]

Yet the immigrant extra may make a parallel space of exception. In *On the Shores of Politics*, Jacques Rancière describes the immigrant as the "worker who has lost his name," as well as any means of resistance. Yet the extra is also the indicator of a structural problem that political consensus tries to overlook.

As such, in Rancière's terms, the extra has the potential to be a kind of "correction" to the wrongs that hide within democratic consensus. Extras provide the extrinsic information, the contradiction that troubles consensus, materializing human rights abuse as well as fallacies in labor and immigration laws.[24] As a consequence the immigrant is both a necessary character and an object of hatred.

Still, consensus can mask its problems without necessarily acknowledging its damages. For instance, Spain has begun to legislate its own purity indirectly by curating its immigrant population. Eastern Europeans are gradually replacing the North African greenhouse labor. Before the 1970s the Spanish were often European immigrants themselves, leaving the country to do menial work elsewhere. The UN predicts that Spain, with its aging population, will have the highest percentage of old people by 2050, and may require as many as twelve million immigrants over the next thirty years to maintain population levels.[25] The Spanish association of towns against depopulation looks for people with work permits and at least two children. They provide five-year contracts, jobs paying 600–840 Euros a week, schools, and medical care. Many of the applicants are from Eastern Europe or South America.[26]

The people of Salé had always welcomed Moors from Spain into the community both before and after 1492. In the first decade of the 17th century, a new type of immigrant began to appear. The last Moors of Spain, whether holdovers still adhering to Islam (Mudejares), or "Moriscos" (called "Andalusians" in Salé), nominally converted to Christianity, had been goaded by the racist and revanchist policies of Spain into a series of revolts and had been expelled en masse by Philip II in a series of edicts between 1609 and 1614. One of Salé's traditional historians tells us that when these new refugees showed up and tried to rent houses there, "because of the non-Muslim ways, Spanish dress, language, and manners, their lack of shame and dignity, they were not allowed" to stay. . . .

The newly arrived Moriscos were even more outlandish . . . [they] had to content themselves with land below the casbah . . . where they constituted a wholly separate group unto themselves. They thirsted for revenge against Spain and quickly became enthusiastic corsairs.

—Peter Lamborn Wilson[27]

Ironically, the invisibility and compatibility coerced from Muslims and Jews in Spain has, over time, sharpened their profile in the region. The chant of the recent rioters, "Moros out!," sends the story streaming back into other agricultural histories of the Iberian peninsula, as well as tales of pirates and aggressions on the Mediterranean sea.[28]

In the early eleventh and twelfth centuries, Muslim communities that occupied the areas now cultivated by greenhouses, landscapes, and political organizations were reciprocally structured. Berber tribes or clans settled in the valleys and on the coast in small groups around a small castle and tower. Fields of fruits and nuts like grapes, figs, apples, and almonds occupied land near sources of water. These were grown together with vegetables and other crops. Historians speculate that growing perishable crops was a means to prevent the rise of a ruling class. Given this type of cultivation, expansion simply ended when each of the valleys and water sources had been developed.[29]

Although it is arid, everything about this particular region of the Iberian Peninsula has, for centuries, amplified the understanding of landscape technologies and agricultural urbanism. Gerald Brenan, a friend of the Bloomsbury Group, who lived between Granada and Almería for six years between 1920 and 1934, wrote that the "view of mountains, valleys, villages and distant sea lay spread out like an illustration of the features of the world in a child's geography book."[30] As in any agricultural area that must negotiate altitude, the growing seasons were dated to the week, and even to the day, with crops ripening later and later in the season as they climbed the hill: four days for every three hundred feet.[31] As if available by some miraculous feat of remote engineering, melting snows from the same mountains continually replenished the Dalias Aquifer, making water freely available. The aquifer has permitted the region to irrigate crops of grapes and tangerines consistently, despite drought or political difficulty.

While the Romans, Greeks, and Arabs left their traces throughout the area in place names and infrastructures, the Arabs and Berbers from North Africa left a truly refined tradition of irrigation, one that molded the landscape into the intensive and tidy agricultural urbanism that the Spanish inherited. When Ferdinand and Isabella captured Granada in 1492, the same year they were exploring other prizes further west, Alhambra, a city of irrigation and gardening, was the jewel of this horticultural science. Before they expelled

Boabdil, the last Muslim king in Granada, they agreed to a coexistence with the Moors, but quickly reneged on this agreement, insisting instead on conversion to Christianity. The forced conversion devolved into a revolt, followed by an all-out war that the Spaniards won. The Moriscos, Muslims who had converted to Christianity, were deported as laborers to the northwestern provinces of Spain. Yet then as now, there was a need to cheat, to keep something extra. In each village two Moorish families were permitted to remain behind to tutor the traditions of silkworm breeding and, of course, irrigation.[32]

After the expulsion of North Africans, all along the sparsely settled coast of Andalusia, from lookout towers that were erected by the previous Arab settlers the Christians kept watch for pirates well into the eighteenth century. A common Andalusian saying, Brenan writes, was "Hay Moros en la costa."[33] Those expelled who turned to piracy took the turf war over the Iberian peninsula to the seas and their elastic jurisdictions. Some of the Andalusians regrouped in pirate North African enclaves like Salé, plotting bitter revenge on Spain, while others played the seas for shifting advantages and allegiances that might be profitable. Privateers contracted with city-states all along the Mediterranean coastline, developing complex commercial networks and soaking up the [see *Pirate*] aggressions that did not culminate in all-out war between nations.[34]

Twenty-first-century forms of piracy and trafficking now haunt the western Mediterranean. Today, Mafia groups respond to covert "calls" for workers among the growers.[35] Thousands of potential immigrants—as many as 25,000—and wait in the Spanish enclaves of Ceuta and Melilla, and thousands die attempting to make the Mediterranean crossing, having paid as much as $1,500 for their passage.[36] The Spanish Canary Islands, visible from the African Coast, are also only a twelve-hour boat ride away, and smugglers often charge from $500 to $2,500 for the trip.[37] As counterpiracy measures, the Spanish use special high-tech sensing devices, radar, and heat-sensitive equipment to catch *clandestinos* as they come in.[38] The gardens of El Ejido have also attracted various underworld groups that organize more intense forms of violence. In July 2001, a Moroccan mafia of smugglers and extortionists were caught in the town attempting to extract a ransom for kidnapped Moroccans who thought they were coming to Spain for work.[39] There are also reports of militant Muslim groups in North Africa—like the AIG, or Armed Islamic Group—collecting a so-called "revolutionary tax" from workers in El Ejido.[40]

Now an Eastern European mafia attends the newest non-African workers. Brokers of contemporary slavery, this mafia retains passports, takes a cut of the profits, and generally treats the agricultural worker as it would treat its brothel workers.[41]

The pirate and the immigrant are both contradictory and necessary to the state. The pirate is at once a criminal and a secret agent of the state. Similarly, the immigrant is both a secret desire and an absolute contradiction. Both are valence agents on which the state is willing to gamble for an extra quotient of uncontrolled revenue. Moreover, the most dangerous organizations are those that oscillate between games, playing a reciprocal network of piracy as well as seeking protection within the fierce righteousness of the state. High-tech agriculture itself coopts fluidity opportunistically, selectively enforcing laws and soliciting loyalties. It is a "war machine" which, as Deleuze and Guattari suggest, maintains a special relationship with the state. It gambles with impunity on the high seas, but periodically runs for cover under the guise of propriety and national identity.[42]

As traditional farming gives way to high technology, Almería now shares many of the same problems plaguing California. Towns are bursting at the seams with urban blight. Ocean water is seeping into the upper reaches of the area's aquifers. Ragged plastic sheets litter the countryside; only a small portion are recycled. Local farms pump out far more water than the aquifer can naturally recharge, while fertilizers appear to have tinged some underground water supplies with nitrates. In 1986, the authorities declared the Dalias aquifer—the principal source of water for El Ejido—over-exploited, and curbed the expansion of intensive agriculture.[43]

The vagabond is the alter ego of the tourist. . . . The line which divides them is tenuous and not always clearly drawn. . . . There is this abominable likeness which makes it so hard to decide at which point the portrait becomes a caricature and the proper and healthy specimen of the species turns into a mutant and a monster.

—Zygmunt Bauman[44]

Many towns all over the world are named El Ejido. El Ejido means "cooperative" or shared agricultural space, and such spaces were typically part of Spain's colonizing formulas in the New World. Today, another spatial product colonizes some of the same parts of the world. Almería, perhaps now developed to capacity, exports not only tomatoes but also a development cocktail of industries that settle in similar atmospheric conditions. Tutored by the success of places like El Ejido, global growers are attempting to reproduce agripoles elsewhere in similar latitudes and bands of sunshine.[45] Seed companies that serve Spain, Jordan, and Asia also provide expertise in Mexico within bands of sunshine and atmosphere very similar to those of North Africa and the Iberian Peninsula. Foreign growers now populate the central regions of Mexico in Sinaloa, Jalisco, Sonora, Querétaro.[46] Although the numbers occasionally dip in response to trade fluctuations, greenhouse production has more than doubled in Mexico.[47] As high-tech agriculture spreads to many new locations, [see *DPRK*] the same mix of tourism and agriculture appears.

All over the world, vegetables, fruits, and flowers have become the subject of fierce export wars and trade agreements between nations. Within this species of war one chooses enemies opportunistically, cooperatively rotating them at intervals.[48] The United States, Canada, and Mexico fight over tomatoes. In an another longitude Spain, Morocco, and the Canary Islands are agricultural adversaries. The combat, called "dumping," is usually an offshore bombardment of very inexpensive tomatoes. After steaming into port, the inexpensive tomatoes simply refuse to leave. Throughout the world, any product whose price approaches zero, and is therefore almost free, is a notorious sign of aggression.

The bundled programs of tourism and agriculture have provided an interesting tactic in the vegetable wars. For instance, former Spanish Prime Minister Aznar's "Programme of Integrated Action for the Development and Order of the Mediterranean Region of Morocco," signed in 2000, translated Moroccan debt into Spanish investment, and suggested that Spain might lend to Morocco expertise in tourism and building infrastructure. By offering development incentives and debt relief to Moroccans, Spain hopes to preempt the possible success of Morocco's own tomato production, and establish settlements on the opposing shore that provide some remote control of the most crowded launching points for illegal immigration.[49] Racial turmoil and the xenophobic sentiments surfacing across Europe have sponsored additional labor legislation: for instance, a deportation and repatriation act which, in the end, did little to reduce the immigrant population.[50] Diplomatic instruments of control may prove to be more successful.

Zygmunt Bauman conjures up a grim comparison between the tourist and the immigrant as alter egos. Desire and consumption are so addictive that the tourist is compelled to look for new territory, while the immigrant or refugee must travel to another territory to survive. Tourists are uncomfortable with the vagabond as a "flawed consumer." In their utopian world, there would be no immigrants. Bauman's premise prompts the contemplation of an inverted corollary within which the migrating worker is in the position of power, traveling to different countries and gambling with currency differentials. Yet the state, in collusion with capital, has cleverly seized the tourist protocol as a masquerade of cooperation that allows it to keep the vagabond in place and in service of the tourist's mobility.[51]

Developers of engineered crops are bracing for further protests in the upcoming growing season. More than a month ago in South Korea, police arrested students and environmental activists who occupied a greenhouse where scientists were developing gene-altered varieties of Chinese cabbage, tobacco, cayenne and other crops. And last month in Auckland, New Zealand, protesters destroyed a test plot of potatoes that reportedly had been genetically enhanced with a gene taken from an African clawed toad.[52]

In a quiet village on the outskirts of Zurich, a genetically engineered strain of rice that its creator says could save millions of children's lives is locked up in a grenade-proof greenhouse as if it were the Frankenstein monster that some critics contend it is. Unlike any other rice on earth, this so-called golden rice produces beta carotene in its seeds, thanks to genetic instructions that scientists added to the rice from a daffodil, pea, bacterium and virus.[53]

The plastic constructions propagated in El Ejido cultivate almost 200 square miles of greenhouses. On the one hand, the peninsula represents a massive exploitation of resources. Yet it also hallucinates the spread of any contagious detail that is intensely interactive with climate—one that might, under different circumstances, possess an alternative intention. Such an invention, an exploitation of exploitation, could tip the fulcrum toward very different political and environmental issues.

Near Mini-Hollywood is a solar experiment with very different politics. The Plataforma Solar de Almería is the European Union's most extensive solar installation, with a large solar array and a number of additional experiments with small mobile dishes, homes, and agriculture. The sun is used to store energy, purify water, or dry food. The United States joined the experiment during the oil crisis, but withdrew once it had satisfied itself that the crisis had subsided. The EU, on the other hand, has set new standards for harvesting sun and wind energy. Southern Spain is not only one of the sunniest places on earth, but also one of the windiest. Offshore wind farms may be its next lucrative *Landschaft.*[54]

Another experiment near Manzanares, fifteen kilometers south of Madrid, rehearses the essential principle of greenhouse design for energy collection rather than horticulture. The German government has sponsored a solar chimney in the area. The chimney is positioned at the center of a large circle of glass roofs, relatively close to the ground. Heat collected under the glass or plastic travels up through the chimneys, activating a turbine. Black tubes filled with water continue to give off heat, and activate the turbine at night. The 80-megawatt project, built in the 1980s, was used to project designs for much larger 100- and 200-megawatt chimneys under consideration in several locations around the world. The towers themselves would be the tallest structures in the world, measuring almost one kilometer in height, and surrounded by a diameter of glass several kilometers in diameter.[55]

Energy consciousness is also a clever masquerade. Energy companies like British Petroleum, Areva, and a host of others wish to promote themselves as a benign global force. They are not hawking a product but, rather, providing a larger, mysterious service for all companies. Nuclear reactors and genetically altered crops may be the company's central focus, but images in television advertisements often feature wheat harvests at sunset and offshore windmills, while the voice-over makes claims about feeding the world's hungry, or replacing the problems of oil with renewable sources.[56]

The Almerían peninsula is a global fulcrum of labor, food, waste, and human rights issues. The agripoles of plasticulture urbanism transform landscape

2.4 Aerial view Plataforma Solar de Almería. Image courtesy of Plataforma Solar de Almería/Ciemat.

soil, sunshine, and wind into commodities and, in so doing, place them on the political bargaining table as alternative variables in the world's fuel and resource wars. As the fortunes of tomatoes flourish and fail, intensified agriculture aggregates with, for instance, tourism, solar energy, water, desalination. Any one of these extends leverage, and provides additional ingredients in the unlikely mix of variables from which change might emerge. High-tech agriculture is constitutionally incapable of acknowledging its human rights abuse. Mobile and seasonal, it flies under the radar and within the shelter of political consensus. It even uses, as leverage and camouflage, the less noxious programs that are bundled within it (e.g., tourism) as camouflage. While regular political channels have little hope of altering the feigned innocence of consensus, the same associated programs might also camouflage a bait and switch that indirectly relieves abuse. The tomato world, like other worlds that try to remain undetected, attracts unusual or extreme contingencies that make it vulnerable to ingenious pirates of the Mediterranean Sea and the global sea of photosynthesis.

Offshore

"Hoteliers are worried that news of the influx, and of the corpses of drowned migrants that have washed up on beaches, will frighten them off."[57]

A Moroccan goat owner intends to sue Spain for the deaths of 10 of her goats during the conflict over the islet of Perejil, the daily *El Mundo* reported Wednesday.[58]

Continental islands are accidental, derived islands. They are separated from a continent, born of disarticulation, erosion, fracture; they survive the absorption of what once contained them.

—Gilles Deleuze[59]

In July 2002, a rock or islet the size of a football field became the offshore site of a military skirmish between Spain and Morocco, one that reinforced the ancient tensions between the two shores.[60] Islands are often not only ambiguous territorial claims, but also extensions of the troubled boundaries associated with landed conflict. Whatever truce or distance waters bring, an island may trouble the ocean boundaries between competitive countries.

Known as Perejil in Spain and Leila or Tourah in Morocco, the rock is only 200 meters off the coast of Morocco. A dozen Moroccan soldiers occupied the island, reportedly to monitor drug trafficking and illegal immigration, yet the occupiers did raise two red flags, as if symbolically reclaiming the territory for Morocco. Spain and the European Union sent navy gunboats and special forces to reestablish Spain's sovereignty over the island. While it appeared that diplomatic dialogues, some with US Secretary of State Colin Powell, easily resolved the military crisis, tensions erupted again the following September, simply because of the presence of a Spanish military helicopter on the island. This incident is only the latest in a centuries-old struggle between small but strategic islands of European and African territory around the Straits of Gibraltar.[61]

Continental islands, as well as ocean islands, contributed to the hostility. Ceuta and Melilla, two Spanish territories on the African mainland, are classic examples of continental islands. Predating the contemporary free trade zone (FTZ), they are isolated zones with special legal or political conditions. They are very similar to microstates, or what are called small states and territories (SSTs), like Malta, Monaco, the Vatican, or Gibraltar, many of which are sovereign states or states previously under colonial rule. While Ceuta and Melilla have sometimes been called autonomous communities, they are not colonies that will eventually contract for their independence. They are the extra ingredients to which the state feels entitled. Both have been under Iberian control since the fifteenth century. While Spain claims that they have possessed these territories since before the establishment of Morocco, Morocco claims that this constitutes only a long occupation, not a property right.[62] Spain remains bitter about Western Sahara, another continental island and a former Spanish colony, rich in natural resources of phosphate, which was annexed by Morocco in 1975.[63]

[see *Seas*]

Fueling Spain's desire to remain in possession of the enclaves is the need to control illegal immigration, but illegal immigration would not be such a problem were it not for the tremendous economic inequalities between the two countries. Moreover, the cities are potential points of entry for legal visa-holders, immigrants who "disappear" through a network of friends, and immigrants who travel in a network of drug-traffickers. Thousands attempting these forms of passage are caught each year. As the only two extracontinental European territories in Africa, Ceuta and Melilla are natural bridges to Europe. While the enclaves are increasingly Muslim in population terms, Muslims are still in the minority.[64]

Through stiff, tense smiles, negotiations between Spain and Morocco are often protracted and inconclusive. Spain usually wins, although Morocco has found some leverage points with fishing rights and agricultural imports. Yet Ceuta and Melilla are also bargaining chips in a number of negotiations that are potentially beneficial to the development of the Moroccan economy as well. Some shared projects involving tourism or infrastructure are negotiated as a form of consensual colonization. Long-range plans for economic cooperation and assistance, among them a new gas pipeline and a bridge, are intended to help stabilize relations. One of the many negotiations included plans to make the enclaves into contemporary free-trade zones by 2010. Yet Melilla and Ceuta have been duty-free zones, or trading zones of a sort, since 1868, and they have always been conduits of goods from Europe to Morocco.[65]

The Spanish territory of the Canary Islands—a destination for British tourists, as well as immigrants and stowaways—provides another stark picture of tourists and vagabonds traveling in similar waters. The Canaries form an enclave of tourist utopias and colonialist architectural nostalgias in the form of resort hotels, homes, and wildlife parks such as Europe's largest dolphinarium.[66] Meanwhile, these islands are not only a jumping-off point for refugees attempting to cross the Mediterranean to Spain, but also a place where global refugees and stowaways from as far away as Senegal or South Korea are discovered or deposited, dead or alive.[67]

Contemplation: Seas

According to the medieval interpretations put forth by the cabbalists, world history is a combat between the strong whale, leviathan, and the no less strong behemoth, a terrestrial animal which was represented imaginatively as a bull or an elephant. . . . According to the cabbalists, behemoth tries to tear leviathan to pieces with its horns and teeth, while in turn, leviathan tries hard to stop the land animal's mouth and nostrils with its flaps and fins, in order to deprive it of food and air.
—*Carl Schmitt*[1]

Landscape

Landscape challenges and tutors philosophical and political contemplations. It is land, sea, and air, politicized territory and topological terrain. It is both *landskip,* the terrain evaluated according to visual aesthetics, and *Landschaft,* a terrain understood in relation to its cultivation and organization over time. It is environment, microclimate, and organism. "Scape" has become a suffix that lends to any line of research fluidity, elastic boundary, or the sense of a discontinuous dispersal of some quality or content within a field.[2] Landscape is a physical territory, as well as a model for theoretical territories and political constitutions. Landscape is a diagram or repertoire—a set of events and behaviors unfolding over time.

Territory, as the word finds its most fertile usages in common parlance, describes both domains and unknowns, fixed geometric areas and indeterminate spaces or places as yet unexplored. It is a term saturated with desire, propriety, and conquest of the unknown, a term that transposes organizational logics to include political logics and political milieu. As it is associated with behavioral repertoires, from those of wolves to those of salesmen, a territory is an area bounded by changing markers and attitudes. Using a network repertoire, territory may be the remote extension of a home turf, such as a colony or protectorate, held within a web of associations and dependencies. A landscape repertoire lends to territory several additional activities. Land as landscape often appears to hold still long enough to sit for our planimetric or perspectival portraiture. We often believe boundary to be most clearly made in relation to this static turf. Simultaneous deadlocked claims hammered out across geometries make boundaries, and shape their regulatory juridical structures.[3] Wars and conflicts often mark their progress with techniques similar to those used to mark property boundary. While this turf is as obdurate as any substance on earth, tempered and made stronger by contestation, properties of that same land are capable of eluding the most fixed and static claims to property. Landscape is so often finally not static, but kinetic—the areas of animals, waters, sands, and atmosphere. Sound, smell, tidal limit, or current offer attributes applicable to elastic rather than static boundaries.

While most landscapes are kinetic, in so many historical and philosophic reveries about the political constitution of shifting territories, it is the sea that is the favorite model of active territories, the sea as the alter ego of the land. The sea is the stuff of epic tales, the mother and the femme fatale, the stage for the heroic historians of world systems or the solvent capable of dissolving landed logics. It is often characterized as a primordial, natural, even innocent, territory in the world that is pliable to the righteous demands of ambition. Contemplations of the sea often test the political constitution of warm seas and cold seas, inland cities and maritime cities, as well as the motives of the pirates in these waters. The repertoire of the sea reciprocally formats the behaviors and political constitutions of naval theaters. Moreover, in maritime literature, the behaviors and masquerades of the sea reciprocally merge with those of the characters that inhabit it: sailors, pirates, and magistrates. Consequently, these tests of the water also yield evidence of disposition, of varying degrees of violence and honesty, productivity, and destruction.[4]

Maritime metaphors are favorites of both neoliberals and super-Marxists. In the neoliberal portrayal, a globalizing frictionless sea carries virtual packets of information that accomplish a one-world economy. The sea naturalizes the assumed human right to a frictionless free market. Alternatively, for the super-Marxists, the sea is the site of biopolitical groundswell, possessing the potential utterly to disrupt market forces. In its various evocations, it may be soft and hard or frictionless and slushy—a place of lawless exception and a cauldron of democracy.

It could be that, little by little, it [the strategic] will exhaust its capacity to transform itself and constitute only the space (just as totalitarian as the cosmos of ancient times) in which a cybernetic society will arise, the scene of the Brownian movements of invisible and innumerable tactics. . . . When one examines this fleeting and permanent reality carefully, one has the impression of exploring the night-side of societies, a night longer than their day, a dark sea from which successive institutions emerge, a maritime immensity on which socioeconomic and political structures appear as ephemeral islands.
—Michel de Certeau[5]

Every insurrectional event provokes a shock to the system in its entirety. . . .

It becomes even more difficult for Empire to intervene in the unforeseeable temporal sequences of events when they accelerate their temporality. The most relevant aspect that the struggles have demonstrated may be sudden accelerations, often cumulative, that can become virtually simultaneous, explosions that reveal a properly ontological power and unforeseeable attack on the central equilibria of Empire.
—Michael Hardt and Antonio Negri[6]

Only there does the cry resound: "Everything is equal!" and "Everything returns!" However, this "Everything is equal" and "Everything returns" can be said only at the point at which the extremity of difference is reached. A single and same voice for the whole thousand-voiced multiple, a single and same Ocean for all the drops, a single clamour of Being for all beings: on condition that each being, each drop and each voice has reached the state of excess—in other words, the difference which displaces and disguises them and, in turning upon its mobile cusp, causes them to return.
—Gilles Deleuze[7]

Monistic

In many formulations, the sea works in tandem with the land as a regulatory device. One classic setting of these historical tales, shared by many who write about the sea, is Fernand Braudel's Mediterranean, where waters are used as *mise en scène* and organizational model for great campaigns of deterritorialization and reterritorialization. Pirates and privateers fight the unofficial wars between the wars, stoking the unofficial commerce, slipping between the national and urban jurisdictions with a shadow set of laws in constant motion and flux.[8] The pirates operate in an enclosed sea, a room surrounded by city-states and powerful families.

Michel de Certeau describes a sea that swells with a flood of individual tactics, "a maritime immensity on which socioeconomic and political structures appear as ephemeral islands." The sea floods the islands that, in de Certeau's reverie, seem like isolated rocks or the last exhausted, remnant tips of entire continents. His characterization of a "cybernetic society" seems to emphasize the power of a population of small influences, the "Brownian" motion of a thousand fluid molecules defying containment and nearly overpowering the land. Yet the island also works in tandem with the water, providing the hard moments, the outposts of the strategic, obdurate, or official powers that both challenge and justify the deluge of water.[9]

Many of the oceans of philosophical speculation further escape the hold of the land. They are filled with white whales, renegados, and pirates that never go home. Deleuze and Guattari write: "The sea is perhaps principal among smooth spaces, the hydraulic model par excellence."[10] In this and similar contemplations, the sea is often used to imagine the dissolving of national, familial, or other territorial boundaries. These waters model a space of impossible elegance which moves through an archipelagic network of power, decoding hierarchies. Deleuze has used the sea to model a perfect anarchy where "a single and same voice for the whole thousand-voiced multiple, a single and same Ocean for all the drops, a single clamour of Being for all beings."[11]

In *Empire,* Michael Hardt and Antonio Negri treat the sea as the mixing medium of politics. Better "seascapes," they say of Arjun Appadurai's cultural "scapes."[12] Hardt and Negri argue that it is not only the classic forces of resistance that adopt the fluid and slippery constitution of the sea, but capital itself, capital in league with the state. Capital, they write, "tends toward a smooth space defined by uncoded flows, flexibility, continual modulation and tendential equalization." In "this smooth space" of the empire, "there is no place of power—it is both everywhere and nowhere."[13] Far from being satisfied with the fixed boundaries of nations and families, smooth organizations build Empire that is essentially sanctioned by the state, but only occasionally touches down within legal jurisdictions. Market and capital, fully metastasized into each other, even switch positions with resistance. Like a colloidal liquid that suddenly clarifies as a solution, or a solid that transforms into a gas, capital is not dead but incarnate as another entity, bearing some of the traits or costume elements of its resistance as a masquerade.

Hardt and Negri treat "Empire" as a noun/verb, a pervasive force that is always referenced as singular. *Empire's* description of a "plural multitude" with "productive creative subjectivities of globalization that have learned to sail this enormous sea" bears some resemblance to de Certeau's sea of multiple tactics, a population contributing nourishment and insurgency, support and friction. The sea that Hardt and Negri describe does not follow the logic of any single political theology: "The relationship between 'system' and 'asystemic movements' cannot be flattened onto any logic or correspondence in this perpetually modulating atopia."[14] Nevertheless, matching the epic logic of Marx, there are some acts of resistance that have the power to affect the system as if it were singular or whole, with insurgency that "provokes a shock to the system in its entirety." Hardt and Negri speak not of recycling regulators, but of "shocks" to the system, and unpredictable "explosions" capable of rocking "the most central equilibria of Empire."[15] Empire is a conglomerate of "fault lines," but the argument sometimes seems to imply that the fault lines are so numerous that they become indistinguishable within the entire constitution. The Empire is matched by the "multitude." The multitude, as a population of the many, expresses the power of the one and the many, and ultimately, the one.[16]

All of this getting even for epistemology is not innocent.
—Gilles Deleuze and Félix Guattari[17]

The cold monster of the state has never ceased working for the hot monster of society, for the desirable objects that society exhibits as critics of appearance and felicitous resolutions of otherness. . . . The folly of the times is the wish to use consensus to cure the diseases of consensus. What we must do instead is repoliticize conflicts so that they can be addressed, restore names to the people and give politics back it former visibility in the handling of problems and resources.

—Jacques Rancière[18]

The sea is perhaps principal among smooth spaces, the hydraulic model par excellence. . . . As Virilio emphasizes, the sea became the place of the fleet in being *where one no longer goes from one point to another, but rather holds space beginning from any point: instead of striating space, one occupies it with a vector of deterritorialization in perpetual motion. This modern strategy was communicated from the sea to the air, as the new smooth space, but also to the entire Earth considered as desert or sea.*

—Gilles Deleuze and Félix Guattari[19]

There is not one of you who does not openly proclaim that every man is entitled to manage and dispose of his own property; there is not one of you who does not insist that all citizens have equal and indiscriminate right to use rivers and public places; not one of you who does not defend with all his might the freedom of travel and trade.

—Hugo Grotius[20]

Hard/Soft/Elastic

Yet to believe that any of the maritime songs is a liberatory reverie of a warm and amniotic sea, approaching homeostatic equilibrium, frictionless resistance, or spectacular revolution, is to bump up against the side of the tank.

Through both the content and the temperament of their argument, Deleuze and Guattari communicate that this smooth sea is also very hard. Fluid models loosen ideas, but they also provide the means to confound or further deterritorialize. When Deleuze and Guattari write in "The Smooth and the Striated" that "smooth spaces are not in themselves liberatory," and caution against believing "that a smooth space will suffice to save us," the water becomes hard not because of the caution expressed but because the caution seemed necessary to express in that moment.[21] As promised, the authors demonstrate, with the translucency of their own intent, that this deterritorializing is reterritorializing, and that the decoding does not imply innocent frictionless passage but, rather, shifting aggressions and adversaries.[22] The philosopher's own score-settling is another necessary piece of information: a trap door from a smooth war to a slushy ocean. Even deterritorializing and destratifying is a competitive aggression. Smooth decodes with a variety of motives, many of which are not liberatory. The smooth sea is also hard.

Capital borrows a smooth maritime repertoire, not to deterritorialize or even to experience elegant frictionless passage. Capital is smooth and elastic to avoid detection or perpetrate a confidence game. Growth proceeds by means of subterfuge. Elasticity appears to offer flexibility, even though the boundaries of the organization remain.

Soft is a clever masquerade of this hard sea, one that uses landscape in all its incarnations as a convenient prop. It is similar to the portrayal of the sea as a regulating system or smooth, free, frictionless medium. Naturalizing the market, *soft* borrows an ethos about penetrable organizations that grow and learn by accepting contradictions. Hybridized into corporate names, it may indicate a company following after a new organizational paradigm—not the corporate hierarchy but an open, fluid, feminized, connected structure. *Soft* executives are enlightened team players. They speak of synergy and feedback, often pretending that this internal regulation of information represents a kind of differentiation. Yet the desire for information is really a desire for optimization, and the illusion of an inclusive disposition masks an exclusive disposition. Recursivity produces an organization with its own steady state, and even its own catastrophes. The goal of *soft* is to devour extrinsic information, remain intact, and avoid contradiction.

Claiming that the opportunistic desires of a nation or private concern reflect the world's true nature is a long-standing strategy. Hugo Grotius's hilarious dissertation *The Freedom of the Seas* (1633) piously and innocently appeals to the world's legal and theological conscience to recognize that the sea, by virtue of its God-given nature, welcomes the Dutch Navy into its waters. The sea is free, and not the exclusive sovereign territory of the Portuguese who have unjustly impinged on the Dutch right to open relations with other countries. Breaking through these barriers, the Dutch eventually assumed the natural state of their freedom, and demonstrated their rights by pirating Portuguese ships in the Straits of Malacca, where contemporary piracy continues to this day.[23]

I've been told, for example, that the cost of transporting tea to England has fallen a hundredfold since the days of sail, and even more in recent years. There are similar efficiencies across the board. But the efficiencies are accompanied by global problems too, including the playing of the poor against the poor and the persistence of huge fleets of dangerous ships, the pollution they cause, the implicit disposability of their crews, and the parallel growth of two particularly resilient pathogens that exist now on the ocean—the first being a modern strain of piracy, and the second its politicized cousin, the maritime form of the new, stateless terrorism.

—William Langewiesche[24]

Plural/Resistant

Beyond the monistic sea or the dialectic between land and sea is another geography of *multiple* seas on land, air, or water—seas that do not naturalize a single epic logic. Worlds and empires shelter and fatten offshore, dropping into protected enclaves, free economic zones, and paper sovereignties long enough to avoid taxes, engage inexpensive labor, or launder an identity. Streamlined logistics and loosened legalities are among the bullet-pointed features of every logistics park and free economic zone in the world. Their segregation from other worlds and other nations helps them to garner power, and shapes them into distended and dominating territories that are constantly expanding and excluding. They are worlds with their own seas.

These new seas and the boundaries between them are arguably some of the most politicized and conflicted places on earth, all laying simultaneous claim to oil-drilling rights or protective zones of security. The United Nations' new Laws of the Sea (1982) thicken the extended and overlapping boundaries at the edges of nations, or in the tangle of archipelagos.[25] These waters are slushy, violent, conflicted, and dangerous, and they are, once again, clogged with traffic.

[see *Park*]

Islands, historically associated with escape, exception, or exemption, are still places of resort, summit, illicit behavior, tax exemption, streamlined paperwork, and cheap labor. Yet, once treated as "the outside," they now only confirm that there is no outside. Archipelagic networks of "offshore" activity may be the primary points between overlapping jurisdictions where laws collide and erupt. Territorial conflicts that have historically focused on landed properties now primarily concern waters and overlapping jurisdictions.[26]

Boundaries between segregated worlds and their segregated seas become more pronounced as they attempt to remain pure and intact. Even when masquerading as soft, they are rarely so elegant or flexible that they can avoid conflict. Even for the nations and worlds that have learned to avoid political constraints, the most highly charged turf wars arise, sometimes even in response to that segregation. A labor law, a global juridical compact, or a better product from another world may release overcharged frictions between worlds that have sheltered for too long in isolated safety.

Empirical politics, that is to say the fact of democracy, is identified with the maritime sovereignty of the lust for possession, which sails the seas doubly threatened by the buffeting of the waves and the brutality of the sailors. The great beast of the populace, the democratic assembly of the imperialist city, can be represented as a trireme of drunken sailors. In order to save politics it must be pulled aground among the shepherds. . . .

The sea smells bad. This is not because of the mud, however. The sea smells of sailors. It smells of democracy.

—Jacques Rancière[27]

Hardt and Negri argue that the repertoire of Empire, smoothly amassing power outside of law, also belongs to "counter-Empire." The perennial comparison between emperors and pirates that characterizes the emperor as merely a pirate on a gigantic scale is fascinating in the context of this Empire/counter-Empire formulation. Contemporary pirates resist or undo the dominating powers of the Empire with the Empire's own tools. Resistance might "ride the wave" while playing the same trick or perpetrating the same masquerade. Introducing the image of a snake as the replacement for Marx's mole, Hardt and Negri, write, "Today's struggles slither silently across these superficial, imperial landscapes."[28] The snake, better than the mole, can navigate the slippery surfaces, identifying a slipstream between entrenched worlds or seas.

In Jacques Rancière's speculations, the sea is a medium of insurgency and democracy. Rancière's sea is not a frictionless space but, rather, a rough space of contention: "It smells of sailors." The sea is capable of enriching and disrupting the landed politics of consensus. Once on shore, political organs dilute the sea's raw democracy, as if secretly wishing for the end of politics or a delivery from the sea's unknowns. Land and sea again appear to be a pair, or two halves of a single world. Yet the site of this contemplation is the shore, the interface between raw democracy and political organization. Wherever that interface exists, there is platform from which to counter what Carl Schmitt called the "shoreless sea" of legal exception.[29] In Rancière's characterization, this slipstream is not a space of least resistance but, rather, a space of traction and contention.

The sea invents or discovers its political context both in its actual terrestrial conditions and in the reveries those conditions inspire. Multiple seas and multiple worlds focus not on recycled information, or on feedback within the domain, but, rather, on the spaces of friction at the edges of segregated logics that introduce extrinsic information. Like shores, these areas of intolerance between worlds sustain and are sustained by error piracy, or the contentions of democracy. As interfaces between worlds, they form a perpetual wilderness with limitless surface area—always newly minted, and often underexplored. However rough they may be, these seas are also spacious, mixing different waters and different political constitutions.

Franchise

Hazards of Architecture could be further aggravated by negative effects resulting from inauspicious qualities of the site, inauspicious slope and shape, inauspicious placement of water bodies as well as other factors. . . .

In many cases, it may be necessary to abandon one's present home and move into a properly designed building with an ideal.

—Sthapatya Vedic Design Principles[1]

Access to this Unified Field brings mastery over Natural Law. . . .

Ideal education—Vedic Education—delivers the fruit of all knowledge: mistake-free, problem-free life—action fully in accord with all the Laws of Nature.

—His Majesty Raja Raam[2]

Ranking among the world's great builders and real estate investors are two species of organization that supposedly possess very different goals: commercial chains or franchises, and spiritual organizations. Yet both are believers of a sort, sharing that common desire of planning prophets to repeat their spatial milieu in strategic locations all over the world. The ideal towns of Roman expansion, European colonial expansion in the New World, or the Laws of the Indies, together with the crafty and orderly real estate formats of America's defecting religious groups, are only more distant echoes of the perennial desires of similar organizations to reinforce their hold on a soul or a market by way of physical territory and spatial imprint. Utopian belief systems love real estate. In the case of Wal-Marts, tabernacles of the Church of Latter-Day Saints, a Japanese cream puff chain called "Beard Papa," Baha'i temples, or an organization from the UK that exports Southern Fried Chicken restaurants (SFC), beliefs and rituals are spatialized with prescriptive planning formats.[3] Reliant on an elaborate syncretic pastiche, both species of real estate product also explore hyperbolic forms of sovereignty and franchise as they colonize a totemic marketplace.[4]

The commercial and the spiritual are provocative in comparison, because they borrow each other's repertoires. Commercial organizations borrow the proselytizing techniques of spiritual organizations, and spiritual organizations borrow from commercial organizations spatial products such as malls and office towers. Taken together, they highlight both the liturgical rituals of spatial products and the territorial ambitions of religious organizations. Ideology, whether about nirvana or coffee, wants to expand into under-marketed or under-spiritualized territories. Both commercial orgmen and spiritual gurus expand, affiliate, and optimize.[5] Both types of organization are able to collect and disburse large amounts of money. Moreover, both use architecture as part of the symbolic capital necessary to colonize time, styles of living, beliefs, or marketing strategies. To increase influence, these must be constantly renewed with new affiliations and psychologized spatial scripts.

Whether commercial or spiritual, these global conquests of space are either overtly or covertly politicized. The all-too-easy McWorld characterizations of these commercial formats and the automatic immunities that accompany spirituality obscure the politics that many such organizations do possess. They are filled with political persuasion for which the organization usually wishes never to be held responsible, insisting on a separation between church and state—lifestyle and politics. Global conquest, whatever its political consequences, is even characterized as a way to maintain the organization's purity or entitlement to sovereignty that is exempt from official consequences.

Among the many chains, franchises, and spiritual organizations that possess territorial ambitions, two—the Maharishi Global Development Fund (MGDF) and Arnold Palmer Golf Management (APGM)—permit a comparison between the dramatic rituals and potent fictions of both brands and gurus.[6] Maharishi Global Development Fund wish to build not only buildings and enclaves but also cities and countries. They have developed spatial products as well as bids for nationhood that seem destined to land them in some of the most politically extreme locations in the world. Arnold Palmer Golf Management operates all around the world, spreading an urbanism of landscape in large increments.[7] The words "Arnold Palmer Golf" and "Transcendental Meditation" are registered trademarks and, as such, are ideologies and practices that are regarded as, among other things, commercial products.[8] The comparison leads naturally to a discussion of other believers, more religious and commercial organizations with ideological and territorial ambitions.

Larry King: *You have no children of your own?*

Maharishi: *That is what a family means—all the children of the world.*

Larry King: *I know, but I'm just asking if you have children from your loins.*

Maharishi: *I am a single person. I'm a Purusha. I'm a—what you call it—sanyasi, if you understand the word. I'm a monk, if you understand it. . . .*

Larry King: *You're a bachelor.*[9]

When Maharishi Mahesh Yogi, the same giggling Yogi that introduced meditation to the Beatles, appeared on Larry King live on May 12, 2002, he was dressed as a holy man, in white robes, and set in a radiating formation of pastel pinks and yellow flowers. Although he appears every day on TV via his own satellite channel, the interview marked his first appearance on mainstream media in twenty-five years. The TV audience was given a primer in the Maharishi's techniques: a secular practice, not an evangelical religion, with some additional paragovernmental and educational functions. Like other Vedanta spiritual organizations, it references the Vedic sciences of ancient India (*Veda* means knowledge), and occasionally comes cloaked in costumes referencing Hinduism, although it makes no direct references to the religion. The five million followers of Transcendental Meditation (TM) in the world believe that it provides as the Maharishi has said, "a means to do what one wants to do in a better way, in a right way, for maximum results."[10]

The occasion of King's interview and pilgrimage to the Maharishi's residence in Vlodrop was the re-release of his book *The Science of Being and Art of Living,* but the Maharishi reported that in the intervening time he had been working on the revival of the Vedic sciences and on "the effect."[11] The "Maharishi effect," as the TM group describes it, is a field of influence radiating from a meditating group that lends to that field harmonious effects. The predictions are quite explicit. If the square root of one percent of the world's population is gathered together to practice the highest forms of meditation (this includes yogic flying, a form of levitation in the lotus position), there should be an "upsurge of harmony and orderliness in society."[12]

This "Maharishi effect" fuels a fundamentally urban and architectural desire to organize the world in specific spatial increments—evenly distributed outposts from which to broadcast "the effect." The TM formula for community plays a role in this attempt at global coverage. Just as meditation is part of the ancient Vedic sciences, and *Ayur Veda,* for instance, is a *Veda* related to herbal treatments, *Sthapatya Veda* is "the most ancient and supreme technology of architecture and planning. Maharishi *Sthapatya Veda* uses precise mathematical formulas, equations, and proportions to design homes and offices in perfect harmony with Natural Law."[13] Adjusting *Vāstu,* or orientation, provides the most significant benefit. For instance, rooms facing east, with bodies of water to the south or east, are most auspicious. Sleeping with the head facing east or south is more auspicious. Kitchens are best placed near entries. One arm of the organization offers consulting services to help design structures as well as evaluate sites. Adjusting orientation affects not only a sense of harmony but an increased business productivity.

The TM organization has rehearsed these principles in a new town called Vedic City near Fairfield, Iowa. There, on flat agricultural land in a region that has been host to over a century of settlements by spiritual organizations, including Mennonites and Quakers, two large domes gather the inhabitants for daily, collective meditation and special events. In fact, in 1984, a gathering of 7,000 yogic flyers in Fairfield was used to determine the percentage of the population necessary to produce the Maharishi effect.[14] Vedic City is developed with houses and office buildings designed according to Sthapatya Vedic principles, and it is also home to the Maharishi University of Management. Houses are small and vaguely neotraditional, and commercial structures are often rendered as bar buildings to maximize auspicious, east-facing real estate. Except for an occasional glint from the kalash, a golden ornament that tops each building and marks its sacred center, the buildings are camouflaged in this prairie with a naked sun. As an intentional community, the town epitomizes the notion of TM as a personal and communal practice whose best hope

3.1 Dreier Building, Maharishi Global Construction. Image courtesy of Maharishi University of Management.

is to offer a sense of well-being.[15] John Hagelin, a Fairfield resident, has run for President of the United States several times as candidate of the TM organization's Natural Law Party, but Fairfield was also an epicenter of support for Dennis Kucinich, the sympathetic underdog in the 2004 presidential election. Kucinich, a congressman from Ohio and a vegan, proposed ideas, such as a Department of Peace, that appealed to Natural Law followers.[16]

Vedic City is, on the one hand, a modest representative of national political interests and templates for community reform. Yet as the center of TM's "Global Country of World Peace," it is also a reflection of the organization's persistent interest in a benign form of global sovereignty. Over the years, various TM shadow governments have been announced by proclamation. The Maharishi created the "World Government for the Age of Enlightenment" (1976), the "Ideal Society Campaign" proposed for 108 countries (1978), the "Master Plan to Create Heaven on Earth" (1988), an "Absolute Theory of Government" (1993), and "Global Administration through Natural Law, with twelve Time Zone Capitals" (1997).[17]

Pursuit of this Maharishi effect has led the $3.3 billion organization to attempt everything from heroic feats of building to the establishment of an independent nation.[18] One plan for the new global government proposed a series of twelve global capitals in each of the time zones, as well as 435 Vedic centers in the United States. Another divided the nation into the congressional districts, while yet another focused on 3,000 of the largest cities around the world, all to achieve the correct distribution of the effect. Some of these global schemes have been beautifully illustrated with one-line books. Pages framed by Hindu-inspired columns pictured colorful world maps divided into time zones, or diagrams of principles of *Sthapatya Veda* that unfold in sequence like a story.[19]

The first architectural expressions of this global initiative received a great deal of attention as not only a capital of the Maharishi's Global Country but as a super-tall skyscraper aspiring to be the tallest in the world. MGDF chose Yamasaki Associates, architects of New York's World Trade Center, to design the tall tower, and sought investing partners for the multibillion-dollar project. The "Peace Tower," as it was sometimes called, resembled a gigantic Hindu temple. Positioned in the twenty-four time zones, these towers would collectively create a global "country" of world peace. The 50,000 TM practitioners living, working, and meditating in the tower would, in theory, broadcast peace to one-twelfth of the world, or one entire time zone. The program cocktail was typical of those currently circulating around the world. In addition to almost a quarter of a million square meters of residential, hotel, and real estate space, the tower was designed to house office and convention space, a calling center, and a university. The total topping one million square meters was to climb forty meters taller than the Petronas Towers.[20]

The MGDF proposed towers in São Paulo, Dallas, and Johannesburg. As each of the projects was canceled, a new one appeared in a different location. The São Paulo tower was to have a sister project called the Transworld Complex, offering conference centers, a resort, a university, a golf course, and even a theme park spread over 150 acres of gardens and waterfalls. By May 2000, the Maharishi's various funds had already purchased 329 acres of land in The Colony, in Plano, Texas, a suburb of Dallas, and applied for zoning changes there.[21] This time, the Federal Aviation Administration canceled the project due to the risk related to heavy air traffic in the area.[22] Plans for the building were canceled in October 2000.[23]

The Peace Tower and the World Trade Towers, both by Minoru Yamasaki, expressed sympathetic sentiments about the power of buildings to inspire collective peace or serenity while also being productive in business. The Maharishi's tall buildings would proliferate just like World Trade Centers, cathedrals of a global trade ethos appearing in locations all around the world. Each in its own way sought separation from the requirements of the state. The TM organization no longer proposes the super-tall tower projects. Especially stunning in light of the FAA's fears concerning the Dallas project, the MGDF was inaugurated on the top floor of New York's World Trade Center in 1997, and had offices there on September 11, 2001.[24]

No one loves and respects the game of golf more than Arnold Palmer. This devotion has been instilled in every employee of the companies that make up the Arnold Palmer Group. It's in every product we make, in every service we offer.[25]

. . . the holes that have tamed the tiger, molded the bear and taught the hawk how to fly.
—Description of Tour 18 golf, a special course design from APGM[26]

For two centuries of westward (and Western) expansion, the grid served as a durable and generous device of speculation, planning and development. With the passing of modernism in the late 1960s, the grid lost its pervasive power, indicted as an emblem of inhumanity and homogeneity. Now, with the rise of golf space, the grid as a neutral tool of planning has been replaced by organic figures of development such as the sand trap and the water hazard. . . . Golf space offers the perfect petri dish for business transaction, a self-reproducing site where tomorrow's resorts are conceived and negotiated today. It grants people the power to venture ever inward—manifest destiny in reverse.
—R. E. Somol[27]

Pride, excellence, character, tradition. Does the golf course reflect its creator? It should.[28]

Arnold Palmer's career as the "king of golf" coincided with golf's expansion from a game for club members to a television sport played everywhere in the world.[29] Palmer's rivalry with Jack Nicklaus, the "golden bear," enhanced this evolving prominence. Today, both Palmer and Nicklaus lend their name to the design and management of golf course communities, leading two different but complementary sects of the golf market. They remain as competitive twins or doubles, enhancing each other by naturalizing the celebrity golf course formula. Arnold Palmer's personality shapes his company's guiding principles, and is ineffably reflected in the course itself. A celebrity endorsement is worth approximately one million dollars per course. In return for the loan of his personality, Arnold Palmer receives eighteen million a year in endorsements and promotions related to his various golf enterprises.[30]

Like any evangelical promoter of spatial products, APGM and other course designers recognize golf as a global real estate phenomenon, an addictive game for developers as much as it is for foursomes of men and women in the afternoon. APGM expands by rescuing foundering golf courses as well as establishing new ones. The larger it gets, the more it is able to handle the steep debt that is incurred by the development of a course and its surrounding property. APGM has designed over two hundred courses in the United States and around the world. Palmer Design courses appear in Japan, Thailand, Korea, China, Taiwan, The Philippines, Guam, Malaysia, Sarawak, Singapore, Indonesia, Ireland, Italy, Germany, Spain, Australia, and Canada. The largest concentrations of courses associated with the Arnold Palmer Golf organization are in Japan and Florida.[31]

Golf developers maximize profits by manipulating not only business strategies but also the parameters of the game itself—a game that seems to be infinitely stretchy and adjustable. The pieces of that game include not only golf balls and fairways, but also houses, clubs, resorts, and roadways, all of which thrive on four-hour periods and a series of tee times throughout the day. Yet the length of play can be altered, as can the physical length of the course. There are executive courses, and courses made up only of par three holes. There are nighttime courses with lighting and altered durations. Cayman golf even adjusts the game by manipulating the interior of the ball to shorten its trajectory. Golf also insinuates itself into building interiors and multistory indoor driving ranges.[32] Each manipulation of the game has a complementary effect on the arrangement of the surrounding acreage for resorts, housing, and edge-city developments. These must offset the financial risk of buying large amounts of land. Course designs are evaluated in terms of acreage and frontage for lot sales. Single fairways use more land, but provide more frontage than double fairways. Core courses, a knot of fairways, provide the least amount of frontage, but are the most suitable for courses that host televised tournaments with aerial views. Small courses facilitate profits in more expensive or smaller urban parcels.

While in Asia and elsewhere the golf course can be a feature of an urban park, in America the surface area of a golf course is homesteading territory that is carefully timed and phased. New housing developments bask in the country club aura. A giganticized version of the Radburn superblock has been put to use to generate large arterials with discrete cul-de-sac pods of development. Unlike the grid that requires more even, comprehensive development, these cul-de-sacs can be phased as the arterial grows. The golf course is gradually surrounded with lots that continue to grow in value, thus quickly relieving the large debt incurred by land purchases. APGM collects statistics about the power of golf to add value to real estate. They use a Harvard Business School study to demonstrate that branded courses and golf products generate a premium of up to 20 percent on the value of surrounding real estate. The company can also demonstrate that potential homeowners are more responsive to advertisements for branded golf communities.[33] Companies like Arnold Palmer Golf also operate within the durations and specialized spaces of entertainment. Temporal management of revenues continues into the daily operations and efficient scheduling of tee times and turnover. Many of these management processes have been automated with special software like LinksTime.com or Liquidgolf.com to choreography tee times and *après*-golf entertainments.[34]

We banned smoking before it became a national trend. We ask our partners to refrain from using perfume or cologne. We won't sell chemically flavored coffee beans. We won't sell soup, sliced pastrami, or cooked food. We want you to smell coffee only. . . .

The sounds that fill our stores also contribute to the brand image . . . music is only one element of what you hear. After you place your order, you'll usually hear the cashier call out the name of your drink and then hear it echoed back by the barista. The hiss of the espresso machine, the clunk-clunk as the barista knocks the coffee grounds out of the filter, the bubbling of the milk steaming in a metal pitcher, and, at the bean counter, the swish of the metal scoop shoveling out a half-pound of beans, the clatter as they hit the scale—for our customers, these are all familiar, comforting sounds.

—Description of Starbucks interior scripting[35]

Name a major player in men's apparel, and chances are he's got a line of sportswear designed for, or at least "inspired by," golf.[36]

Given the similarity between nurturing brands and nurturing beliefs, the Maharishi and Arnold Palmer, in their respective organizations, play very similar roles in reinforcing duty to a cultural bond. In addition to offering charismatic leaders, every aspect of a spatial format, from aromas to colors, costumes, and sentiments, is scripted. The theater, strictly choreographed and ritualized, is quite elaborate. The logistical no less than the emotional terms for space have a degree of fictional content, faith, or belief.

Just as the Maharishi has his own television channel, so Arnold Palmer, as a co-founder of the Golf Channel, quickly and fortuitously discovered the territories of television that congeal a market and an audience.[37] Many contemporary spatial products have an analogous space on TV that helps them to conquer not only time frames and geographic territory, but also states of consciousness. Both MGDF and APGM sponsor ritualized experiences not only in person but also on television—rituals that are generally protracted, quiet, and meditative, with the occasional celebratory burst of activity. TM calls for at least one session of daily meditation, although it provides several ambient environments on TV each day. Golf, too, commands a large radiating landscape of concentration, even meditation. It requires the introspective rehearsal of extremely subtle modulations of balance, vision, and strength that can be experienced corporeally but also vicariously in the meditative, whispered environment of the television golf tournament.

When the aging Maharishi named his successor, there was a coronation of sorts, one that was heavily reliant on costumes, rituals, and architectural décor adorned with various vegetal or architectural patterns in pastel polychromy. In 2001, the MIT-trained Tony Nader was crowned "First Sovereign Ruler of the Global Country of World Peace."[38] Touted as the "world's foremost neuroscientist," Nader posed for coronation pictures legs akimbo, on an oversized scale that balanced against his weight in gold. The gold was his reward for having made a "historic discovery" that human brain physiology corresponds to and is capable of acquiring a total knowledge of the universe.[39] He often appears in ceremonies and within the web pages wearing a crown and white robes, attended by surroundings of floral pastel and gold. On October 17, 2000, he structured his government into forty ministries corresponding to "the forty values of Veda." In his first decree as king, His Majesty Raja Raam set out the currency of the Global Country of World Peace. One Raam is equal to ten US dollars. The Raam has been in circulation in Vlodorp.[40]

Similarly, golf sponsors a line of succession as a game played between fathers and sons breathing deeply in the open. APGM creates an emotional, genteel form of family urbanism around the traditions of the golf game. It must establish a company patina with a misty legend. Players walk the greens, merging with advertisements for banks and insurance companies. Often commended for their courage, they embody an athletic or paternal spirit that must go on despite dangers and risks. The rewards must involve more than a return on their investment. The trappings of Arnold Palmer Golf are the rewards that the privileged give to themselves for bearing the responsibilities of leading a privileged life. In this way they produce an urbanism similar to that of most evangelical orgmen. Like the Raam, celebrity endorsement is legal tender within the organization, associated with a quantifiable enhancement profits. The Jack Nicklaus organization, with an even closer match, offers its own Nicklaus credit card.[41]

In millions of interiors, golf on the TV mixes with the somnambulant sounds of air conditioners, tinkling ice, and grass being watered or mowed. APGM leaders have pride, integrity, and "fighting heart." Costumes rely on a very specific short-sleeved silhouette, and they must be garments fabricated as athletic gear with special performance characteristics. Endorsements of Ford Motor Company or Nike are advertised on the golfer's clothing and gear. Armani, Hugo Boss, Tommy Hilfiger, and Ralph Lauren have all designed golf apparel.[42] Additional crests and emblems appear on special vestments, like the jackets or hats that signal membership in a club or brotherhood of champions.

Association with the Maharishi or Arnold Palmer could be construed to be a distended version of "commodity fetishism" and its "accidental" values.[43] Yet values attached to the Maharishi or Arnold Palmer are also easily associated with the irrational activities of symbolic capital. Like Pierre Bourdieu's example of the extra yoke of oxen bought *after* the harvest to make a family appear prosperous, these gurus, without exertion, miraculously and irrationally produce value.[44] The logistical and the liturgical, in equal proportions, can be quantified and accompanied by currency, credit cards, and lending points. The product does not become something almost mystical because a profit motive separates it from use value. It begins with an almost mystical belief that is quickly commodified.

Baby Busters claim to be the most "authentic" in relationships yet they are more likely than any other generational segment to engage in sex outside of marriage, less likely to devote time to serving others, and the least values-driven . . . "downscale" people are less likely to discuss their feelings, values and beliefs with others, and are more open to advice from non-traditional spiritual sources.

—Market research for spiritual organizations[45]

We had been warned that, culturally, the Japanese refuse to carry to-go food or beverages on the street. Yet many customers were walking out the door proudly carrying their Starbucks cups with the logo showing. I stood there watching with Howard Behar, architect of our international expansion. He turned to me with tears in his eyes.
—Howard Schultz, chairman of Starbucks[46]

Phase I will feature the world's only "levitating" building—a 42-ton structure that appears to float 15 feet above a lake. Guests will ride flying chariots that shrink and dive into the molecular structure of a rose. They will plunge down a swirling golden whirlpool and emerge in a crystal city miles within the earth. The world's greatest magic show will prove that nothing is impossible.
—Description of proposed Vedaland amusement park[47]

Commercial organizations and spiritual organizations deploy similar business strategies for survival and success. Both APGM and MGDF inherit from companies like Wal-Mart a reliance on the ability to optimize data with tracking software and special logistics. Religious organizations may consciously borrow the same business practices, even marketing their organization not only to increase the flock but also to understand how religious practices compare with popular commercial activities and other cultural preoccupations. Many have their own marketing gurus to help them design the influence of a congregation or spiritual grouping. They may tabulate, for instance, tithing patterns, "faith trends," or "technology usage of born-again Christians."[48]

Both the Church of Latter-Day Saints and the Unification Church reinforce the long-standing copresence of spiritualism and business. The LDS organization is worth billions of dollars, and would rank among the Fortune 500 companies. It has built temples in 245 countries and 300 cities. Indeed, 88 of the 112 revelations delivered to Joseph Smith, nineteenth-century spiritual leader of the Church, were related to the Church finances.[49] The Mormons also established their own independent state in Utah, and considered their various outposts around the world to constitute the sovereign state of Zion. Similarly, the Unification Church, often referred to as "the Moonies," has a multibillion-dollar global business in shipping, automobiles, arms, and communication. [see *DPRK*]

In addition to sharing business strategies, commercial and spiritual organizations have also occasionally used precisely the same spatial formats and marketing techniques. One unusual example was the TM organization's plan for Vedaland, a theme park to be designed in collaboration with the late magician Doug Henning, who died in February 2000. The original idea, as Henning described it in *Life Magazine* in 1990, was to provide a park for which "the themes of the attraction will be knowledge, enlightenment and entertainment."[50] Initially the theme park was to be located in Florida, on 450 acres near Walt Disney World, at a cost of one billion dollars.[51] Developing the concept further, without Henning, the International Maharishi Vedaland board was, as of summer 2001, making plans for a scaled-down version near Niagara Falls in Canada that never materialized.[52] The park was to be the world's only levitating building, presumably achieved by its reflection in a body of water.

Another "Vedanata" organization, focusing on practical, secularized versions of the Hindu Vedas, Art of Living (AOL), also deploys spectacular techniques seemingly borrowed from the entertainment industry. AOL's leader, Sri Sri Ravi Shankar (TM's Jack Nicklaus of sorts), was an early follower of Maharishi Mahesh Yogi who comes complete with a beatific autobiography. Even as a child, he could be "discovered chanting the shlokas of the Bhagavad Gita." His followers write that, in adulthood, "Joy, love, playfulness, poetry, deep wisdom and a twinkle of mischief have all come together in the person of Sri Sri Ravi Shankar."[53] The AOL meditation hall of their ashram near Bangalore, for instance, is a large structure with a computer-programmed lighting show that is visible for miles.[54] Nevertheless, Art of Living's focus is slightly different from that of the TM organization. It claims to be one of the largest NGOs in the world, working in over 140 countries to provide relief and aid to the poor.[55]

After houses of worship or meditation, perhaps the most striking development format shared by many spiritual organizations is the university. The Maharishi's organization has numerous universities. Soka Gakkai, a Buddhist lay group founded in 1930, has recently built Soka University of America in Aliso Viejo, California, a private liberal arts college. Designed by Hardy Holzman Pfeiffer, it was intended to resemble a Mediterranean hill town.[56] Ave Maria University, a Catholic college in Florida, will be built with funding from the billionaire who founded Domino's Pizza.[57]

Megachurches, a widespread phenomenon in America, have begun to organize their ministry with spatial products like malls, television studios, food courts, and fitness centers in large enclosed complexes. There are hundreds of megachurches in the United States, serving 150 denominations. Texas and California are each home to over a hundred megachurches. Some—like the Willow Creek Community Church, the Community Church of Joy, or the Lakewood Church—are complexes in which the congregation lives, shops, exercises, and dines. They may have a gym, a McDonald's, or a rock-climbing wall. They are active seven days a week, with a charismatic leader and a very large congregation engaged in many events devoted to both worship and social interaction. The Lakewood Church, like many megachurches, also televises in a massive studio sanctuary, which features all the flags of the world around a large pulpit stage. Megachurch books and CDs are often distributed by retailers like Wal-Mart and Costco.[58]

Just as spiritual organizations have adopted commercial business strategies, so New Age CEOs have likewise adopted techniques associated with self-help and spirituality. They have replaced the word "monopoly" with "family," "sharing" intelligence by entering into massive affiliations that numb the competition. Many of the companies want their spatial brand to mean everything, to encompass an approach to living, often by affiliation with other spatial products. Not only more divisions, but also more products come into the constellation, and more potential competitors are converts to the fold. Associations with infrastructure, advertising, entertainment, or celebrities provide flattering accoutrements to serve a company that no longer wants to look omnifunctional and self-sufficient. This often means, however, that the constellation of spatial products is simply going through another cycle of expansion, incorporation, and risk-spreading. These affiliations enhance the brands, extend contact time, or expand the market by associating with other similar companies. An anticompetition stance masquerades as an antimonopoly stance. In addition to handling real estate, merchandising and advertising divisions, retailers often find themselves actually adopting the methods of their affiliates to form increasingly hybridized products and services. Chains, franchises, and brands affiliate, timing their offerings to deliver and disgorge audience members from meals to movies to shopping, styling and coordinating all of life's accoutrements from evening dresses to potting soil.

While APGM's primary affiliation is with its celebrity, like any contemporary commercial organization (or spiritual organization) it exists as a "family" of partnerships stretching into several different areas of commerce, including TV tournaments and products bearing the celebrity name. The affiliated companies include Palmer Course Design Company, Arnold Palmer Golf Academy, the University Clubs of America, Arnold Palmer Golf Tournament Services, Arnold Palmer Enterprises (licensing and endorsements), and Tour 18 Golf. Through the Golf Channel, APGM is associated with televised tournaments like the Bob Hope Chrysler Classic.[59] APGM managers have grasped every possible opportunity to merchandise golf products and accessories bearing the Arnold Palmer name, including footwear, clothing, and even self-help programs.[60] Jack Nicklaus's global company, run by father, sons, and sons-in-law, has a number of affiliations, including golf academies, clothing and equipment, art and memorabilia, books and Golden Bear Realty.[61]

Even commercial organizations without a totemic leader like Arnold Palmer, Maharishi Mahesh Yoga, or Martha Stewart may develop psychological profiles for their company. Wardrobes, architecture, or an inevitable autobiography of the CEO are crafted into self-reflexive promotional devices. This psychology then extends to a set of ambient urban protocols and narratives conducive to consumption. In the typical CEO profile, information is drawn into one of several hackneyed plot lines chronicling an unlikely ascent to power based on a simple dream to sell at a discount to "just plain folks" in rural areas, or to sell a "hand-made" cup of coffee with feeling and heart.

Wal-Mart's leader, Sam Walton, now deceased, was a mascot of sorts for the company, leading cheers like the one that begins "Give me a W, Give me an A," or the one that ends "so help me Sam." He inspired the kind of company loyalty seen, for instance, in the employee's willingness to procure pens from conferences to save money.[63]

Meanwhile Wal-Mart, no longer a suburban legend, has been naturalized as a global force. The company is China's fifth-largest trading partner, and it has expanded into Argentina, Brazil, Canada, China, Germany, Mexico, Puerto Rico, and South Korea. Wal-Mart has released a statement to the effect that "The United States has only 4.5 percent of the world's population, so the way we see it, that leaves most of the world as potential Wal-Mart customers."[64]

Although it was voted down, Wal-Mart has also tested its sovereignty by attempting to legislate its own jurisdictional area in Inglewood, California. The so-called "Wal-Mart, California" would be exempt from local laws that would conflict with Wal-Mart's development protocols.[65]

Starbucks chairman Howard Schultz wrote a psychologized and soul-searching autobiographical account of the company's development, *Pour Your Heart into It,* that follows Clintonesque plot lines. Schultz makes mistakes. He retreats to the wilderness. He comes back and asks for forgiveness. After his own father dies, he is mentored by other former executives of gigantic companies. He cries with his employees, and gives them dental coverage. He needs to reach everyone, one cup at a time. Shultz is a righteous leader with an ex-hippy-entrepreneurial ethic, prepared to promote new myths about authenticity. Situated perfectly between the neotraditional boomers and the younger hipsters, he is not like those big chains: McDonald's and Wal-Mart. Detractors hurt his feelings, but the mass conversion to drinking his coffee and its mystique fills him with a wistful pride. Starbucks, the cloying "new urbanists" of the American hypermarket, generate their own form of urbanism through stores so numerous and repetitive that they cannibalize each other, or operate like TV commercials. With the chain sometimes expanding by one store a day, there will eventually be more Starbucks in Asia than in North America. Starbucks will be the new Coke, and the stores will be the new "third place" or "front porch."[66]

Today, Maharishi University of Management celebrates the dawn of a New World Order of Peace, as demonstrated by the invincibility of President Fidel Castro of Cuba, the freedom of President Robert Mugabe of Zimbabwe, the Divine Rulership of President Abdurrahman Wahid of Indonesia, and the casting off of corrupt democracy by President Robert Guei of the Ivory Coast.[67]

Israel is a child of America. I have forgotten about Israel because when people are murderers, who can bother about them? All that is happening in Israel is the doing of America. Wherever there is destruction, it's the doing of America. For the sake of politeness, one may not say that, but those are my thoughts.

—Maharishi Mahesh Yogi[68]

The purpose of the Parliaments of World Peace is not to compete with, or replace, the current functions of government, whose primary focus has been coping with the nation's critical problems. . . . The purpose of the Parliaments of World Peace will be to prevent problems from arising. We will make the administration of every nation simple.

—Dr. John Hagelin, "Minister of Science and Technology" in the "Global Country"[69]

The MGDF's attempt to identify and control the world's trouble spots has entangled the organization in several political misadventures. At one time, the Maharishi regularly took stands concerning global leaders or forecast political trends. In 1978, armed with the "scientifically" verified numbers required to make the earth "invincible," the Maharishi's "World Peace Project" dispatched 1,400 TM experts to Nicaragua, Lebanon, Iran, Cambodia, Zimbabwe, the Middle East, and Iran.[70] According to predictions, the "effect" would reduce crime, war fatalities, regional conflict, and terrorism, while improving foreign relations.[71] In the late 1980s the TM group monitored crime rate, occurrence of fires, traffic accidents, and rises in the stock market in Israel to find a correspondence between meditation and improvements in each of these indices. They even published their findings in the *Journal of Conflict Resolution.*[72] In 1994, President Joaquim Alberto Chissano of Mozambique began ordering his military and police to meditate for twenty minutes each day. While initially reported as a success, the plan was discontinued for "administrative reasons."[73]

As part of the effort to influence global politics, the TM organization also made several attempts to establish a sovereign nation. In 2001, the organization targeted 3,500 hectares (8,645 acres) of space within the South American country of Suriname. The organization planned to lease the land for two hundred years in exchange for $1.3 billion dollars' worth of investment and ten thousand jobs. It would establish an agricultural community there as well as a central bank, with the new Raam currency.[74] On June 23, 2002, TM's Global Country of World Peace announced the establishment of a state-within-a state called Rika Shanti Rashtra among the BriBri people of the Talamanca Indian reserve in Costa Rica. One of the members of the tribe, Epe De Awapa Lisandro, was named king. The TM group offered the tribe $250 dollars a month per family, a "trouble-free" administration, and investment in organically grown products that, together with Indian crafts, would be marketed under the Global Country label. Perhaps not sufficiently tempted by the offer,

Costa Rica's President Pacheco reportedly asked the Global Country adherents, including the prime minister of the Global Country of World Peace, Emmanuel Schiffgens, to leave on July 19, 2002.[75]

In a broadcast on July 10, 2002, the Maharishi's organization announced that it would stop trying to persuade world leaders to adopt its policies, and attempt instead to pursue another component of the Global Country of World Peace: its Peace Palaces. According to the plan, the Peace Palaces, planned for 3,000 of the world's largest cities, would be placed in prominent locations, controlling some agricultural land that is either adjacent or nearby. Some renderings of the Peace Palace resemble early American primitive paintings of rural communities, many of which were also based on development guidelines that extended into the spiritual realm. The simple isometric drawings show long white bar buildings, not unlike those that have been developed in the flat farmland of Vedic City in Iowa. A typical Peace Palace would organize 6,300 square meters (almost 68,000 square feet) of building and 1,500 hectares (3,750 acres) of agricultural land. Ten wealthy individuals, the "distinguished founders," would purchase land and finance improvements. The start-up investment of almost $4 million, including the expenses of the peacekeeping experts who would be farming and marketing the organic crops, would begin to be repaid within the first three years, after the first harvest. Surplus profits could be shared among the initial sponsors and managing directors.[76] Currently there are plans to build Peace Palaces in Canada, the USA, and Australia.[77] The Los Angeles site drew David Lynch, Laura Dern, and Heather Graham to an opening celebration.[78]

Having worked internationally in Japan, Thailand, Korea, China, Taiwan, The Philippines, Guam, Malaysia, Indonesia, Ireland, Italy, Germany, Spain, Australia, Venezuela, Canada, Costa Rica, Portugal, Puerto Rico, Venezuela and India, Palmer Course Design can provide its clients with unsurpassed knowledge and products specific to their needs with a sensitivity to cultural and political differences.[79]

The Chinese have a hunger for the Western lifestyle and golf is a game where you must be in the privileged class to play. . . . Like people who drive Mercedes Benz or BMWs, you have "arrived" in society if you play golf.[80]

The Arnold Palmer organization designed the first golf course in China in 1984: Chung Shan in Guandong Province. In twenty years, over a million Chinese have taken up golf, and in China the political and environmental problems associated with the game in the West are exacerbated. Golf is an economic indicator, tied to growth, hierarchies of wealth, and landownership issues.[81] Requiring so much land, golf is indexed in relation to grain shortages and desertification in China.[82] It has also been a contentious and empowering issue for farmers, whose complaints about losing land to golf developers without adequate compensation have gotten the attention of the central government as well as promises of compensation. The Ministry of Land and Resources, in some newspaper reports, has targeted golf in its concerns about land abuse, claiming to have approved only a fraction of the courses in China.[83]

Moreover, golf, like World Trade Centers, appears in free trade zones and oil fields, port and other enclave forms. A massive Jack Nicklaus-designed complex of ten golf courses and communities, Mission Hills, has also appeared near the port and free trade zones of Shenzhen.[84] Golf courses accompany most American military installations in the South Seas or the Arabian Peninsula. The horizontal golf landscape joins and, in some cases, replaces the high-rise silhouette of a Hilton hotel as a symbol of aspirations to Western culture. A licensed Arnold Palmer T-shirt appeared in a duty-free shop on the southern edge of the Korean DMZ, as if signaling, as does the Maharishi, that the game of golf is poised as peacemaker on the edge of a belligerent country.[85]

Golf first appears to be a gymnastic version of diplomatic protocols. Its association with landscape, and so with tranquility, has even sponsored the ironic speculation that it appears with greatest frequency not in belligerent countries but in stable, peace-loving ones.[86] Sporting events are the tools of diplomacy, but golf is the sport that the diplomats themselves play. Especially on American soil, foreign leaders are expected to be able to summit in special confines of the golf course.[87] The World Golf Village in St. Augustine, Florida, is further evidence of golf's self-portrayal as a global unifying force. Approached via the International Golf Parkway, the World Golf Village grows radially from a central circular lake within which islands are shaped like the edges of North and South American continents. The town even conjoins the rival twins, Arnold Palmer and Jack Nicklaus, in a single course called the "King and Bear."[88] Yet Osama bin Laden reinforced a broader public opinion about

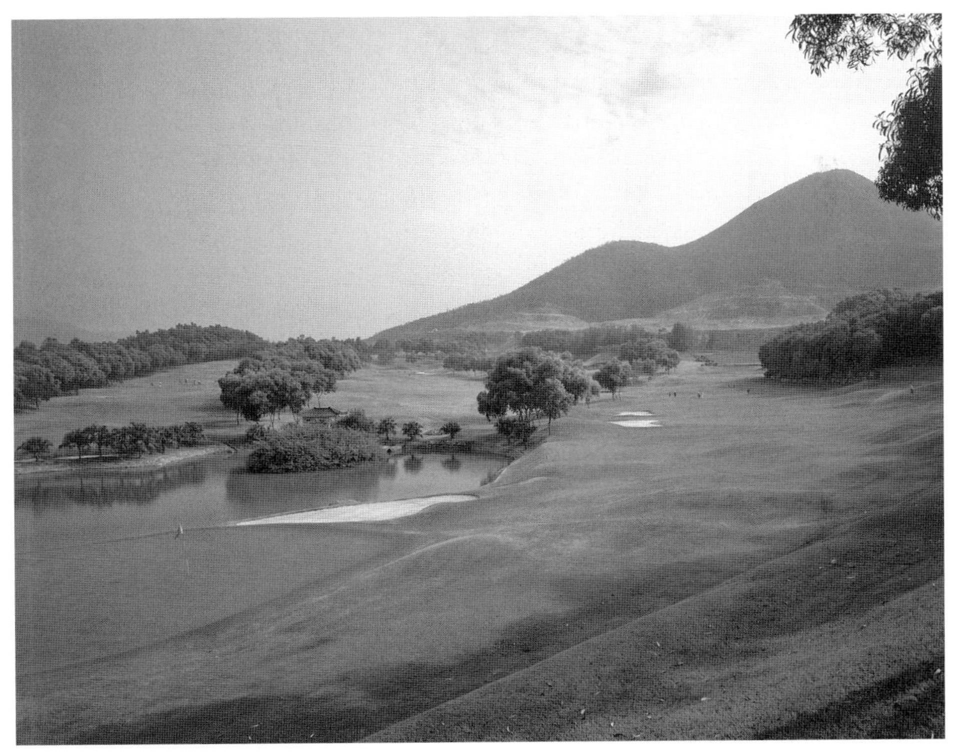

3.2 Palmer Design's first golf course in China: Chung Shan Hot Spring Golf Club, Zhongshan City, Guangdong Province. Image courtesy of Palmer Design.

3.3 Aerial view of World Golf Village in St. Augustine, Florida. Image courtesy of World Golf Village Hall of Fame.

golf as a game associated with politics when he included in one of his training sessions the assassination ambush of a golf tournament for global leaders.[89]

To combat the scourge of golf, the Global Anti-Golf Movement was founded in 1993 by Japanese market gardener Gen Morita after he discovered that his crops were contaminated by chemicals from the water draining off a nearby golf course. GAGM has beeen observing a "World No Golf Day" since the 1990s.[90]

The most important technique for both APGM and MGDF in their pursuits of real estate, political influence, and spiritual persuasion is the maintenance of a partial story, the brand amnesically refreshed. In the case of both TM and golf, a generational line of succession is part of this refreshment. Both organizations make stories, accompanied by cash deals. The fictional content of the story is essential to the organization's transcendent success. Multiple masquerades strengthen it, making it both more elusive and more pervasive. The ambivalent status of these organizations in terms of taxes or international jurisdiction protects them from most reprisals. The Maharishi's various programs are often replaced before they reach fruition. For instance, the global capital, or the center in which the Peace Parliaments are to be convened, remains unclear. Vedic City is certainly one global center in some readings of the literature. Other readings would suggest that the global capital is to be on the banks of the Ganges, where 10,000 (the number varies from 10,000 to 40,000) Vedic pandits would reside.[91] Nevertheless, no explanations about an alteration of plans accompany any of these changes—just a new installment in the story, and a rearrangement of the statistics, with a few numbers changed. Each new scheme is usually just a few billionaires away from spiritual perfection and world peace.

In this mixture of commodity fetishism and symbolic capital, the enhancements to products are continually removed from associations with labor or rational business techniques. Yet as branding develops techniques for quantifying ineffable beliefs and rituals, symbolic capital becomes more than auxiliary insurance to the workings of material capital, more than a psalm dropped at the altar. Beliefs, associations, and rituals become the material of capitalist exchange—sometimes the more ephemeral the better. These fabrications are at the heart of production. If the strategies of both believers and cheaters are successful, because one presents only the tautology of belief and the other presents a proliferation of stories, the mutual mimicry between spiritual and commercial organizations achieves the best of both strategies.

Both the TM and Palmer organizations share a gently unrelenting political disposition. One of the TM logos pictures a map of the world over which the Maharishi's head hovers, and from his head spotlights of satellite TV beam down to a below. Golden starbursts surround this galaxy. Arnold Palmer Golf similarly features Arnold Palmer's face expressing both introspective concentration and a scan of the horizon. He is surrounded by a timeless green landscape that spans generations, and is covered with patches of saturated sun and shade. In this ephemeral space of meditation and afternoon walks, cohesion relies on fiction camouflaged into a broader landscape of persuasion in which all things, however unrelated or unfinished, might be construed to be progressive steps toward innocence and perfection.

Offshore

Kish was barren and deserted before Mr. Sabet started this place. Our religion favors pleasure and entertainment as long as it is not provocative. Plus, he has created jobs, and tourists are bringing money to the island. There is nothing un-Islamic about that.

—Religious leader in Kish[92]

Islands are ideal sites for the TM organization's aspirations toward nationhood. The MGDF offered Tuvalu, a collection of coral atolls in Oceania, two million dollars annually in exchange for the right to make the island a TM state. The offer was rejected.[93] The TM organization also offered the island of Rota in the Mariana Islands a similar arrangement: an investment of over a billion dollars, gardens, and a university if it would secede from the rest of the islands and become a sovereign nation. The Global Country of World Peace held its parliament on the island, which it called the "Capital of the Global Country of World Peace," in March 2002, but by April 2002 Rota had decided that it would remain within the Commonwealth of the Northern Mariana Islands, and maintain its association with the United States.[94]

The island of Kish, off the coast of Iran, is becoming increasingly attractive for its loosening of Islamic rules of conduct, including headscarves, touching between couples, and the consumption of alcohol. Some of those Iranians who might have vacationed in Dubai are now vacationing in Kish. While the beaches are segregated, couples mix in jet-ski or speedboat rides. They shop in malls, and sneak liquor into their hotel rooms after all-night entertainments. There is even prostitution on the island. A developer of one of the island's Grand Dariush hotels, Hossein Sabet, also owns hotels on the Canary Islands. The dramatically lit hotels feature gigantic marble halls and massive Persian statuary. Nearby resort programs include an aquarium, an amusement park, and a dolphinarium.[95] Sometimes called "Kish free zone," the island permits offshore banking and supports business, trade, and tourism.[96] While citizens of most countries of the world do not require a visa for entry, Israeli citizens are not permitted on the island.

Similarly Dubai has been designed to provide a largely secular environment for its many tourists and businessmen. The United Arab

Emirates is already an offshore island of sorts for the entire world, and the capital and headquarters of all global offshore activity—from cloning experiments to data storage to an outpost of America's homeland security.

Since 1999, it has also begun to build island formations that are so large that they will be visible from space. Promoted as the eighth wonder of the world, one of these formations, The Palms, actually takes the form of date palms in silhouette. Each of the fronds emanates from a trunk of entertainment and resort buildings and extends out into the water like a peninsular cul-de-sac, adding in all over 120 kilometers of expensive coastline. Encircling the entire formation of fronds is an outer breakwater. In this engineering feat, each of the shapes is made by compacted sand and rock dropped precisely from boats, while divers conduct the necessary underwater structural and environmental work. Houses are townhouse mansions similar to those that might be sold in North Dallas, Texas. Tourists and Western expatriates populate the advertisements.[97]

Another island formation, The World, using a similar engineering technique, creates an archipelago that takes the shape of the world's continents. On these islands, owners from anywhere in the world may create anything from a private compound to a resort. Some will mimic the glamorous global locations to which they correspond geographically. The World also advertises complete privacy and safety for its offshore owners and tenants by providing a small fleet of security boats charged to continuously troll the waters between islands.[98]

Park

*Korea Container Terminal Authority will make every effort possible to achieve the goal of Korea becoming the most wealthy logistics nation in the new millennium maritime era. Looking forward to readers' bundless [*sic*] love, concern and unsparing lashing and encouragements to us.*

—Kim Kwang-Soo, President, Korea Container Terminal Authority[1]

In the imagination, e-mail and airmail come to bracket the totality of global movement, with the airplane taking care of everything that is heavy. Thus the proliferation of air-courier companies and mail-order catalogues serving the professional, domestic, and leisure needs of the managerial and intellectual classes does nothing to bring consciousness down to earth, or to turn it in the direction of the sea, the forgotten space.

—Allan Sekula[2]

The sea, no longer the peripheral territory of the state, now carries over 95 percent of the world's freight, and sloshes up against a gigantic new form of global city—the logistics city.[3] The now-familiar container, filled with flip-flops, panties, animals, tangerines, and microelectronics, is the germ of a surprisingly excessive urbanism. "Parks," orgman patois for campuses or headquarters, and "distriparks" are the aggregate units of this new global conurbation—often automated enclaves that sort and redistribute the contents of containers for e-commerce. Global trade involves not simply the control of virtual packets of information, but also the movement of enormous amounts of material between port installations and the logistical fields that form around them. Whatever the flicker of media persuasions, or the instant transfers of virtual wealth, parks are the materializations of digital capital that reside on the network side of the computer screen. They are the back lots of heavy manufacturing that thrive in the slippery space between national jurisdictions.

From New York to São Paulo to Tokyo, vertical circulation generated the skyscraper urbanism of the most familiar form of global city, the global city as financial center. From Singapore to Rotterdam to Hong Kong, automated sorting devices organize a horizontal global city, the global city as logistics center. These automated devices, necessary for the seamless and increasingly efficient movement of goods, conflate the long-standing aspirations of cars, elevators, and rapid transit to achieve omnidirectional movement. Automated guided vehicles (AGVs), matured in the military, are now the devices of peacetime logistics, currently deployed in what the industry calls "materials handling." Throughout their history, these conveyance germs have been components of various futurologies with different political dispositions. While most of these future projections typically intone utopian scripts of frictionless passage and perfect responsiveness, most actually arrive with their own forms of friction, congestion, and failure.

The world's top ports—Hong Kong, Singapore, Pusan, Kaohsiung, Rotterdam, Shanghai, Los Angeles, Long Beach, Hamburg, and Antwerp—continue to vie for top rank.[4] Rotterdam is forty square miles in area. Hamburg is twenty-eight square miles. Conurbations of free economic zones (FEZs) in China and Russia spread over hundreds of square kilometers.[5] Port conglomerates such as Singapore's PSA, the United Kingdom's P & O, Hong Kong's Hutchison Port Holdings, and Europe's ECT are reminiscent of the mercantile companies of another time as they develop multiple high-tech installations all over the world.[6] Megaships that populate these ports have, in recent years, gone from carrying 6,500 TEUs (twenty-foot-equivalent units, or the equivalent of a 20-foot-by-8-foot-by-8.5-foot container) to carrying 9,000. As they increase in capacity (some are over one thousand feet long), they must also be unloaded even more quickly.[7]

Distriparks cluster not only around seaports but inland next to airports, free trade zones, or UPS/FedEx hubs. They may attract not only warehouse space but intelligent office space, export processing centers, IT campuses, calling centers, conference/exhibition centers, and other programs. The Taisugar Kaohsiung Logistics Park, Tsurugashima City near Tokyo, the Airport Logistics Park serving Singapore, Schiphol's Y-town, or any number of formations from China to South America have been planned around the park model.[8] AllianceTexas, just north of Fort Worth, spreads an airport, intermodal hub, and warehouse parks over sixty-five square miles.[9] Transpark in southern North Carolina is over 15,000 acres, and its developers are considering additional parks in Thailand, The Philippines, and Germany.[10]

The logistics city has done everything it can to remain undetected by and independent of any political jurisdiction. It is not sited in its locality but, rather, positioned within a global network of similar enclaves serviced by autonomous infrastructure.[11] The city typically streamlines customs and lifts taxes in special economic zones (SEZs), or export processing zones, even trading on these loopholes and benefits transnationally to, for instance, launder the identity of a product, or employ cheap labor. Although they are spaces of exemption, the world's major inland and oceangoing ports are also spaces of piracy, refugees, tax sheltering, and labor exploitation. Moreover, they have now also become the locus of global anxieties about security. Consequently, despite all attempts at immunity, the logistics city is a powerful global entity, in the crosshairs of political conflict.

We have now moved beyond the simplistic arguments between, on the one hand, a "Silicon Valley" replica and on the other, a financial centre. Instead there has now emerged, we believe, a consensus that Hong Kong should position itself as the world-class city of Asia by, inter alia, making better and more sophisticated use of technology. The latter should not be developed for its own sake but as an important ingredient in the integral development of Hong Kong as a world city. . . .

If all the above developments are put together, we believe a strong case can be made of developing Hong Kong into the world's leading logistic hub of a global scale.[12]

On the main floor the mechanical tedium is relieved in three ways: in the build-up of single pallets, with workers arranging dozens of small packages trimly in an eight-by-ten-foot-square load . . . by the loading of oddly shaped or remarkable objects—a matched set of four, dark blue Porsche 911s, a complete prefabricated California ranch-style house; and by the sheer variety of goods—bins of chilled horsemeat, Persian carpets, diplomatic mail bound in sisal twine and sealed with red wax, bear testicles, museum art exhibits, cases of explosives.[13]

Cultural addictions are found not only in intoxicating and liberatory landscapes, but also in the environments of the compulsive workaholic. The urban addictions of the logistics city are associated with obsessional stacking and sorting behaviors. This, in turn, fuels the tabulation of tonnage, berth length, and throughput that the port can handle. Commodity chains undercut the competition by searching the world for the cheapest labor, unfilled quotas, and efficient material-handling. For instance, global commodity chains may take cotton from Savannah, send it to the Pearl River Delta to be spun into fabric, then on to a factory in India, and finally to a processing zone in Bangladesh in the hunt for ephemeral savings. Spices from Hungary mixed with pork from Mexico to make Vienna sausages in Long Beach may represent another triumph of orgman efficiency. Ports, the capitals of trading regions, are competitive rivals. Extreme in their desire for accomplishment and overachievement, most of the terminals are completely wired, producing and correlating data about every aspect of shipping. A statistical swagger is invariably part of their bravado and bluster.[14]

The ECT Delta Terminal in Rotterdam and the Hong Kong Air Cargo Terminal (HACTL) are among the most automated terminals in the world. The Delta terminal operates twenty-four hours a day in order to compete with the relatively cheap labor of the stevedores.[15] A driverless ballet of automated stacking cranes (ASCs) and AGVs wait, receive cargo, and glide along, at eleven miles per hour, moving containers from ships and pallets to warehouses. Transponders in the pavement and a remote monitoring system provide redundant controls. Otherwise the vehicles and their cargo are the only citizens of this kilometer-long terminal, observed by a small team of operators in a control tower.[16] Obdurate physical material ideally behaves more like information, sorting itself and thus further enticing the distribution addict to his obsession. In this landscape of machines and vehicles, materials are not belts or cogs in the machinery, but chips or bits in an information *Landschaft.*

Just as acres and acres of outdoor space can be transformed into a machine, the warehouse is also becoming an automatic building. Within each supply chain, the movement of containers is just the first stage in an extended choreography of storage and retrieval that descends in scale to the pallet and the individual unit for sale. The internal mechanisms in the eight-story spaces of warehouses eliminate the need for floors, substituting instead mechanical

4.1 Field of containers and AGVs at the ECT Delta Terminal. Image courtesy of ECT Delta Terminal <www.ect.nl>.

stacking devices and pallet racks that may extend several stories in height. Storage and retrieval devices ride along tracks in the floor and lift materials from the pallet racks. Pallet forklifts, intricate networks of belt and skate wheel conveyors, horizontal and vertical carousels of stacked racks and drawers, work with robotic gantries and AGVs of all kinds to constantly redistribute the contents of the box. The floor, more than merely the durable surface underfoot, is the map or infrastructure holding the other half of an intelligent navigation system. FROG, a company that develops vehicles for industry, transport, and entertainment, has developed an AGV with internal mapping able to navigate areas of 100,000 square feet. It uses steering angle, wheel rotation, and odometry to navigate while occasionally double-checking the course against graphic or electronic detectors in the floor.[17] Automatic warehouses also literally perform like the motherboard of a computer, combining and redistributing goods as bytes and containers like software containers.

Once we visualize cars as chips with wheels, it's easier to imagine airplanes as chips with wings, farms as chips with soil, houses as chips with inhabitants. Yes, they will have mass, but that mass will be subjugated by the overwhelming amount of knowledge and information flowing through it. In economic terms, these objects will behave as if they had no mass at all. In that way, they migrate to the network economy.
—Kevin Kelly[18]

Academia-level award winning programmers with PHD degrees guarantee to deliver what you need in shortest time on your budget.
—SoftAcademia.com, a company providing automated logistics programming[19]

Organizational paradigms that control AGVs reflect the political disposition of the logistics orgman and his park *Landschaft.* The fleet of AGVs typically links decision with position in a dance of cooperation and avoidance. Control systems are decentralized, since centralized systems are more difficult to expand. Although it is hierarchical, the system does not generate an arborescent organization. Rather, the hierarchy might be described as a layering of subsets of sequenced tasks, thus dividing the problem into manageable

4.2 Control Room, ECT Delta Terminal. Photographer: Andrew Moddrell.

and redundant components. Heuristics are a series of rules or choices along a pathway, and greedy heuristics are the optimal selections from among these choices. Greedy algorithms solve a problem by taking the next step based on local of immediate knowledge. However excessive its sorting behaviors, the fleet of AGVs sets about its tasks, free of neuroses, considering its decisions only when it has arrived at the crossroads. The ground plan outlines a pattern of behavior that involves no advanced planning but, rather, the moment-to-moment recognition of advantageous patterns.[20]

[see *Seas*]

In the world of transshipment, extreme desires for flexibility are actually extreme desires for control. Supply chains need information correlating stock against timing and price. Companies portray themselves as instantly responsive to consumer desires even though, as Manuel Castells has pointed out, these structures of flexibility are really defensive structures for controlling or anticipating the desires of consumers. "'Toyotism,'" he has written, "is a management system designed to reduce uncertainty rather than to encourage adaptability."[21] Within the boundaries of its world, the organization appears to be free of adverse consequence, yet the species of information that it circulates within the system is always completely compatible, combinable, and divisible. The organization attempts to banish the error that it requires for growth. Organizations may control so much, so effectively, that they find it difficult to admit contradictory information. The inability to learn is referred to, in the industry, as a control error. A control error typically precedes a failure of greater-than-normal magnitude. Yet transshipment logisticians seem to have developed a combination of absolute control that scours the process for information. They require information of others not so that they can alter themselves, but so that others can alter themselves to conform to their protocols. The control organization can then demand compatibility, or predict the most opportune moment to abandon one organization or identity for another.

For instance, Wal-Mart, one of the original innovators in computerized stock-keeping, continues to insist on more and more data, as new devices for tracking inventory and customizing goods attempt to contain errors. Beyond bar codes, Wal-Mart has now begun to require from its suppliers the installation of radio frequency identification (RFID) or smart tagging microchips on its products. With their own antennae, these chips broadcast location, timing, and expiration in the supply chain. Wal-Mart's volume of sales can command supplier compliance even though the supplier will only be permitting Wal-Mart to better monitor any errors it makes.[22] [see *Error*]

The logistics city shields the modern dream of comprehensive statistical feedback in a zone of political quarantine where data function beautifully and the world is a spreadsheet. The logistics orgman is a believer in robotics and organizational paradigms found in popular books and CDs. No longer the ham-faced backslapping wharfie, transshipment specialists all around the world are techies—not hackers or system administrators, but precision technicians with the can-do of the military. Kevin Kelly's terse *New Rules for the New Economy,* praised as "required reading for all executives," is an orgman literature of sorts, written in the tone of one who is not presenting his father's version of the future.[23] Deriving rules from the digital and neobiological fascinations of complexity theory, cybernetics, and self-organizing systems, Kelly's paradigms favor "plenitude" and resilient, redundant organization. He argues that networks with large populations, whether organisms or markets naturalized as organisms, nourish themselves and grow more rapidly by relinquishing control at the top.[24] Yet the orgman, using the politics of greedy heuristics, determines his temporary loyalties and attentions in response to information that must wait on the decisions of a control organization with a singular purpose.

This superb one-directional highway with its seven lanes. . . . at designated speeds of 50, 75 and 100 miles per hour is engineered for easy grades and for speed with safety. . . . Traffic moves at unreduced rates of speed. Safe distance between cars is maintained by automatic radar control. Curb sides assist the driver in keeping his car in the proper lane under all circumstances.

—Narration from To New Horizons, *a film accompanying the Futurama exhibition for the 1939 New York World's Fair*[25]

Technology. . . . There are two areas in which recent inventions can make a radical difference, control and transport. . . . Robotics replace laborious, unwieldy processes of storage, retrieval, sorting, and reshuffling with smooth movements of frenzied ease that force us to rethink entire systems of classification and categorization. . . .

The second innovation is in transport. As more and more architecture is finally unmasked as the mere organization of flow—shopping centers, airports—it is evident that

4.3 Warehouses, AllianceTexas. Image courtesy of Hillwood, AllianceTexas <http: //www.hillwood.com>.

circulation is what makes or breaks public architecture. . . . Two simple, almost primitive, inventions have driven modernization toward mass occupancy of previously unattainable heights: the elevator and the escalator. . . . One moves only up and down, one only diagonally. . . .

At the dawn of the 21st century, a number of advances in vertical transportation are being made, from cableless self-propelled elevator systems to Otis' . . . Odyssey, a small train, platform, or large box that moves horizontally, vertically, and diagonally—literally opening up new architectural potential: to extend the urban condition itself from the ground floor to strategic points inside a building in a continuous trajectory.

—Rem Koolhaas[26]

When J. C. Penney moved its mail facility from Manhattan to Plano, Texas, it deployed a fleet of transcar vehicles of different types that moved through the building delivering mail, alerting employees of its arrival with a "friendly chime."[27]

The park landscape seems almost to achieve the perennial transportation dream of omnidirectional, automated, intelligent streams of movement instantly responsive to need like the bloodstream, or like a network of electronic circuits. In the air-conditioned Futurama Exhibit at the 1939 New York World's Fair, one of the first dramatizations of this dream, a circular ring of seating slowly rotated around the central model, gradually revealing the projected rural and urban landscape of 1960. Its radio-controlled cars, seemingly dispatched from position to position, subsequently inspired heavily funded experiments of the automobile and aerospace industry to pursue automated transport systems. In the ultimate—and as yet unfulfilled—future, cars, beloved by all, would aggregate or separate according to the whims of passengers, getting through the congestion of the city as mass transit and then morphing into individual vehicles to deliver passengers to their front door. Bruno Latour's *Aramis, or the Love of Technology* recounts one such tale of the irrational romance of the most rational scientists with Aramis, a similar dual transport or personal transport system.[28]

Although it differed significantly from the traffic engineering of automobiles, elevatoring also contributed to the dream of automated conveyance. Elevators, the box from which one enters briskly in science fiction, shed their operator, and were treated as a population of vehicles that could be timed and synchronized to work independently and in concert.[29] Both elevatoring and robotics start with a population of dumb identical objects that have only to accomplish one simple task, such as moving up and down. While a single algorithm for distributing hundreds of people through a skyscraper for ten hours a day would be difficult to devise, breaking down the problem into a set of simple activities with slight variations creates a field of objects that are, as a population, intelligent.

Architectural proposals for kinetic or robotic environments resonate with automated logistics as well. Still, park landscapes are quite different from, for instance, Archigram's portable bots (e.g., Logplug, Rokplug, and Cushicle) that would provide individual mediated environments in a wilderness. Nor are AGVs analogous to the gizmos of Reyner Banham's fascinations: the gun, portable motor, or other devices to be slung over the shoulder and used to format a new territory. The park's automatic warehouses do resemble some of Cedric Price's proposals for the Potteries Thinkbelt, Phun City, or the Twenty-four-Hour Economic Toy. Price imagined universities, performance spaces, and houses with traveling programs and scheduled responses to the inhabitant's wishes, so that one's classroom or office could simply arrive by gantry at the desired moment. In these constructions, just as in the warehouses, the object of transport is not a passenger, but the building itself.

Ironically, two eccentric inventions originating in the back lots of the US Interstate Highway system, a system that chose not to incorporate either automation or intermodality, initiated the growth of multimodal transshipment urbanism in ports all around the world. In the 1950s, the very decade that the Interstate was legislated, Malcolm McLean of Sea-Land, a cargo shipping company, introduced the idea of a transferable container, one that could be moved from a rail car to the back of a truck, and onto an oceangoing vessel. Pursuing the project as a private venture, in 1957 McLean launched the first container vessel, which traveled from Newark, New Jersey, to Port Houston, Texas. In 1966, he shipped to the first European container port in Rotterdam. Almost concurrently, in 1954, the Cravens Company at Mercury Motor Express of South Carolina installed in their factory the first AGV that operated from a ceiling guide-wire. Although similar arrangements were broadly used in other American factories, the AGV industry did not take off in the United States, and was supported instead in Europe.[30] The port of Rotterdam, a leader in automation today, started the first container transshipment company in 1966, and received Sea-Land's USS *Fairland* in 1967.

By combining the repertoires of cars, elevators, robots, and rapid transit, the AGV descendants of these devices are returning to passenger applications those behaviors originally conceived for human transport, but best rehearsed with cargo. For instance, FROG has proposed that their logistics vehicles be used as personal rapid transport prototypes, experimenting with these devices as parking lot or transit shuttles in enclave formations between Schiphol and the port of Rotterdam.[31] With Yamaha motors, FROG has also developed and tested an automated Cybercab.[32] Schiphol, like many global hubs, is also proposing an underground logistics tunnel between trade and infrastructure within which AGVs would deliver storage and freight as if in a utility network or pneumatic tube system.[33] Otis Elevators marketed an elevator-car hybrid, the Odyssey system, designed to move horizontally and vertically through buildings—from, for instance, parking lot to office.[34] In a similar project, SchindlerMobile, now called SchindlerEurolift, and Porsche (automobile companies often reenter the story) collaborated to build another horizontal/vertical vehicle—the so-called "slowest Porsche on earth."[35] Translogic/Swisslog has designed a battery-operated, infrared-controlled AGV, called the Transcar, that self-navigates the logistical spaces of hospitals, universities, and mail centers. Completing the recombination of automobile and conveyance ambitions, the Transcar is able to call an elevator, select a floor, and exit on that floor by means of infrared signals from the controlling computer.[36]

Encoded with the means of inflating or deflating a building envelope or recalibrating associated spaces, conveyance devices are germs or technological imperatives that shape larger urban fields. The elevator traveled through urban fields with the speed of an epidemic, propagating cities in block after block of towers in less than a half century. Just as an elevator must be added for every two floors of skyscraper height, escalators and moving sidewalks index the world with expressions of building height to elevator core to traffic flow per minute, or corridor length to travel time to airplane wingspan.[37] Controlled by infrared, laser, radio, transponder, or even GPS, these elevators that can take an elevator, or cabs that can take a cab, are components of a larger field of broadcast signals, suggesting ways in which buildings and urban spaces surfaces might be more readable and navigable.

4.4 Interior, automated warehouses, J. C. Penney. Image courtesy of J. C. Penney.

Whatever their utopian or dystopian portrayals, the percolation of transportation inventions and devices through culture is often errant and complex. The smart vehicles of the Futurama exhibition and its descendants could exist only in the absence of contingencies. As with many romantic dreams of modernism, the explanation for their failure could only be that they had not been fully perfected, or that the data had not all yet been received. With its repetitive, modular problems, logistics perhaps more closely matches the organizational paradigms and algorithmic capacities of automated control vehicles than did the highway, with its impossible number of contingencies. Still, the park only *aspires* to be free of contingencies, just as traffic engineers hoped that statistics would predict the movements of cars in perfectly synchronized streams. Dystopian visions of a control society in which robotic devices form their own world of cybernetic communication are also too simple and too singular—perhaps too consistent with the predictions and paradigms of the org-man himself. However ingenious they are, the movement of these automated germs through culture follows an eccentric and jagged path through the back lots of the market, transferred and retransferred, rejected and rediscovered. Even embedded in a landscape designed for perfect self-reflexivity, AGVs, like ships they serve, encounter their own politics and traffic jams that will not adhere to singular logics and perfectly synchronized feedback.

In the park's sterile political zone, its own civilization may begin again from the beginning, and its germ of automated conveyance can adapt to other purposes. While large areas of the Keppel Distripark, in Singapore, require no human being, a neighborhood for logistics or transport business offices is part of this automated urbanism. One primordial cultural offering there is an air-conditioned cafeteria serving Muslim, Chinese, and Indian cuisine.[38] In other parks there may be special AGVs accommodating passengers as well as cargo. For instance, one AGV on the market is fashioned as a clear plastic cylinder, gliding on wheels hidden under its skirt. It is designed to permit managers and overseeing businessmen to navigate the space. In this safety bubble, visitors to the installation, standing up and clutching the handrail, can progress through the same slow choreography that the other vehicles share, inspecting even the hazardous manufacturing or materials-handling installations.[39] From this hermetic bubble the logistics park citizens wish to encounter only their own errors and catastrophes.

The AirportCity is an environment where you can stay with the commercial dynamics and allure of a world town.

—G. J. Cerfontaine, president and CEO, Schiphol Group[40]

Rapid expansion of air travel, container shipping, and fiber-optic telecommunications links and flows across national boundaries make borders more of an opportunity than a barrier.[41]

The boundaries of the region state are not imposed by political fiat. They are drawn by the deft but invisible hand of the global market for goods and services. . . . Region states are natural economic zones.

—Kenichi Ohmae[42]

The organizational and political constitution that attends flexibility and greedy heuristics extends from the scale of an automated device to the scale of the city and region. Management guru Kenichi Ohmae has identified large cities or "power corridors" within nations that were more distinct as trading powers than the nations themselves. He also identified cross-national "growth triangles" that exist in the interstitial space between national jurisdictions. His taxonomy classifies these "region states" as areas of five to twenty million people, with an airport, a port, and container-handling capacity. With the usual conflation of liberalized economies and openness, Ohmae, writing in the early 1990s, characterized these trading areas as fair, disinterested, and flexible. He encouraged countries toward "relaxed control," a means of relenting to the "invisible hand" and enabling an "exorable drive for prosperity."[43]

If a "region state" is, morphologically, an aggregation of parks, legally it is an aggregation of free economic zones that encourage foreign investment and trade. The free ports that have existed since the sixteenth century evolved into free trade zones between the world wars, and at mid-century began to adopt special parameters. The first export processing zones (EPZs) were established in the 1960s in Kandla in India, Mayaguez in Puerto Rico, and Kaohsiung in Taiwan. *Maquiladoras,* the often foreign-owned assembly plants on a twenty-kilometer-wide border between the USA and Mexico, were also established in the 1960s. In 1979–80, China initiated the first special economic zones (SEZs) in Fujian and Guangdong in the cities of Shenzhen, Zhuhai, Shantou, and Xiamen. Eastern Europe established it first free economic zones at approximately the same moment. Science-based industrial parks or technopoles (SIPs) may also take on the legal status of a free trade zone.[44]

[see *Shining*]

Viewed as economic stimulants for developing countries, export processing zones became a global contagion, increasing in number from seventy-nine in 1975 to three thousand in 2003.[45] EPZs are segregated areas where raw materials or the contents of the containers are further developed, branded, or packaged for movement onto the next container in the supply chain. They take advantage of cheap, typically female, labor to perform a repetitive task or translate a product from one organizational regime to another. Some EPZs prohibit strikes or unions. Large countries like South Korea often use export processing zones as economic generators to benefit their own manufacturing base. Smaller countries, like the Dominican Republic, may only be able to make of these zones areas of quarantined wealth and exploitation. Nations, their consultants, and their analysts struggle over ranking evils and gains in countries with severe economic problems, as if the exploitation of labor were the result of poor management or improper implementation of advice from the World Bank.[46]

As special economic zones have begun trading with each other, they have generated international zones—cross-national political orders—that thrive on a cocktail of exemptions. Most visible along the Asian-Pacific coast from Russia to Indonesia, these zones are becoming central rather than littoral. Singapore and Hong Kong are, in a sense, capitals of cross-national regions or growth triangles. Xiangming Chen identifies three growth triangles in particular to illustrate this transnational phenomenon: SIJORI, the transnational region between Singapore, Johor, and Riau (an Indonesian province); the Tumen River Regional Triangle on the border between China, Russia, and North Korea; and the Greater South China Economic Region (GSCER), which has experienced enormous growth since the late 1970s, when it opened its first four special economic zones. Cars, clothing, and athletic shoes circulate in these waters, their supply chains acting as a bond between ports that may supply raw material, labor, or management. These cross-national zones are not simply open networks but, rather, special instruments in a complex game of filling quotas, circumventing labor restrictions, and finding favorable logistics.[47]

Looters broke through the wall around Haiti's main port Friday and pillaged containers. As violence spread, at least four people were killed.[48]

To enhance navigational safety and port security, MPA and Temasek-linked research and development (R&D) company Growth Venture Pte Ltd have also been jointly developing a cost-effective, transponder-based vessel identification and positioning system that would allow enforcement agencies to determine the identity of ships within the port waters.[49]

[In April 2002] ten Shell employees, including an American, were taken hostage from their oil-rig supply ship off the swampy coastal village of Amatu. The forty youths, ethnic Ijaws, were apparently retaliating for the destruction, by Nigerian security forces, of their boats, thought to have been used in pirate attacks. Shell, which negotiated for their release, has often been the target of attacks by locals who claim they get little of the revenue from the resources.[50]

At least five states (China, Malaysia, the Philippines, Taiwan and Vietnam) have established military bases and naval stations in the Spratlys, and fighting has erupted on several occasions when one or another of these states has sought to expel the forces of another.[51]

The masquerade of openness effected by the lifting of any restrictive national loyalties or tariffs turns very easily to evasion, closure, and enclave.[52] The free economic zones (FEZs) and EPZs of the world.

They cheat, just as most maritime city-states have cheated for centuries. Like the Mediterranean city-states of the thirteenth to the eighteenth century, with their extended networks of aggression and contraband, the port cities generate a constellation of surrounding interdependencies that may take advantage of geographic proximity, but may also develop in response to distant supply chains.[53] Yet the comparison between maritime cities and inland capital cities that characterizes the capital city as the control organization and the maritime city as a more fluid, complex market organization may still hold in some cases.[54] Still, whatever ancient patterns of trade and piracy reappear within the context of deregulated shipping, the port city is no longer a cosmopolitan marketplace but, rather, a society of hyper-control. It constantly oscillates between closure and reciprocity as an open fortress of sorts that orchestrates controlled and advantageous cheating.

An export processing zone in Saipan or the thickening border of *maquiladoras* are constitutionally comparable to the camps and borders of warfare. Nevertheless, given the infancy of international law, POW camps and detention centers may be the subject of more regulation than export processing zones and other special economic zones. There is very little agreement or enforcement concerning, for instance, labor standards. Environmental issues such as oil spills, or human rights issues such as the passage of stowaways in containers, also await more global regulation and international law.

Zones of exemption around the world must occasionally approach a legislative or judicial body for permissions, or for a day of reckoning. Given the influence of lobbyists on legislators, the courts have increasingly become the organ of resistance and representation in cases related to international law. For instance, the huge trade volume that allows Wal-Mart to command new levels of service and information from its suppliers would seem to immunize the organization from control errors. Yet the same scale and volume has exposed and amplified a control error in another area of the company's operations. The recent class-action lawsuit against Wal-Mart modifies the expectations of accumulation and concentration of workers associated with organized capital. The suit, which brings charges of sexism against the company, is powerful not because of a concentration of workers capable of protesting, unionizing, or striking. Not concentration but bigness threatens the company with a catastrophe of sorts. The size of the company multiplies the plaintiffs in the case. The control error, an attempt to avoid complaints from women about their pay, has led to a lawsuit that finally involves 1.6 million women, and damages in the billions of dollars. The plaintiffs are not voting for new legislation but, rather, being counted as a multiplier of damages in court cases.[55] Still, a much larger Wal-Mart workforce, operating through suppliers, remains unrepresented. [see *Error*]

Although international labor abuse may not always draw the attention of juridical bodies, the threat of terror and the need to secure the safe passage of goods have galvanized global cooperation, regulation, and enforcement. The International Maritime Organization (IMO) and the International Maritime

Bureau (IMB) have issued many security measures against piracy in, for instance, the Malacca Straits. Now, since September 11, 2001, together with Homeland Security agencies directed by the United States, these agencies have brokered national and international agreements to fight terror on the high seas. Port security schemes deploy physical searches, X-rays, infrared, and biometrics within an impossibly huge population of containers. An extremely small percentage of the millions of containers in the major ports are scanned for suspicious contents. The transponders, GPS, and electronic signals, the very devices that control the warehouse and the distripark, now extend further in scale to control the security of open ocean. Ships are tracked by transponders when they are at sea, just as airplanes are tracked in the sky or AGVs monitored in logistical fields.[56]

[see *Pirate*]

On land, the airplane is a potential bomb aimed at skyscrapers. In the ocean, the analog of the airplane as bomb is the oil tanker. Moreover, the South China Sea is an oil-rich basin. The success of container manufacturing only raises the stakes in territorial conflicts over new exclusive economic zones. Every country on the rim of the South China Sea now claims this new 200-nautical-mile territory at its edge, and China hopes to claim it at the edges of outlying archipelagos such as the Spratlys and the Paracels.[57]

The success of the park has also generated congestion that exacerbates new security concerns. While the automated container fields in Rotterdam and Hong Kong are compact, the footprints of US ports continue to spread. They absorb the world's inexpensive manufacturing but return the containers empty or, when it is too expensive to do otherwise, abandon them in gigantic fields. A pile-up of traffic waits to get into port, and a pile-up of empty containers collects on its land side. In some projected solutions, the ocean itself becomes the container field, unloading in offshore locations and perpetually moving within the already striated sea.[58]

The park is a warm pool of past and future urbanism. The automobile formatted the landscape of highways and sprawling suburbias. The elevator formatted the tall building, not as an architectural endeavor but as a real estate formula for the global city of skyscrapers. Conveyance devices that mix these and other transportation repertoires might have enormous consequences for the morphology and use of buildings. Still, they might also be the coveted objects of control. North of Fort Worth at AllianceTexas—on land that fronts the US Interstate—Hyundai, Daimler-Chrysler, Honda, and Kia sort their vehicle production through the gears of a 735-acre intermodal hub. The hub translates the labors of *maquiladoras* between air, rail, and highway.[59] The hub hallucinates the gigantic switches and gears that might have been part of a more intelligent mid-century highway network. In the surrounding warehouses, untroubled automated vehicles provide cheerful, tireless labor. Residential communities called Heritage and the Circle T Ranch are included in the master plan. The runway and warehouses are landscaped with manicured green lawns that epitomize the clean workings of the distripark's office park antecedent—a collection of "research and development" facilities, with its inevitable pond and duck. Complication is vacated or remote. For all the claims of connectivity or information saturation, when the self-promotion is written, the park might choose to exclude information about the origins of its products.

Networks of global logistics cities, presumably immune from contradiction, begin to play a much more complex and less predictable political game broadcasting territorial desire into an already contested sea. Their embryonic culture, full of potentially potent inventions and spatial germs, has also begun to attract international legal standards and regulations that might embed labor and human rights issues into the techniques of building and urbanism. The quarantined territories of ports and parks are, strangely, another iteration of the dream of optimized frictionless passage. Yet, like the maritime metaphors for globalization, they encounter both hard and slushy waters. Whatever their mixtures of greedy heuristics—perfect closure with reciprocity, excess without neuroses, or cheating with absolute control—parks are the likely targets of the very political contingencies they have supposedly banished.

Offshore

Fact blurred into fiction as delegates at an international conference on piracy in Kuala Lumpur watched a mock-up of a hijack rescue set to the James Bond theme tune. Meanwhile Indonesian security forces stormed the hijacked tanker *Selayang* for real after a high-seas chase off the coast of Borneo.[60]

In troubled times it's good to know the best are there to help. Our operators are the best military counterterror, counterpiracy, and maritime security professionals there are in the private sector . . . period. With skills honed in the elite military units of the world—the U.S. Navy's SEAL Team Six, the U.S. Army Delta Force, the Royal Navy's SBS, and others—the Coriolis operations staff can ensure your government or company the quality and results it demands.

—Promotional material from the Coriolis Corporation[61]

The ship is sailed out to sea, and for the price the syndicate will change its identity and deliver it to some mutually agreed location within three days. This could never happen in the aviation industry. One wonders what the reaction would be if a crewed 747 carrying cargo—DHL or FedEx plane—were to disappear.[62]

[see *Pirate*]

BritAm taught the Singapore SWAT teams to board ships using the pirates' own tried and proven techniques, with a little modern technology thrown in. There is the Plumett system, a shoulder-fired grappling gook with a line connected to a nylon ladder, ideal . . . for scurrying up the side of a ship. And there is a series of four small, powerful magnets that a commando uses to walk up a hull: "Rather Batman-like, but effective."[63]

Haunting the waters and archipelagos where piracy has been successful for centuries, contemporary high-tech piracy corresponds to the recent explosion in oceangoing trade. For instance, the Malacca Straits has always been a treacherous area, because when ships slow down to navigate through the straits, they become especially vulnerable to attack. In the late 1980s, there were usually fewer than ten pirate attacks per year, but in the 1990s this rate began to rise.[64] The IMB reported a 56 percent increase in global piracy in 2000 over that in 1999.[65] The ancient pirate belts around the world—the South China Sea, the Brazilian coastline, the West African coast, and Kandla and Chennai in India—are active once again.[66] Piracy often flares up in response to trading monopolies or embargoes. Early-seventeenth-century piracy in the Malacca Straits surfaced in defiance of a Dutch trading monopoly in the area. Similarly, the apparent impenetrability and dominance of contemporary global trade practices, signaling both largess and exploitation, incites the opportunist to acts of "counter-violence."[67]

A few barefoot men in speedboats are often able to board and take control of gigantic ships and oil tankers. They may rob the ship of money and equipment, murder the crew, take hostages, or cause the entire ship to simply disappear. It is remarkably easy to board even the largest ships. The hulls are often equipped with anchor chains, and the pirates are incredibly adept at climbing. While there may be no striped shirts, wooden legs, and parrots, there are hoods, masks, guns, and knives. Some have special equipment, like a $30,000 titanium grapple to use in boarding the boat, or a GPS device like the very instruments used in attempting to detect pirate activity.[68] The IMO and IMB have issued guidelines establishing reporting procedures, and recommending extra watches and lights in areas typically haunted by pirates. They also caution against resistance. Consequently, shipping companies gamble with small crews, and may even use dummies to stand on deck and create the appearance of an extra watch.

Many small bands of pirates are simple thieves, intent only on robbing the safe. Here piracy is usually an act of desperation. Pirates may even steal nautical rope to use in making fishnets in their home village. A band of women off the Nigerian coast pirated a ship and stole all of the clothes that were in the ship's washing machines.[69]

Pirate syndicates also perpetrate more complex confidence games with shipping and cargo. They may pose as a shipping contractor in a stolen ship with an illegal registry. The cargo is unloaded in a port different from the agreed-upon destination, and sold as contraband. After changing their identity, pirates may resell these "ghost ships" or "phantom ships." Organized crime rings actually openly inspect and identify potential victims while in port, thus permitting clients to make their selection from the available stock. Hijacking a ship can bring profits of up to three million dollars, meaning that pirates must complete only a few raids per year to maintain a lucrative business.[70]

Like the mercenary soldiers or privateers of another time, ex-soldiers and special-forces experts are available all over the world as antiterror and antipirate forces. These private contractors may be well armed, deadly and, occasionally, unpredictable. One such company, the Control Risks Group, seems to merge the roles of the counterpirate and the insurance specialist. CRG provides both enforcement and consulting, detecting risk in port facilities and supply chains.[71] The waters host a complex mixture of mercenaries, international law enforcement, private contractors, and criminals—all wishing to exploit a logistics apparatus that is, by turns, information-rich and information-poor.

Contemplation: Error

Since I have a Judeo-Christian religious background, it is obvious to me that one must link any definition of the accident to the idea of original sin. The content of this idea is merely that any person has the potential to become a monster. Now, this idea of original sin, which materialist philosophy rejects so forcefully, comes back to us through technology: the accident is the original sin of the technical object. Every technical object contains its own negativity. It is impossible to invent a pure, innocent object, just as there is no innocent human being. It is only through acknowledged guilt that progress is possible. Just as it is through the recognized risk of the accident that it is possible to improve the technical object.

—Paul Virilio[1]

Error is only the reverse of a rational orthodoxy, still testifying on behalf of that from which it is distanced—in other words, on behalf of an honesty, a good nature and a good will on the part of one who is said to be mistaken. Error, therefore, pays homage to the "truth" to the extent that, lacking a form of its own, it gives the form of the true to the false.

—Gilles Deleuze[2]

Philosophy has been asking around about stupidity; at least, a need has been expressed to enrich the concept of error by determinations of a different sort.

—Avital Ronell[3]

Mistake

In common parlance, errors are wrong answers. They produce shame and embarrassment for those who make them or discover them. Error must be contained to prevent it from disrupting our logical proofs. We even treat it as the destined antithesis that proves the assumed conclusion. Or we impose some means of returning error to a determinate system, calling it part of a chaotic or entropic order, something that, like Satan, will stay in the family of the whole. Virilio called error "the original sin of the technical object."[4] Baseball games tally and maintain statistics of all of the minute split-second failures of men standing alone in a field. These errors determine a player's rank, and the amount of money he can provide for his family. Error is not rewarded but rather, often, punished.

Declaring error, misdirections, and wrong choices to be pathological is even a source of pleasure. Yet the most logical systems and the most earnest attempts to forestall uncertainty with elaborate planning and prediction may yield the most profound error, a kind of catastrophic false knowledge. The fantasy is that, by controlling and constraining extrinsic desire and activity, we can keep the organization intact. We dress the cat to make him into an object that can be named within our cultural constructs rather than an animal that is always an infinitive of sorts. This is the power of errors and accidents to overturn our keenest desires for order, optimization, and purity. Error is the beautiful improbability that escapes fortifications of logic.

To focus on the word error would seem, at first, to confirm the dominance of logical thinking by focusing on the species of fault that it sanctions. In "The Image of Thought," Deleuze characterizes error as a "dogmatic image" when it is recognized as the only possible "misadventure of thought."[5] Here the word "error" is used as one might use the word "mistake" or "miscue," an obstacle to exploring other sorts of confusions or ways of not knowing. Continuing this train of thought, Avital Ronell writes about stupidity as that rich vein of activity too long subsumed under the rubric of the error as mistake. Stupidity in all of its forms—from straying to cruelty to delusion to the seeming simple-mindedness that sometimes accompanies cunning—cannot be contained within the puniness of faulty logic. One of the greatest stupidities would then be the dismissal of stupidity.[6]

In this contemplation, the word error is not used as a logical fault, as one might use the word "mistake." Instead, it looks for the enriched notions of error that take advantage of its usages in many other disciplines, from networks to genetics. In this discussion, error is the valence electron of organizational constitution, a common expression for naturally occurring extrinsic information, the germ of many disruptions and misadventures. Error is a fascination of all those who study organization and behavior. Intelligence related to the constitution of groups, whether they be groups of cells or neurons or individuals, enters into the deliberations not only of social scientists and behaviorists, but of philosophers, anthropologists, political theorists, and economists. An organization's tolerance for error is critical to its disposition, a factor capable of relaxing or intensifying that constitutive agency. All borrow and adapt models and constructs among their various disciplines to discuss not only human and machinic interaction but political, economic, and military organizations as well.

There is no universally agreed classification of human error, nor is there one in prospect. A taxonomy is usually made for a specific purpose, and no single scheme is likely to satisfy all needs. Nearly everyone who has published in this field has devised some form of error classification. Consequently, the literature abounds with such taxonomies, reflecting a variety of practical concerns and theoretical orientations and ranging from the highly task specific to broad statements of underlying error tendencies.

—James Reason[7]

Error is a straying from the truth, something believed wrongly; it is a mistake, a misplay, a deviation from a standard of expectation or judgment; it is the result of ignorance, inadvertence, or the inability to achieve what is right.

—Guy Benveniste[8]

The performance of the model [Kan-Ban, Toyotism, just-in-time] relies also on the absence of major disruptions in the overall process of production and distribution. Or, to put it in other words, it is based on the assumption of the "five zeros": zero defect in the parts; zero mischief in the machines; zero inventory; zero delay; zero paperwork. Such performances can only be predicated on the basis of an absence of work stoppages and total control over labor, on entirely reliable suppliers and on adequately predicted markets.

—Manuel Castells[9]

Control

The specialists in culture who attempt to taxonomize error are acutely aware of their own proliferation of error with each attempt. Equally poignant is the work of scientists studying industrial management whose writings attempt an error taxonomy of sorts. In these studies, as in common parlance, an error is not only something that obstructs efficiency or costs money; it is something that causes an employee to be judged harshly. An error is something to hide. However dry or analytic, these discussions of error retain a peculiar capacity for pathos and hilarity.

In an attempt to predict more accurately when an error might occur, an error specialist might first distinguish between two types: *constant* and *variable.* Constant errors are those where the subject consistently makes the same mistake over and over again, while with the variable type, the error is a measure of the inconsistency of action, the "spread" between attempted shots at a target, for instance.[10] Equally useful is the distinction between slips or lapses and mistakes. Slips or lapses represent the inability to complete the planned activity, whereas mistakes represent an ill-conceived plan or an inadequate objective.

In another taxonomy of networked industrial organizations, four types of industrial error are found: *marginal, common, articulation,* and *control* errors. A *marginal* error is entirely circumstantial, the failure of one of many possible contingencies. Marginal errors are tolerated as long as they do not recur too frequently. *Common* errors are the result of a third party that generates obstacles in an industrial process through legalities or regulations. Global networked industries are often subject to more regulations, but they are also better equipped to organize internally so as to avoid them. An *articulation* error occurs when a product is completely mismatched to its market, or simply has no market. It differs from a marginal error in that it is not isolated and circumstantial, but produced in large quantities. It is error that is even occasionally mass-produced. The maker may not be able to respond to fashion, or to force the changing trends. The company may try to avoid the dangers of disarticulation in many different markets, or it may retreat and attempt to control its customers. *Control* errors describe the temporary success of companies in managing to sell or force the acceptance of unwanted goods. The company denies or hides the inappropriateness of the product, keeping secrets from the public and deluding itself. It will deny the addictive properties of tobacco, or the accident statistics associated with tires for SUVs, assuming that these problems are merely articulation errors or isolated problems. The company will attempt to diffuse responsibility, in the hopes that the error will not be detected. Someday, the consumers it longs to control will finally come around to seeing things its way. When the product is finally rejected, it becomes an articulation error, and the company can decide whether or not to recognize the failure, learn, and adapt.[11] In this information paradox, a great deal of intelligence is required to nourish the hermetic and maintain stupidity.

The hucksters and orgmen annually fill many millions of square feet of warehouse-style retail outlets with millions of unwanted items that must be reduced in price until they are almost free. For organizations like Wal-Mart, this near-failure constitutes success. The company demands information that will protect it from articulation errors and common errors, so that it can continually approach failure in order to produce products at their lowest possible cost. The production must slide between the trivial errors and the massive control error. Yet even Wal-Mart's avoidance of real failure by the cultivation of compatible error inevitably encounters error that the system does not recognize. The attempt to avoid sex discrimination lawsuits by virtue of its corporate size, for instance, has resulted in a control error commensurate with that size.

Chasing after error in a networked, automated world is a beautiful comedy. Organization and optimization designed to reduce error usually also produces it, since error is always escaping its cage. Building logical structures to avoid or camouflage error simultaneously generates more profound error from the other end.

A spinster is a bachelor's wife.
—From a collection of children's misspoken words[12]

The phrase "in the mind" can and should always be dispensed with. Its use habituates its employers to the view that minds are queer "places," the occupants of which are special-status phantasms. It is part of the function of this book to show that exercises of qualities of mind do not, save per accidens, *take place "in the head," in the ordinary sense of the phrase, and those which do so have no special priority over those which do not.*

—Gilbert Ryle[13]

. . . game theorists do not not attempt to exploit their opponent's folly.

Since it takes no great insight to recognize the existence of folly in this world, and since the game theorist purports to be influenced by the world, why this puristic attitude? The answer is simply this: it is much easier to recognize the existence of error than to fashion a general, systematic theory that will allow you to exploit it. So the study of tricks is left to the experts in each particular game; game theorists make the pessimistic, and often imperfect, assumption that their opponents will play flawlessly.[14]

The truth of the matter is that every circuit of causation in the whole of biology, in our physiology, in our thinking, our neural processes, in our homeostasis, and in the ecological and cultural systems of which we are parts—every such circuit conceals or proposes those paradoxes and confusions that accompany errors and distortions in logical typing.

—Gregory Bateson[15]

The alternative to the freedoms introduced by paradox is the rigidity of logic.

—Gregory Bateson[16]

Joke/Exception

Whatever the desire to eradicate error, it is also treated as an enriching ingredient that an organization or a mind must continually cultivate. If error is considered to be the trap door from which to escape or renovate a logical construction, it is also the threshold to meaning in an active fluid register. Freud collected errors as an entry to the unconscious mind. Collections of malapropisms, misspellings, juvenile writings, and other errors of language constitute an underground genre of sorts. These collections look, not for flaws that fit the logic of a tragic riddle, but for the accidental predicaments that are the foundation of comedy and the precious evidence of a human imagination. Error may be an indication of multiple and often incompatible logical types.

Henri Bergson locates laughter in a release from the mechanistic, or a confounding of the mechanistic in confrontation with life and its accidents.[17] Similarly, philosophers like Deleuze have abandoned the more litigious forms of analytic proof, looking not to contain or correct error but to enter a different form of contemplation that recognizes the world's fictions rather than privileging its logics.[18] For Guy Debord, the inadvertent moment or *détournement* was a kind of straying from the dominant cultural script of the spectacle. This *dérive,* this wandering away to another side of a cultural logic, served as an antidote to topple accustomed constructs.

One of Gilbert Ryle's most memorable formulations in *The Concept of Mind* describes an error in logical constructs that he called the "category mistake." In examples of this "looking for the wrong type of thing," he notes the identification of a parade of "battalions, batteries, squadrons *and* a division," when it really should be a parade of the "battalions, batteries, and squadrons *of* a division."[19] A category mistake is limited in its exploration of error, in the sense that it is a short-term error confined within the boundaries of language and logic. Yet when the imagination takes hold of the error, it may manufacture extra hilarity from felicitous misuse. Ryle also makes distinctions between ways of knowing—between, for instance, "knowing how and knowing that"—and between the more deliberate and overt forms of knowing and the various "ghosts in the machine" that resist knowing. He identifies meaning expressed in an active register that cannot always be reconciled against familiar forms of symbology or semiotics.[20]

Many organized systems, from games to electronic circuitry to genetics, behave in ways that run counter to our common notions of order and efficiency. Messy redundancies, generally thought to inhibit streamlined organization, multiply possibilities for trial and error; accidents broaden the base of responses, because they introduce new information that the system needs in order to grow. Losses, accidents, inversions, jokes, and tricks introduce extrinsic information or error that makes organizations robust. Exceptions and mistakes in organizations like networks, for instance, increase pathways, acting as new material that skews and grows the network. Sloppy programming is productive. Error is the antigen that reseeds a network, a wild card that, matching many formats, has unintended effects.

The game theory situation called "Prisoner's Dilemma" describes players arranged symmetrically, with only a few logical options to sway the game. A more productive game for modeling a buildup of error and circumstance might be Parrando's Paradox. Parrando's Paradox claims that although two losing games played independently will always lose, two losing games played alternately may generate a winning streak.[21] The losses in one game, like the small repetitive supports of a ratchet, seem to prevent downward movement or losses in another. Since two games, when cross-referenced, seem to multiply intelligence, Parrando's Paradox encourages a gamble with losses that would generally be considered unproductive. Yet perhaps even more important than the number of players or the accretion of circumstance is the recognition that game theory itself presumes no "folly," affect, or bluff that does not register as logic.[22]

Cyberneticians often treated information as the universal unit of translation between disparate pieces, thus fueling a fascination with the possibility of looping systems within which the feedback of information automatically regulated the organization. One of their more eccentric practitioners, Gregory Bateson, was fascinated with unities and recursive systems as well, but was equally intrigued by the instrumentality of exceptional phenomena or extrinsic information within an organization. His catholic style of thinking circulated ideas between, for instance, networks, mechanisms, animal behavior, or global politics. Whether he applied this to analysis of tribal behavior in New Guinea, a digital language for dolphins, or processes of addiction and fellowship in Alcoholics Anonymous, Bateson articulated expressions of process, the architecture of active regulating relationships within a heterogeneous population of subjects. He recorded complexity in organization by observing and experiencing the resistances between people and groups of people. For instance, within the cybernetics conferences themselves, Bateson was fascinated with the coexistence of resistant categories of information that resulted when representatives of so many different disciplines gathered. Moreover, he observed that it was the comedy of the collisions between their various logics that led them on.[23]

For Bateson, involutions, reversals, and catastrophes in life were the pivotal moments that sent the story outside of itself, beyond its accepted level of abstraction or logic. Joining others who have speculated about operatives of humor, Bateson understood it to be, like error, a disruption of cultural logic. Laughter was a "convulsive" moment or a cultural paradox caused by mixing information from one type of logic and reality with another. Bateson even speculated that one could produce electronic circuitry that responded to contradictions in this way—a cybernetic machine propelled by its own humor.[24] Humor was a source of learning that repeatedly enriched and shifted the rules of the game, saving minds from "the rigidity of logic."[25]

Bateson's theories of schizophrenia were related to his theories of humor and fantasy. He used communication theory to describe the schizophrenic's mental conundrum when attempting to classify information or juggle multiple levels of abstraction. The uncomfortable coexistence between these levels of meaning sent the schizophrenic into a "double bind" or a site of contradiction that was visited repeatedly and for which various coping mechanisms developed that confused a commonly accepted reality.[26] Bateson described the theory of the "double bind" as a "language," that is, a practice or an epistemology that cannot be proved true or false.[27]

In the 1940s, 1950s, and 1960s, Bateson rehearsed this language in a series of dialogues that were "conversations about some problematic subject." He called them *metalogues* because they incorporated into the overall shape and interplay of the dialogue an abstract architecture that revealed something about the content of the discussion itself. Bateson and his daughter Catherine were the speakers in these dialogues. Often they were titled "Why do things have outlines?" or "Why do Frenchmen?", or began with a query from Catherine like "Why do things get into a muddle?" or "What is instinct?" The dialogues rehearsed a discussion about the coexistence of resistant orders or categories of information. Each portion of the conversation would either stumble into its own exception or wrap itself around some non sequitur or category mistake, sending it into yet another contradictory strain of reasoning. The conversations were constantly inverting and undoing themselves with information outside the proposed system of language or behavior.[28]

D: *What are we talking about?*

F: *I don't quite know—not yet. But you started a new line by asking if the game of croquet could be made into a real muddle only by having all the things in it alive. And I went chasing after that question, and I don't think I've caught up with it yet. There is something funny about that point.*

D: *What?*

F: *I don't quite know—not yet. Something about living things and the difference between them and the things that are not alive—machines, stones, so on. Horses don't fit in the world of automobiles. And that's part of the same point. They're unpredictable, like flamingos in the game of croquet.*
—Gregory Bateson[29]

How then are we to revolutionize an order whose very principle is self-revolutionizing?
—Slavoj Žižek[30]

Error Language

Just as Bateson described not a logic but a language of the double bind, so one might also contemplate a language of error. An error language is inadvertently discovered, as well as deliberately cultivated, and it cannot be proved or disproved as a logical fault. Error requires a field guide to its many species and flavors. Like the books that rehearse strategies in chess or tsugis in Go, the field guide would operate like a playbook of error. Error includes accident, trick, wild card, joke, or *détournement.* Some entries would footnote Huizinga or Bakhtin, De Certeau, Debord, Bateson, Bergson, or Ryle. The field guide would include exit, catastrophe, involutions, and reversals, but it would also include gigantic, central species of error that lie somewhere on a continuum between tactic and strategy.

While various cultural mixtures of complexity theory and cybernetics have searched for predictability and recursivity in organization, one might look instead for foreign ground, resistance, discontinuities, and unpatterned multiples—no homeostasis, but other inexplicable and even cruel buffooneries in organizations that are continually exiting their own logic. In this theory of error, it is not the reductive, corrective, or recursive that nurtures intelligence. Rather, it is that which multiplies and adds improvisationally, outside of the single frame. It is not the one or the many that must reconcile to a whole, but only the many. Error, comedies, and broad gaffes are evidence of having exited a self-reflexive logic. Error exists in the misalignment between formats, the space between the indices. Error is not the shameful, unwanted, catastrophic event, but the cultivated crop. It is not the exception in industry but, rather, the only thing we manufacture—a solid crop of errors.

Perhaps error is more constantly and abundantly present in a world that attempts to foreground the stability, unity, and recursivity that it does not have. Orgmen everywhere give hilarious Powerpoint presentations on a new streamlined distribution or retail scheme, boasting of an optimization that will inevitably implode as a result of attempts to control the unpredictable. Cheerful and long-winded explanations of the organization's righteousness, gentleness, and friendliness may fill the air to obfuscate meaning and defer a reality check. Alternatively, subterfuge accompanies the cheating, and various alias identities replace the absolute evangelical character to create the smokescreen or diversion of disguise. Both forms of masquerade, however different, are often successful. They cultivate not the exceptional, unusual, or contradictory circumstance, but the exception as exemption from law or democratic reckoning to foster a "special" stupidity.

The conflation of these two meanings of exception is potentially productive. On the one hand, exception means exemption, and an attempt to keep error and regulation at bay. Exception triggers a critique of the island or legal lacuna. On the other hand, exception describes the unavoidable error that will eventually infiltrate an organization. A collapse between both forms of exception creates an opportunity. Both the volatile comedies of the orgmen and the apodictic expressions of more extreme splinter groups are, from a vantage point outside the organization, error-rich. The collapse marks an opening, and invites the countermasquerades of piracy to respin the psychological weakness of the believer or the secrets of those undercover. Jacques Rancière, for instance, has written about the immigrant as an element that contradicts or corrects political consensus.[31] De Certeau has described the cumulative political power of tactical tricks or *perruques* that the worker or consumer perpetrates on the powers that be. As a political imagination works on error, it transposes and amplifies tactics to the status of counterstrategies.

Capital has no one essential tragic contradiction. It does not follow the structure of a tragic riddle. Indeed, contradiction and error may make capital more robust, giving it more platforms within which to shelter multiple masquerades. In a super-Marxist formulation, market and state are fully metastasized into each other. Rejecting singular logics associated with the perfect negation of organized capital, opportunity may reside in the elegance of negation itself. A multitude of potential negations replaces the single contradiction. In a formulation that is somewhat less tragic than the Debordian cultural spectacle, the market is perhaps not monolithic and impenetrable. Rather, both Empire and counter-Empire are armed with similar instruments of change. It is a spongy organizational paradigm, at once monolithic and porous to the individual, encouraging a more active ethical struggle in a world where many more sites are political fronts and there is no definitive revolution, only the possibility of continual revolutionizing.

An error language is a language of urbanism, but also a landscape of politics. Cities succeed when they make a deliberate gamble with exceptional conditions, amassing an excess of circumstance, error, and contradictory evidence. The sense of that language is centered around multiplication—multiplication of meaning, enemies, friends, and differences. Expertise in this language might involve the practice of knowing nothing rather than the practice of protecting an accepted set of skills. The elements that fall between the rubrics and between the indices, the pathologies and eccentricities in culture that do not stay in their place, are constantly undoing an information paradox or loosening the boundaries of knowledge with extrinsic information.

Shining

Imagine a scenario where you, a guest in a top hotel in the US, make a call for room service. The call is routed to India, because your hotel has discovered the cost-advantages of outsourcing this customer interface to a lower-cost English-speaking locale. . . . Though this is a rather simplistic analogy, it shows how India is very well positioned to become the "Wal-Mart" of the global service sector.

—Ramalinga Raju, chairman of Satyam Computers and Satyam Infoway[1]

For today, gentlemen, whether you intend it or not—whether you wish it or not—you have signed far more than yet another intergovernmental agreement. You have just signed the first draft of the Articles of Federation of the United States of Earth.

—Arthur C. Clarke at the signing of the first Comsat agreement[2]

In the 1960s, Western leaders promised to use satellites to create a "global village" but ended up using them in ways that reinforced global inequalities, carving the earth into spheres of north and south, developed and underdeveloped, and fast and slow.[3]

Satellites named Optus, Telstar, Eurobird, Hot Bird, or Atlantic Bird beam down overlapping spots of microwaves to the receiving territories below, transmitting Zee TV, STAR TV, and Al-Jazeera to Abu Dhabi, Bombay, or Singapore.[4] These supposed instruments of the fabled global village have produced not a single global village, but a number of global villages. National and commercial consortia stratify the microwave sea of transmissions, making it increasingly more dense, codified, and politicized. While transmissions from extraterrestrial devices orbiting the equator are still often treated as if they were magically immaterial, microwaves rely heavily on the physical plant of architecture and urbanism for their function and political persuasion. Indeed, satellites arguably transmit a form of urbanism, a *broadcast urbanism* that is bundled together with television, telephony, and data.

Satellite fleets of the most developed nations are soaking heavily populated regions with microwave transmissions that are largely redundant to the landed grid. In response to Sputnik 1 (1957), NASA counterlaunched an experimental satellite in 1961, sanctioning the subsequent legislation of the Communication Satellite Corporation (Comsat). Early Bird, launched in 1965, was the first of Comsat's six-satellite system. Its earth stations in the United Kingdom, France, Germany, Italy, Brazil, and Japan broadcast the first global village transmission of the moonwalk in 1969. While it was developed with military or space-race technologies, Intelsat—a descendant of Comsat, and the most heavily subscribed satellite consortium—now collectively owns its own infrastructure.[5]

Now not just a "US military fiefdom," both publicly and privately owned regional satellite fleets have formed all over the world, and they sometimes transmit not redundant but primary broadcast and broadband infrastructure to some of the least developed places on earth.[6] Among these are RSCC, serving Russia and the Commonwealth of Independent States (CIS), Arabsat (1967), serving the Middle East and North Africa; Indosat (1967), serving Indonesia; and Insat (1975), serving India.[7] Entrepreneurial companies with offshore pads along the equator now replace ex-Soviet launch contractors with Cold War military remainders.[8] Using on-line trading markets like E-Sax, customers can buy bandwidth, a satellite, parts of an earth station, or other Cold War remainders found among the 26,000 orbiting mechanisms and bits of space junk.[9] Any new merger of military and media can sell services such as bomb-damage assessments, or found a new city-state in the satellite sea.[10]

Futurologists imagined that satellites would allow developing countries to leapfrog into the developed world, bypassing investments in a conventional infrastructure grid by simply beaming down a communication infrastructure. Satellites would produce a transmitting pollen or weather, of sorts, that would not be magnetized to any existing metropolitan formations. In the same way that dam-building was thought to reorient infrastructures around a natural resource, satellites might be a resource stored in the air, returning benefits to

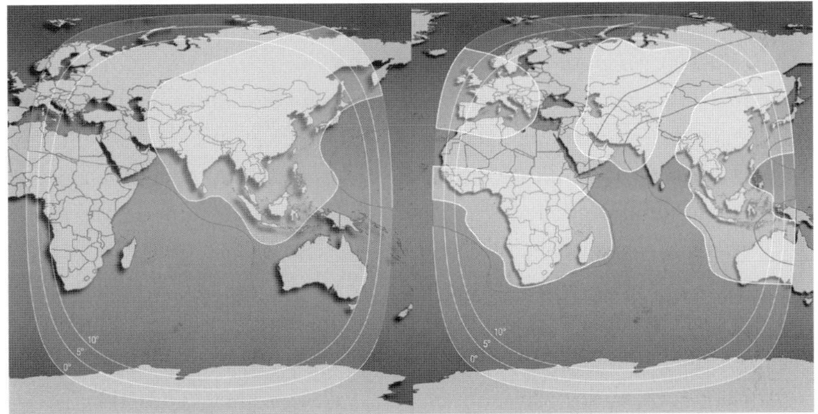

5.1 Intelsat footprint maps. Image courtesy of Intelsat.

all they touched regardless of previous urban and political structures. In *The Third Wave* (1980), in a chapter titled "Gandhi with Satellites," Alvin Toffler projected India's use of satellites as a possible exemplar. Correcting the mistakes of military industrial infrastructures, the fleet would insert high-performance technologies into very primitive rural environments to act as economic catalyzers. With the elegiac and emotional tone favored by futurology, Toffler called for an agrarian democracy, a Gandhian pastoral or rural village served by satellite communication.[11]

Yet since most broadcast receivers also require electricity, and since developing countries such as India have unreliable electrical grids, the very thing that must be done to take advantage of this infrastructure of the air is to build discrete concentrated enclaves with dedicated electrical generation as well as access points to cable and fiber. The satellite sea needs its "last mile" of hardwiring that must be laid next to roads and built into new construction—the last contested, messy outcropping that allows it to siphon attention and revenues.[12] Consequently, in the villages of Insat in India and its neighboring Arabsat and Indosat, the fabled "knowledge parks" or technopoles, styled after the Silicon Valley-style IT campus, replace the utopian plans of visionaries and futurologists.

In India, these IT parks are home to one of the clichéd instruments of one-world globalization—the calling center operators that handle outsourced telephone calls for American Express or Citibank. As globalism's adorable new mascot, they adopt a variety of global aliases to fit in around the world. The operators even, famously, perfect their accents by watching American TV, as the global media love to report. These broadcasts of HBO, STAR, and Zee TV that have supposedly dilated India's nation-centric politics with pop culture may even be bouncing from the same satellite that delivers the calling center's c-band.

The shining temples and palaces of IT parks of Arabsat and Indosat in Dubai or Malaysia seem to clinch the familiar political argument that these enclaves often elude locality, generating apolitical forms of urbanism, incubating or laundering data and resources like a Swiss bank account for technologies. With much less restraint than the CIA-style international modernism of the preceding era of Hilton Hotels, these technology country clubs often express a mixture of enthusiasm for digital capitalism with the reassurances of a five-star hotel or resort. In *Splintering Urbanism,* Stephen Graham and Simon Marvin examine the effects of these "premium and secessionary networked infrastructures," while also measuring their responsibility for the local politics that they elude.[13] For Benjamin Barber, in these high-tech commercial additions to "McWorld," "there is nothing that looks particularly democratic."[14]

While some of the same arguments apply all over South Asia and the Middle East, some IT parks in India harbor more complex and peculiar political masquerades, some of which are broad or overt and some of which are well camouflaged. Wrapped around TV and c-band are not only the politics of digital haves and have-nots, but also various aging disguises for modernism, nationalism, secularism, and futurism that easily mix with more insidious disguises for racism and plutocracy. Any mixture of these may be genially prepared to make the global deal. Any mixture of these may also duck under India's self-styled *über*-disguise of absolute unknowable, perfect complexity. Networking between the Middle East, Malaysia, Africa, and China, India's IT viceroys, both elected officials and entrepreneurs, wield these disguises to colonize a web of IT territories that are discontinuous or remote on the ground, but connected in section by a bounce to the stratosphere.

Architecture and urbanism are accoutrements in the masquerade. While the logistics park is the materialization of software on the network side of the screen, the IT park materializes the media and marketing side of the screen. In India, the architectural face is primarily critical in establishing signals of global satellite contextuality for the almost identical roster of companies that act as the ready-made tenants of IT's favorable legal and infrastructural envelopes. Yet both the inclusion and evasion of democratic institutions in these global techno-mediascapes also have national political consequences. This architecture in media-mimesis may support a globalizing nationalism, or incite democratic resistance, but it may also be merely vestigial to the larger pirate shadow of IT's gray market. [see *Park*]

We will build and construct, so people will come, we will not ask people to come to an empty place.

—Sheikh Mohammed bin Rashid al-Maktoum[15]

Dubai Outsource Zone is both inspired and driven by the vision of His Highness General Sheikh Mohammed Bin Rashid Al Maktoum, the Crown Prince of Dubai and UAE Defense Minister to build Dubai into a global knowledge economy hub.

—Sheikh Mohammed bin Rashid al-Maktoum[16]

Malaysia upholds the virtues of the new world order, believing that the globe is collectively moving towards a "century of the world," a century of world-wide peace and shared prosperity among nations.

—Promotional description of the Multi-Media Super Corridor[17]

Dubai Internet City, the first free trade zone for IT, e-commerce, and media, is a city-state, of sorts, in a global village or consortium between Egypt, the Indian subcontinent, South Africa, and the Commonwealth of Independent States.[18] An outcropping of Arabsat, Dubai Internet City (DIC) allows for complete foreign ownership of property within its boundaries, no taxation, and relaxed local laws governing partnership. Like Dubai itself, DIC has streamlined legal registrations and established flexible labor laws, visa-handling, and fast-track immigration to guarantee "quick access to required talent." Cheap labor comes from the edges of Arabsat's satellite beam in Africa and India. DIC is ready to provide any necessary disguises for e-commerce, domain names, addresses, and servers. Dubai itself is becoming an aggregate of every species of politically exempt zone, including Dubai Outsourcing Zone, Dubai Knowledge Village, Dubai Ideas Oasis, Dubai Healthcare City, Dubai Maritime City, Dubai Humanitarian City, Dubai Textile City, and Dubai Media City. These are only some of the many building projects to be completed in the United Arab Emirates, including Palm Island and Dubailand, a massive tourist compound with two billion square feet and forty-five megaprojects.[19]

At DIC, an abundance of futuristic architectural expression accompanies the knowledge village as resort. Curving streets ease the default expectation of a phantom suburban monotony, and a Bath-like crescent of buildings and walls encircles the rotary. A number of urban faces, tropes, and microenvironments appear: the gates of an Arab city, the office buildings of a Western research and development compound, and the sparkling mirror-tiled palaces of a country club for digital industries. Indeed, DIC is a grand hotel or resort where tenants are alternately called "members," and they speak in an argot of acronyms.

Sited in the Singapore of the Middle East, Dubai Internet City refers to one of the early quintessential technopoles, the Multi-Media Super Corridor (MMSC). MMSC was developed as part of Malaysia's plans for 2020 as both a "physical area and a new paradigm for creating value in the Information Age." Almost 900 companies that roam the world populating IT campuses have located in its 290 square miles of "Multimedia Utopia" bounded by the Petronas Towers on one end and by Kuala Lumpur Airport on the other. The ethos is of liberal business practices, and the city boasts of having "smart homes, smart cities, smart schools, smart cards, and smart partnerships." MSC's International Cybercourt of Justice is developing standards for international "cyber-laws."[20]

Signaling to both of these global digital cities is Hong Kong's project for Cyberport. The city is a venture of Hutchison-Whampoa, a conglomerate controlling container terminals, telecommunications companies, and STAR TV. In the early 1990s, STAR TV (Satellite Television Asia Region) began broadcasting a mix of movies, music, Western TV, and sports to an area stretching from Turkey to Japan. Cyberport is the latest scheme of Richard Li, the young "superboy" heir to the Hutchison-Whampoa fortune, who is notorious for his fictitious claims to have graduated from Stanford University.[21] Dressed in the sculptural formalism and shiny renderings that appear on the computer screens of architecture professionals and students, Cyberport offers a retail arcade, an office complex, and a residential enclave on a 24-hectare (59-acre) site at Telegraph Bay. Despite a bad reputation for wildly risky deals, Li is often compared to the greatest of all IT viceroys: Bill Gates.[22]

Sabri Al Azazi, the Chief Operating Officer (COO) of security service firm Datafort, has become the first UAE national to win the prestigious Certified Information Systems Security Professional (CISSP) certification from the International Information Systems Security Certification Consortium (ISC)2. The (ISC)2 has also nominated Sabri to the (ISC)2 Faculty & Common Body of Knowledge (CBK), the Training Committee of (ISC)2.[23]

There are some who question the relevance of space activities in a developing nation. To us, there is no ambiguity of purpose. We do not have the fantasy of competing with the economically advanced nations in the exploration of the moon or the planets or manned space flight. But we are convinced that if we are to play a meaningful role nationally, and in the community of nations, we must be second to none in the application of advanced technologies to the real problems of man and society.

—Dr. Vikram Sarabhai[24]

The gleaming campus in Bangalore of Infosys, India's third-biggest information-technology firm, has a golf green and a Domino's Pizza as the staff canteen. You might as well be in Silicon Valley.[25]

In India, the often-published portrait of Vikram Sarabhai presides over what might have been a very different pool of microwaves from that in Hong Kong or the UAE. Looking beatifically skyward as the father of an Indian space program in India, Sarabhai, an advisor to Indira Gandhi, hoped to combine high technology with the dream of a rural broadcast. As if designed to fulfill Toffler's satellite projections, this airborne infrastructure was to reinforce a Gandhian or Nehruvian political ethos, like dams on a microwave sea. The India Space Research Organization (ISRO) was established in 1972, not as competition for Russian or US space programs, with their space stations and manned exploration of extraterrestrial planets. Instead, the targeted frontier was nation-building.[26]

In 1975, the same year that HBO broadcast its first satellite downlink of an Ali/Frazier fight (the Thriller in Manila), a USSR Intercosmos rocket launched the first Indian satellite, Aryabhata.[27] The political geography of the launches reflected India's stance of political nonalignment. In 1976, using an American satellite, ATS-6, India began an experimental program called SITE (satellite instructional television experiment) which broadcast TV for a year to 2,400 villages in the least-developed areas.[28] From 1977 to 1979, India used Franco-German technology for another similar experiment called STEP.[29] The Insat satellites, one of which was bought from Arabsat, were launched in the 1980s with the help of the United States and Europe. This system still broadcasts today. Insat-1B allowed Doordarshan, the government television station, to set up a national network that focused not on regional or rural markets but, rather, on those in India's largest cities.[30] These transmissions would eventually mix with global satellite broadcasts from STAR TV and others. While various state-sponsored pilot projects have delivered TV, data, and government information, some of the most recent projects have focused on the software industry and its exports.[31] The government agency, Software Technology Parks of India (STPI), brokers bandwidth and enclave urbanism to a collection of global companies. Twenty-two earth stations generate IT gateways and a bandwidth allotments in time zones that, when paired with the US time zones, provide twenty-four-hour continuities in the workday together with wages that are a quarter of those in the USA.[32]

STPI's architecture offers neither redemptive modernism nor a Nehruvian hybrid between modern and traditional. It is most often a pastiche of exclusive resort and homegrown, science-fiction modernism. Genealogies of modernism track the cross-pollination between South Asian architects and the pedagogical theologies of Western architecture schools, concentrating on valorized mixtures of modern and regional vernacular. Yet the careers of architects like Le Corbusier, Louis Kahn, Balakrishna Doshi, or Charles Correa may be less relevant to the traditions of c-band urbanism, given that it has its own global vernacular. Nor do the architectural signals reference center-periphery patterns of global superpowers. Rather, they are often more fantastical, expressive, and even extraterrestrial, like the broadcast urbanism of c-band itself.

Tidal Park in Chennai, for instance, offers a glass and concrete architecture resembling perfunctory modernist office parks or civic buildings in America. Thiruvananthapuram Technopark, on the other hand, most resembles a resort in the colonial style, with its gigantic landscape of red roofs covering a structure of whitewashed walls. International Tech Park, near Bangalore, with its tall buildings, polished materials, and calling centers, provides architecture signals of foreign investment from Singapore.[33] Bangalore, a city of colonial and postcolonial headquartering by nations and corporations, received its first satellite connection in 1985, when Texas Instruments bought a segment of bandwidth.[34] Nearby Electronics City mixes small-scale office buildings and villas in ad hoc lots that sometimes line well-planted streets, but usually gather informally on nominal roads with little need for shared design presence. The properties that surround flagship buildings combine sci-fi Taj, or the Taj-deco-modern or deco-sci-fi recipes, with varying proportions of each ingredient. Fields of satellite dishes and radio towers are continuous with the gardens of office-villas, isolated cultural offerings such as Domino's Pizza or golf greens, and the tent encampments of the construction workers. Men and women wearing traditional garb work together on the construction line using ancient tools to dig a trench that might hold cable and other transmission lines.[35]

Subhash Chandra is often asked whether he attended a business school. Sure, he says . . . I went to Jaganath Goenka University.

The joke is his way of honoring the entrepreneurial prowess of his late grandfather, Jaganath Goenka, a small-town cottonseed trader who knew a thing or two about business—the kind of street-smart stuff they don't teach at management institutes. If it wasn't for the old man, Chandra might never have become India's first self-made media mogul, a figure often compared at home to News Corporation boss Rupert Murdoch.[36]

Photo opportunities were carefully crafted to provide a colorful spectacle: sadhus in saffron costumes, political leaders wearing headgear out of mythological films, a profusion of marigolds, and paraphernalia such as tridents, daggers, javelins, and bows and arrows, scenes whose "newsworthy" character eluded a simple secular/communal division.

—Arvind Rajagopal[37]

Although he had no previous experience as satellite viceroy, in 1991, just as STAR TV was about to launch, Indian entrepreneur Subhash Chandra asked to rent a channel in their network. Since the national satellite system did not allow private broadcasts, he planned to bounce his own Zee TV channel from STAR's satellite to an audience in India and around the world.[38] Chandra's first enterprise was plastic tubes for toothpaste and other pharmaceuticals, but he moved on to high-tech theme parks, play-win lotteries, and finally satellite TV. Supplementing their strict secular stance and regular diet of documentary political programming, Doordarshan broadcast weekly movies of Hindu epics. Chandra, banking on a hunger for such programming, essentially created a

Hindi station. While STAR's largest market was in India, Zee was eventually more successful locally, even challenging STAR's next owner, Rupert Murdoch. Zee still controls several of the channels available in India, offering soap operas, talk shows, gimmick shows, and reality TV. Satellite TV expanded in India in the 1990s partially in response to the success of STAR and Zee. Yet regional rivals such as Sun TV, Eenadu TV, and Udaya TV, which developed later, catered to even more specific audiences, and managed to take over a good deal of Zee's market share.[39]

Arthur C. Clarke's "Extra-terrestrial Relays" (1945), an early satellite scenario, predicted that global satellite TV would be instrumental in creating a form of global governance. Yet despite the global bounce of satellite transmissions, they have also become the tools of more self-reflexive national political sentiments. In the late 1980s and throughout the 1990s, when no one party had majority support in India, satellite television began to be used as a political instrument. A variety of political persuasions were broadcast from the regional TV stations. While some used Hindu imagery without specific political ambition. Arvind Rajagopal's *Politics after Television* investigates television's contribution to the rise of Hindu nationalism and the success of the Bharatiya Janata Party (BJP) in the 1990s. Rajagopal speculates that these televisual persuasions, such as serialized versions of the Hindu epics and carefully staged political events, have fueled the same anti-Muslim sentiments that contributed to defining episodes like the demolition of the Babri Mosque. That event fueled the popularity of the BJP and touched off a series of aggressions and retaliations between Hindus and Muslims in India.[40]

[see *Subtraction*]

Using the slogan "India Shining," the Hindu nationalist movement evoked traditional values, while it also signaled a readiness to engage in the myths of globalization. Competition with China, India's rival, and expansion of the atomized sovereignty of technopoles in the Middle East and Malaysia were also on the agenda. In this so-called "saffronization," the same glint of gold and vibrant color accessorized the political use of Hindu garb and symbology, as well as L. K. Advani or Narendra Modi.[41] If the country was not going to adhere to its traditional techniques of nation-building, it would find an even more extreme masquerade of traditional values to float over a liberalized deregulated economy. Slipping in anti-Muslim sentiments with the

MTV, the BJP should have had a winning strategy by any standard of global operations. Using a reliable formula of power, they had established the sanctity of a belief system, but maintained a more reciprocal network to keep that hermetic world alive. Believing and cheating should have worked well together, especially when the belief system was so extreme that it camouflaged a more elitist nationalism of privilege and defensive exclusion. Nationalism itself was a masquerade of sorts, and so needed several good disguises.

Still, India's new successful economy seemed to be tied to a nationalist fervor that many of its beneficiaries found distasteful. A huge population of farmers who still look to the weather of monsoons rather than to the weather of microwaves felt that they would be left behind in this new global economy. Yet the world was surprised when the 2004 elections unseated the BJP and Prime Minister Atal Bihari Vajpayee, replacing them with the Congress Party candidate, Sonia Gandhi. Gandhi then asked Manmohan Singh to take her place as Prime Minister. Singh, an economist and Congress Party finance minister, had initiated some of the very "reforms" that had come to fruition during the 1990s.[42] Juggling multiple meanings of "modern," the Congress Party will also float the sanctity of secular political traditions over the new globalizing economy.

My plan is to learn from Singapore, from Malaysia, from Rudoph Giuliani, and to bring change to our 50 year old country.
—Chandrababu Naidu[43]

I want to be Bill Gates.
—Mr. J. A. Chowdary, President HYSEA and former director of Software Technology Parks of India, Hyderabad[44]

India cannot afford to miss the IT Revolution. IT is knowledge, wealth, everything. Those who adopt it will prosper . . . we must have a mega dream and mega vision.
—Chandrababu Naidu[45]

There is a "Feel-Good" factor and I am confident that Vajpayee will become Prime Minister again.
—Chandrababu Naidu[46]

Right now, when you come to our campus, you're leaving India behind. . . . We're living in a make-believe world.
—N. R. Narayana Murthy, chairman of Infosys Technologies[47]

Chandrababu Naidu, entrepreneurial Chief Minister of India's state of Andhra Pradesh, was a special protagonist in the political shift that replaced the BJP. Styling himself as a viceroy of the new cybereconomy for his state, and calling himself Chief Executive Officer instead of Chief Minister, he spoke of wanting to turn Hyderabad into Hong Kong, and his affiliations track the major coordinates of the Asian and South Asian satellite network in Malaysia, Singapore, the Middle East, and China. He became a friend of President Bill Clinton and, through Clinton, a friend of Prime Minister Tony Blair. As one of India's best-known global politicians, he visited Rudy Giuliani and Bill Gates in the United States.[48] He quickly established an alliance with Microsoft to develop the Microsoft Software Development Centre in Andhra Pradesh.[49] A master of the optimistic forecast, Naidu hoped to accelerate growth in his state by using the computer and the TV for e-governance, cutting bureaucratic red tape by allowing citizens of each Mandal, or government subgroup, immediate access to information.[50] By analogy with the promotion surrounding the Multi-Media Super Corridor, Naidu called his government a "SMART" government, standing for Simple, Moral, Accountable, Responsive, and Transparent.[51] Like the CEO leader of any brandlike cultural persuasion, he wrote an inspirational book, *Plain Speaking,* that profiled his approach to life and his plans for the future of Andhra Pradesh.[52]

Naidu retained his position as Chief Minister by generating several different opportune alliances. He entered into power through a curious mixture of national, traditional, and televisual symbology. His father-in-law was N. T. Rama Rao, a Bollywood movie star who gave up his acting career to become Chief Minister of Andhra Pradesh in 1980. The Hindu imagery broadcast on

TV in Andhra Pradesh is often associated with regional political propaganda, not necessarily related to the BJP. Exalted as a film star playing Rama and Krishna, he often appeared in his Rama costume when campaigning, quoting lines from the Mahabharata. Naidu was elected to political posts within the Telugu Desam Party founded by Rao, until in 1995 he actually won the election for Chief Minister of the state, beating out Rao. Capitalizing in his own way on symbols of Hindu tradition, and using a variety of regional persuasions to different ends, he has, over the course of his career, maintained alliances with the BJP, the Telugu Desam Party, the National Democratic Alliance, and the Congress Party in Andhra Pradesh. Playing the young progressive with the laptop under his arm, he typically called for a neoliberal mix of "secularism and development."[53]

In 2000, Clinton visited Naidu's flagship STPI cybercity, HITEC City, a park of 158 acres located a few kilometers away from the Banjara Hills, a wealthy suburb of Hyderabad. Bill Clinton, Tony Blair, and Bill Gates are all honorary diplomats of the global knowledge village. Clinton saw HITEC's first phase of development, the Cyber Towers, a squat, ten-story cylindrical building housing a calling center for GE and offices for 48 companies including Oracle, Microsoft, IBM, and Toshiba.[54] An exterior fishnet of exposed structure wraps the cylinder, and at the entry a missing wedge of that cylinder reveals an inner core covered with highly reflective glass. Phase Two of the project, launched in 2000, is called Cyber Gateway: an 8,600,000-square-foot building with an interior open space the size of three football fields. Cyber Gateway resembles Hollywood constructions in science-fiction movies like *Stargate*.[55] A residential grouping is planned for eighty-seven acres, and ten-acre plots have been set aside for executive villas. Some plans for commercial development so far include a Pizza Hut, a novelty shop, a wellness center, and a tourist car facility.[56] All of these structures seem to land on a dusty ground that, in the rush to the future, is not yet prepared for them.

Naidu had also hoped to agglomerate a collection of technology parks together with a necklace of villages and highways into a mega city project called Cyberabad.[57] A new six-lane highway was to link all of the new development with a new international airport. Balakrishna Doshi, an architect legendary for providing a model of traditional and modern architectural mixtures, was employed as Cyberabad's designer/planner.[58]

5.2 Cyber Towers, HITEC City, Phase I, Hyderabad. Image courtesy of Satya Pemmaraju.

One of the most unusual projects that Naidu supported was New Oroville, a 500-acre IT campus for 20,000–30,000 people. In 1999, three American entrepreneurs, formerly employed at Microsoft, launched the community. Catalytic Inc. found, in Hyderabad, a talent pool for their "just-in-time" software. "We think humans are the rare commodity right now," they said.[59] Building a company town allowed them to offer gradual ownership of scarce housing, while also circumventing long commutes over bad roads to Hyderabad. All 4,230 homes (26 feet in diameter and 32 feet high) are designed as domes of concrete and metal reinforcing formed around an inflated balloon. The provider, Monolithic Dome Institute in Texas, claims to take inspiration from Buckminster Fuller.[60] In addition to the 2,200-square-foot houses, the community will include water and power plants, large domed buildings for offices and shops, a temple, a mosque, a church, a park, a swimming pool, and even an ice rink.[61]

In Cyber Gateway, Cyber Towers, and New Oroville, the architecture of South Asia's c-band urbanism mixes with televisual and media images to make special political signs. In America, television and film store futurologies in ephemeral broadcasts, while architecture stores neotraditional sentiments. In India, television has been politicized by neotraditionalism, while the architecture of broadcast urbanism often embodies futurologies. In India, special effects and ephemeral fantasies accessorize the cultural imagination that makes a business of software exports.[62] Architecture is instrumental in privileging imagery over interactivity. This architectural "face" even sometimes resembles a more primitive still image from the screen itself—a software environment of colors and implied movement.

Months before the election, in the fall of 2003, a Maoist group called the People's War unsuccessfully attempted to assassinate Naidu by blowing up his car while he was visiting a Hindu temple.[63] Naidu's on-line fan club always justified his dubious local support by celebrating his ability to engage global cooperation in development. His vision was certainly not that of the pastoral satellite democracy feeding the rural village, or offering "free rice and dhotis . . . at election time."[64] Still, Naidu's bid to move from an agricultural to a service economy was not popular among farmers who were still struggling with poverty, illiteracy, environment, and problems of inadequate physical infrastructure.[65] In the same elections that defeated the BJP, Naidu's party was soundly defeated.[66]

It will have everything India's best IT resorts have and much, much more. Not just an IT park or an IT resort, it's a fully integrated, self-contained development designed to offer international-quality, ready-to-use office space and social infrastructure for IT industries and IT-enabled services.

—Noida's promotional literature[67]

The new office building of HCL Perot System at Noida, built by architects RK and Associates, is spread over a 25-acre plot. The building, which has 3 wings, houses over 620 employees and has self-service café with vending machines on every floor. . . . The architects have used bright colors for the interiors keeping in mind that most software engineers were young. [68]

Within the larger global satellite sea, India's architecture and urbanism shares some architectural signals with Dubai Internet City, the Multi-Media Super Corridor, and Cyberport. Its newest IT cities may even be cast in the mold of duty-free special economic zones like Shenzhen or Jebel Ali, offering streamlined legal formalities, restricted labor laws, and high-performance infrastructures.[69] One such city, Noida, established in 1991, was another of STPI's fist earth station. The settlement (153 square miles when fully developed) has its own power, water, and telecommunications infrastructure, and is separated from Delhi by a twenty-minute expressway ride.[70] Its several sectors are being developed in phases that include, among other things, large industrial campuses, corporate headquarters, and universities for the Maharishi Mahesh Yogi and Gautama Buddha University. The central district is filling with supermalls, restaurant chains, a Cineplex, and a five-star hotel.[71]

Another such new city in India is Navi Mumbai (New Bombay). Charles Correa, an architect who, like Doshi, is renowned in India for his fluency in both traditional and modern architectural languages, designed the planned city in the 1970s as Bombay's more salubrious and spacious twin, one utilizing planning tools such as the "neighborhood unit" from urban reform traditions in the West. The government of Maharashtra gave the City and Industrial Development Corporation (CIDCO) permission to establish the city on 344 square kilometers (133 square miles) of land across from the Port of Bombay. While it still lacks tenants, developers and investors have begun to call the community a "futuristic technological village." CIDCO, in the meantime, has gained expertise in everything from infrastructure planning to financing and designing buildings, and they are developing more IT installations in India. CIDCO has even begun to advertise itself with the slogan "CIDCO—we make cities."[72] A portion of Navi Mumbai will now become MahaMumbai (MMSEZ), one of a series of SEZs in India brokered by a development company called Sea King Infrastructure Limited (SKIL). SKIL will develop over 12,000 hectares (29,520 acres or 46 square miles) with industries that include IT, biotechnology, microelectronics, and textiles.[73]

India is now launching satellites for other countries, and has the chance to brand its software and consultant services as a commodity for which it sets the standard.[74] The corridor between the Middle East, South Asia, and the Far East is becoming well worn. Joining forces with Intelsat, Thaicom, and the Dutch company New Skies, STPI also supplements its satellite bandwidth with fiber cable. It needs the extra capacity to communicate with neighboring satellite pools, as well as with Australia and Europe.[75] A number of companies are exploring wireless telephony in India (in both the licensed and the unlicensed spectrum).[76] Infosys, Tata, Wipro, VXL, and Satyam are among the automatic tenants of DIC, MMSC, and SAIF, a free trade zone in Dubai. Tata now calls itself not India's but Asia's largest IT company.[77]

In January 2004, accompanied by patronizing reports that it had "overtaken its parent," India claimed to have more computer specialists than Silicon Valley.[78] In the cat-and-mouse game of off-shoring or "right-shoring," Indian companies, including Wipro (Azim Premji, head of Wipro, is, notably, Muslim), have occasionally reversed the flow by buying or outsourcing to Western companies.[79] The young South Asian executives who have served in Silicon Valley are also reversing the flow by returning to India to build suburbs that look like those of southern California.[80] Subhash Chandra now wants to build a global media empire, and his ventures have expanded to include wireless and Direct to Home television.[81] Chandra's most recent enterprise, Agrani Satellite Services Ltd (ASSL), plans to broadcast not only television but remote and rural wireless telephony in an uninterrupted zone between South Asia and the United Arab Emirates. ASSL has completed a contract to become India's first [see *Park*] private satellite organization.[82]

This is a world that is everyday in its imaginary, pirate in its practice, and mobile in its innovation. This is also a world that never makes it to the computer magazine, more the technological discourses dominated by the cyber-elite. The old nationalists and Left view this world with fascination and horror, for it makes a muddle of simple nationalist solution. One can call this a recycled electronic modernity. And it is an imaginary that is suspect in the eyes of all the major ideological actors in techno-space.
—*Ravi Sundaram*[83]

For years now, the effort has been to peddle this technology to all corners of the globe, to achieve the dream of connecting every individual to every other individual in the world. Little attention is paid to the fact that "business at the speed of thought" is a concern that unites Bill Gates and Azim Premji, but is as inconsequential, as it is in any case impossible, for the tea-shop proprietor in the Indore municipality, the herdsman at Khyber Pass, the porter in the Nepali midhills, or the boat people of the Padma.[84]

Two "fables," as Ravi Sundaram has suggested, have been operating in relation to India's new digital capitalism. The elitist fable that imagines India commanding an expansive new market in digital capital is countered by the leftist fable that India will, in this transaction, remain a poor subject of larger global powers. But a vast "gray market" of technology, according to Sundaram, ignores both fables to pirate what it needs from the new digital economy. This force is not the mass of humanity posing with a gigantic public works project, or organizing in revolution against the powers that be. It is the force of the small everyday tactic multiplied in a disorganized groundswell. This perfectly elusive force (perhaps a third fable) invariably enters discussions of South Asian politics as hallowed territory. Existing in the active, infinitive political register, it eludes the declarative or nominative. It even eludes those who wish to romanticize India's boundless complexity. In this way, it is as perfect or utopian as any other naturalization of the market. Yet Sundaram's gray-market characterization allows for simply another imperfect force to be present at another scale in national and global political organization—a shadow force with its own misadventures. In the elections of 2004, the support for the BJP's programs dissolved into its agricultural roots, its global networks, and its gray market. But the crowd into which that support disappeared, when rendered with a piratical independence, is truly another invisible hand, intertwined with the classic invisible hand of capital.[85]

In rural villages, a small group of houses and shops cluster around one of the many STD (Subscriber Telephone Dialup) stations, PCOs (Public Call Offices), or TV receptors, which serve only a handful of people. While government, in partnership with industries, private providers, and charitable organizations, has been working toward rural teledensification, there are still very few telephones and TVs per capita.[86] The problems of software branding and competition do not facilitate a simple and widespread standard that would meet rural problems. There are approximately thirty people per landline telephone in India, and in the whole of South Asia there are between one and four mobile telephones per one thousand people. A computer costs a year's salary, and transportation to a central communication hub is difficult and unreliable.[87]

The pirates of the gray market, about which Sundaram writes, patch together the remainders as a survival technique—old motherboards, manuals, and software writing techniques. Cable television must overcome persistent line-poaching, and violence over that poaching. The urbanism of these operators, found in Delhi or at the Nehru Place market, is not like that of the IT park. "Present here," Sundaram writes, "are the agents of large corporations, and also software pirates, spare parts dealers, electronic smugglers and wheeler-dealers of every kind in the computer world."[88] Although the spaces of this pirate urbanism are marginal, they are everywhere, everywhere where telecommunication and computation is desired or traded. In Hong Kong, perhaps the most notorious capital of software piracy, multistory malls like the Wanchai computer center are filled with small stalls devoted to pirated software which costs a fraction of the retail price, and is completely naturalized despite occasional crackdowns.[89] The Wanchai counterpart in Beijing is the Bai Nao Hui department store.[90]

Another group of pirate survivors in India, GRASSO (Grameen Sanchar Seva Organization), combines activism with engineering ingenuity. GRASSO addresses transportation problems while also mining the unlicensed spectrum, which may be the truly fluid waters of the satellite sea, with new technologies like WiFi, WLL, and VSAT. Among their programs is one in which itinerate bicyclists sell telephone calls using electricity generated from their cycling.

5.3 Cyber Gateway, HITEC City, Phase II, Hyderabad. Image courtesy of Satya Pemmaraju.

Given that sales of motorcycles and mobile phones are often used as indicators of mobility and technological progress, the energy-generating bicycle seems the perfect trope.[91]

[see *Pirate*]

The broadcast urbanism of India's satellite media-technoscape demonstrates the difficulty of classic political characterizations of modernity and market. Like electricity during the TVA period, the new technology was projected to champion the simplest agrarian economies while providing an introduction to modernity. Yet the satellite sea, in either promotional campaign, is fraught with more contradictions and disguises, some of which combine the two visions in a shifting portrait. The digital refreshments of broadcast urbanism reinforce not just a regional but also a global field commensurate with the broadcast dimensions of satellites themselves. They provide vague references to several moderns, any combination which can be laminated with reflective materials to signal a standard degree of readiness. Satellite viceroys like Richard Li, Subhash Chandra, Chandrababu Naidu, or Azim Premji make walk-ons from every direction wearing various costumes. Naidu's costume camouflaged the political sentiments associated with his various alliances, just as the mixture of crisp new media formats and traditional costumes created a mutual camouflage for the BJP. IT urbanism references just enough of either a modernist or a neotraditionalist script to interest both camps, but remain in disguise. The almost aggressive enthusiasm and politeness of the parks fool those who are attracted to their one-world charms, and believe they have found the perfect servants. Indeed, the broadcast urbanism of the new SEZs possesses other global ambitions prompted by competition with China. Microwaves are already the tool of both the market and its resistance. India's bright IT palaces have embodied the disposition of two invisible hands, neither of which is natural or innocent.

Offshore

Ebene CyberCity is a knowledge park providing a single-stop world class facility for ICT companies engaged in the business of IT enabled services, call centres, back office operations, business process outsourcing, software development, intelligent manufacturing, IT education and IT-enabled education. It benefits from the experience of similar technology parks in Chennai, Hyderabad and Bangalore.[92]

India's STPI now provides consulting to the government of Mauritius to help transform its nation into "cyber island," which, along with the "data haven," is a relatively new offshore phenomenon. The descriptions are familiar: a one-stop twenty-four-hour, seven-day-a-week cyberurbanism of "knowledge parks" developed with architectural envelopes similar to those one might find in HITEC City. In fact, HITEC is being used as a model for financing and phasing the project. Operating from satellite bandwidth, Ebene CyberCity's sixty-four hectares would be developed with a Cyber Tower and Multi-media Zone on twenty-seven acres and a commercial area on thirteen acres. An additional fifty-acre area would be parceled in one-acre lots for the individual business headquarters of companies like Satyam, Wipro, Infosys, Microsoft, Hewlett-Packard, IBM, and Oracle.[93]

IT joins the other building blocks of Mauritius's relatively successful and diversified economy, built on new as well as postcolonial enterprises including sugar, textiles, tourism, and offshore banking. Demonstrating that the southern satellite sea is not merely the receiver of Western investment and labor needs, Mauritius is hoping that Indian as well as Western businesses will invest. Also, while India can offer an English-speaking labor force, Mauritius can offer French as well, thus serving other French-speaking Africa nations. As the so-called "beginning of the Indian Ocean," it is situated as a link between Africa and India. Moreover, the southern IT network, establishing its own hierarchies, may treat Mauritius as its offshore facility for outsourcing and networking.[94]

Mauritius, which has long been networked with the rest of the world, both broadly and reciprocally, demonstrates the way in which free trade zones are ancient ideas. Statues and monuments around Port Louis feature both figures of Europeans and Hindu shrines.[95] While the Portuguese first identified Mauritius, the Dutch completed the first conquest in 1598, making way for the Dutch East India Company's sugar plantations and slave trade. The French appeared in 1721, the British in 1814.[96] Citizens of Mauritius are Indians (from Tamil Nadu, Uttar Pradesh, Bihar, Andhra Pradesh, and Maharashtra), Chinese, French, English, and creoles of mixed European, African, and Asian descent. Many of those of African origin were freed slaves who became tradesmen in the nineteenth century. The connection to India was deepened by an early-nineteenth-century episode in which Indian convicts were transferred to the island as indentured servants.[97] Catholics comprise 27 percent of the population, while Muslims make up 16 percent.[98] Creoles seem to have a less stable status in the mix, and while the white French landowners have traditionally exercised political power, Hindu leaders have recently maintained dominance in the government, a fact underlined by Vajpayee's attentiveness to the country. Mauritius has even, opportunistically, made friends with the USA by being a partner in its Iraqi and Gulf War campaigns.[99]

The island is an anomaly in sub-Saharan Africa since, while it has experienced some downturns, its steady economic growth outflanks that of other African countries, with the exception of South Africa and Kenya. Analysts attribute this growth to a number of factors, perhaps most notably the country's establishment of an export-processing zone, which has gradually reduced the dominance of sugar, as will the presence of an IT industry. EPZs, which have not always provided the predicted quick fix for Third World countries, have succeeded in Mauritius perhaps because its ethnic composition has always been global and well disposed to foreign investment. Subhash Chandra's ASSL has holdings in Mauritius, recognizing it as a strategic location.[100] Mauritius is also linked to SAFE, the South African Far East Submarine Fiber-Optic Cable linking Malaysia, South Africa, West Africa, and Europe.[101] The island's long history of trading has steered its course since its independence in 1968.[102]

Yet Mauritius has not simply accepted a submissive role as just another island in the postcolonial confetti of Empire. Since there are already 15,000 offshore banks on the island, it is hoped that they will require internal services from calling centers to support the island's existing enterprises. The offshore island has even begun to export some of its sugar production "offshore"—which means, in this case, to the mainland of continental Africa, to Mozambique and Tanzania, where the labor is cheaper.[103] Mauritius seems to possess, perhaps through mimicry and opportunism, the political cunning of all of those who have used it. The island was a site of pirate escapades where colonial governors could be bribed for favors, but its global heterogeneity also made it attractive as a place of pirate retirement.[104]

[see *Pirate*]

Subtraction

Little specks of the Desert Inn are blowing everywhere. . . . Even though the tower is gone, bits of it will be left all along the Strip.
—Audience member present at the implosion of the Desert Inn[1]

Such a superiority, such an originality, made the moderns think they were free from the ultimate restrictions that might limit their expansion. Century after century, colonial empire after colonial empire, the poor pre-modern collectives were accused of making a horrible mishmash of things and humans, of objects and signs, while their accusers finally separated them totally—to remix them on a scale unknown until now.
—Bruno Latour[2]

Methods for demolishing, imploding, or otherwise subtracting building material are not among the essential skills imparted to architects in training. Believing building to be the primary constructive activity, the discipline has not institutionalized special studies of subtraction. In fact, for architects, the building envelope is almost always the answer to any problem, and subtraction is often understood to be preparation for more building. The demolition plan, one of the first pages in a set of construction documents, provides instructions about the removal of building material, but only building material that presents an obstacle to more building material, the material of a new, superior design. Architectural authorship is measured by building objects rather than the admirable removal of building material, and the general consensus within the discipline is that architectural efforts should be visible in photographs. Architecture permits soulful or brutish carving as well as clarifying essentialism, recognizing these to be artistic excisions or erasures. Still, they, too, should be visible in photographs. Moreover, the arduous task of piling one thing on another in the hopes of engaging gravity with stability becomes a more satisfying and bankable exertion when the object is considered to be durable, or even permanent. Whether for banks or architectural careers, building envelope is currency. Yet the subtraction of building has arguably been at least as important as the making of building during the last half-century. In some cases, building and subtraction are indistinguishable, and either may be equally aggressive, submissive, or constructive.

In the mid-twentieth century, architects all over the world removed their special-order Corbusian glasses and gestured sincerely to a presentation drawing where the words "tabula rasa" were written in cursive under a cartoon *soleil.* In love with the tablua rasa, architects are the perfect moderns, the perfect believers in the purification and obsolescence of successively immanent ideas. Whether the deletion of ruthless moderns or the "healing" and "stitching" of their descendants who profess to be more gentle, the tabula rasa is a seizure or conquest usually accompanying utopia. It is the weapon of delusional superiority in aesthetic generational wars.[3]

More important, the tabula rasa is the weapon of patient urban magistrates whose masquerades of cleansing and purifying diseased fabric often disenfranchise entire populations. The subtractions of planning may be no less violent or deliberate than the subtractions of warfare. Marshall Berman—who has, over the years, exposed several forms of wanton, even casual, forms of urban murder, whether in Sarajevo or the Bronx—has called these subtractions "urbicide."[4] Demolishing areas deemed to be blighted is a long-standing municipal practice used to revalue property or recalibrate parcels. Shifting political climates may also delete ownership, value, or physical property with a slight change of laws or master plans. Although it may hide within the folds of legalities, this covert destruction may be as devastating as wars or natural disasters.

Yet while one view of urbicide renders buildings and populations as victims, buildings and urban formations are often themselves aggressive instruments of subtraction or aggression. The very particular morphologies of high-rise housing and highways, for instance, have been used to clear territory—to simultaneously construct and subtract. Moreover, buildings possess disposition and agency in their organization, and are able to broadcast fields of blight or altered real estate values that begin a process of attrition. Buildings are not only economic indicators, but volumetric reflections of volatile markets, part of a rapidly changing economy of elastic and disposable spatial formats. These ecologies have, arguably, accelerated the animation of making and unmaking building. Accumulation or accretion generally signals growth, and subtraction generally signals loss, but in active urban organizations every building construction is a subtraction or replacement. Subtraction is not simply absence or presence, but a trace in a set of exchanges and advances, aggressions and attritions.[5] The extreme ecologies of development make of deletion a recognizable building activity—even a global industry.

Whatever mobile territories are at stake in the wars between the world's empires, buildings and cities are, as they have ever been, spectacular targets, and building deletions, whether as warfare, urban corrective, or staged explosion, have become cultural spectacles that are all executed with similar engineering techniques. Constructing tall buildings, dams, highways, and other large public works involving dynamite and large-scale movements of material has traditionally provided building spectacles. Currently, however, it is the *deletion* or implosion of housing towers, bridges, sports arenas, and convention centers that provide this theater. Moreover, in this period of Gulf Wars, the precise destruction of physical targets has become an anticipated component of media-savvy warfare. Both forms of subtraction merge with their Hollywood counterpart. An index of the global industry of subtraction encounters planning utopias, political maneuvering, terrorism, and war.

I don't want him always to see everything on the screen at home. It's not the same. I want him to have real experiences. I would really have liked to get him close enough to feel the air currents, to have some dust settle on his head.

—One of the spectators wishing to expose her son to the "E-Ticket" experience of the Disneyland Grand Hotel implosion[6]

The concrete palace along Dale Mabry Highway [Tampa's Houlihan Stadium] was supposed to give way to an implosion at 8 a.m. As 220 pounds of dynamite were ignited with a push of a button by raffle winner Saarin Aukin of Lutz, the sights and sounds were spectacular.[7]

In Las Vegas the pirates always win.
—Steve Wynn[8]

Countless postmodern architects used images of the demolition of the Pruitt-Igoe housing towers in St. Louis (1972) as a polemical tabula rasa, to clear the preceding modernist agenda. Since the collapse of the World Trade Center, the Pruitt-Igoe demolitions have become doubly iconic. Designed by Minoru Yamasaki (as was the World Trade Center) and built in 1955, this wildly dysfunctional housing sustained vacancies of approximately 30 to 40 percent, and was destroyed after only seventeen years.[9] Destruction of the Pruitt-Igoe housing towers also roughly coincided with the inauguration of the World Trade Center. Moreover, one of the engineers who helped to demolish Pruitt-Igoe developed, on that job, a new technique for deleting buildings that has become standard in the global industry of building destruction. This new implosion technique removed lower supports, leaving a top-heavy structure of at least five stories to collapse by gravitational force. The engineer, Jack Loizeaux, began imploding buildings that very year as the founder of a company called Controlled Demolition Incorporated (CDI), now a global company with offices and affiliates in major cities around the world.[10]

CDI provides a special index of the global industry of subtraction. In addition to deleting housing, old factories, department stores, or obsolete Cold War equipment, CDI and other demolition experts remove spatial products that have rapidly lost their currency. As the mirror image or the negative engineering of recent structural achievements, implosion indexes a specific economy of obsolescence. Only those buildings with significant height or particularly coherent structures respond well to this technique. Often the largest and most expensive buildings such as high-rises, sports stadiums, convention centers, and resorts are deleted by implosion, usually in less than thirty seconds.[11]

CDI has described its implosions as "awesome public relations opportunities that would otherwise cost clients hundreds of thousands of dollars," and that will "create instant visibility for their new development projects."[12] CDI designs demolition effects for films like *Lethal Weapon 3, Demolition Man,* and *Enemy of the State.* Yet Steve Wynn, a Las Vegas developer of megaresorts, crafted its most visible publicity. With his help, Las Vegas celebrated the New Year in 1996 by imploding the Hacienda Hotel and Casino for a huge crowd and a live satellite broadcast. Perhaps the most elaborate spectacle, however, occurred three years earlier at Wynn's Treasure Island resort. At the Treasure Island, styled as an eighteenth-century Caribbean pirate village, pirates ordinarily sink a British frigate as the finale to their hourly staged gun battles. In 1993, CDI staged an implosion in which cannon fire from the pirates appeared to cause a complete collapse of the Dunes Hotel across the street.[13]

Resort aggregations in Las Vegas and around the world become obsolete when they are no longer able to optimize space and time to absorb all potential consumption. In addition to the Dunes and the Hacienda, CDI imploded the Sands, Landmark, Aladdin, El Rancho, and Desert Inn in Las Vegas, along with resort hotels all around the world, from Guam to the Caribbean and Dubai.[14] Most of the imploded hotels are approximately fifty years old, slightly above the average age of the imploded housing towers. Megaresorts, with 100,000-square-foot casinos and anywhere from 1,500 to 4,000 rooms, typically replace the demolished hotels in Las Vegas. These gigantic Jerde or Disney-style resorts, like blockbuster summer movies, must not only merge resorts with theme parks, but also generate an enormous enclosure that simulates a world or a microclimate.[15] Robert Venturi's figure-ground drawing of Las Vegas in the 1970s revealed a sea of parking lots supporting a relatively smaller area of building footprint. In Rem Koolhaas's end-of-the-century redrawing of that figure-ground analysis, the vast expanses of parking lots have been filled with a new formula for spreading building enclosures and conglomerate programs.[16]

The program cocktail itself is an instrument of subtraction. Building envelopes are closely tied to economic and logistical formulas for optimizing the consumption of goods or entertainment, and may be as volatile as the market, as slippery as municipal tax structures, as subject to change as the financial health of large corporations, or as ephemeral as the desires surrounding fashion and entertainment. For resorts or hospitals in a multistory building, new

6.1 Implosion of the Dunes Hotel, Las Vegas (1993). Image courtesy of The Loizeaux Group, LLC, Controlled Demolition, Inc. Photographer: Mr. Greg Cava, Cava Photo, Inc., Las Vegas, Nevada.

technical or programmatic needs generate rapid cycles of obsolescence. Yet, remarkably, all that is really needed to topple a building, whether it offers constrained or generous dimensions, is a new wrinkle in consumption logistics or an ephemeral desire in the styling of entertainment.

The expense, monumental size, and structural heroics of sports arenas make them especially satisfying subjects of deletion. They represent temporary stabilizations of the fortunes and allegiances of ball clubs, the ephemeral chemistry of new municipal taxes and rents, as well as revenue from the operation of the arena itself. Upon completion, the stadiums are almost immediately at risk of obsolescence. A large singular figural space cannot simply be inflated. It must be removed and recast to introduce a new program or audience capacity. However massive and durable the construction, some stadiums are torn down within just over twenty years.[17] When it was built in 1976, Seattle's Kingdome, for example, exhibited especially ingenious feats of engineering, and was made to last for hundreds of years.[18] Its implosion in 2000, like most of the others, was a live urban spectacle as well as a media event. In Microsoft's 3D-enhanced cybercoverage of the implosion, chunks of concrete and dust appeared to fly toward the viewer, who was also able to repeatedly reactivate the implosion with a mouse-click on the dome.[19]

Convention centers and malls join the list of demolition subjects, although they are demolished at a somewhat younger age than either housing towers or stadiums. Convention centers may not make it past their twentieth year, in part because they are instruments of pork-barrel funding projects.[20] A twenty-year-old mall in Pasadena fell to the ground while broadcasting *Also sprach Zarathustra* and releasing a flock of doves.[21] Of the 1,500–2,500 working malls, several hundred have been closed or destroyed. So-called "category killers" of big box retailing optimize niche markets, sometimes encircling the mall and eviscerating their older, obsolete patterns of marketing. Another weapon of retail warfare, the "fortress mall," gathers so many valuable stories within a gigantic footprint that it, too, is often able to kill a smaller mall.[22]

Despite its apparent perversity and expense, obsolescence in large public works produces a harvest of jobs, revenue, and campaigning power that are boilerplate ingredients in municipal politics. An arena that is imploded today might have cost $500 million when it was built, with two hundred million contributed by the sports organizations, and thirty million per year recouped by the city in tax revenues from the operation of the arena. In some cases, extra values accrue from a perceived revitalization of older downtown areas. The implosion of these structures is also a multi-million-dollar job, and most of the stadium projects today will be rebuilt at a cost of approximately $1.5 billion.[23] Yet politicians will invariably attach themselves to a stadium or convention center boondoggle, and a city will invariably court sports teams who threaten to shift their loyalties to another city with a better stadium offer. The members of the architecture profession who speak about permanence and *firmitas* at annual meetings of the AIA or RIBA are also overtly harvesting work in this field of subtraction. All over the country new sporting facilities are going up, built by firms like HOK, NBBJ, HNTB, Ellerbee Beckett, and HKS—names styled in the contemporary patois of the acronym. By specializing, these professionals bring expertise to the table, and ensure that the game will be played just as it was the last time.[24]

After campaigning on a promise to raze 5,000 houses by September, Mr. Kilpatrick [mayor of Detroit] has so far seen only about 1,000 come down. He blames lack of money and a diffuse bureaucracy.[25]

The kind of difference that defines every place is not on the order of a juxtaposition but rather takes the form of imbricated strata. The elements spread out on the same surface can be enumerated; they are available for analysis; they form a manageable surface. Every urban "renovation" nonetheless prefers a tabula rasa *on which to write in the cement the composition created in the laboratory on the basis of discrete "needs" to which functional responses are to be made. The system also produces need, the primary "substance" of this composition, by isolating it. The unit is as neat and clean (*propre*) as digits are. Moreover, the lack of satisfaction that defines each need calls for and justifies in advance the construction that combines it with other needs. This is the logic of production; ever since the eighteenth century, it has engendered its own discursive and practical space, on the basis of points of concentration—the office, the factory, the city. It rejects the relevance of places it does not create.*

—Michel de Certeau[26]

With the 1998 demolition of Villa Panamérica and Las Orquideas, public housing in Puerto Rico, CDI broke its own world record for the most buildings imploded simultaneously. In 1996, CDI had simultaneously imploded twelve public housing buildings in Pohang, South Korea.[27] Yet these implosions were just some of the hundreds of thousands of high-rise housing units that have been razed since the destruction of Pruitt-Igoe. From Baltimore to Chicago to Newark to Detroit, municipal governments have voted to replace high-rise warehouses with mixed-income housing, sometimes imploding the buildings before replacement units have even materialized. In 1996, Chicago projected the implosion of 15 percent of its public housing projects by 2002. Most of the towers destroyed are less than forty years old, close to the life expectancy of roofing material on a single-family house.[28] Philadelphia is clearing thousands of row houses, cleaning up vacant lots, and thus creating development parcels sized to meet the demands of new real estate products.[29] In large cities like Detroit, Philadelphia, or Baltimore, subtraction efforts constitute the bulk of public building projects. The act of subtraction itself may significantly raise property values.[30] In Beijing, the disposability of building and the volatility of the building envelope encounter a small-scale, low-revenue residential fabric. Beijing's Hutong alleys are being demolished at a rate of 600 per year to make way for new development.[31] [see *Park*]

When gunmen took aim at the citizens of Sarajevo from the modernist high-rise housing towers lining "Sniper's Alley," they added another episode of urban deletion and death to the several waves of subtraction that most twentieth-century building projects experience in their life span. Marshall Berman's first writings about urban destruction in *All That Is Solid Melts into Air* recount the stories of Robert Moses's systematic subtraction in the Bronx to make way for high-rise housing and highways.[32] "Tower in the Park" high-rise housing, built all over the world, initially sponsored the subtraction of existing tenements. Gordon Bunshaft's model for public housing in New York City demonstrated that additional floors did not significantly increase construction costs but, rather, decreased costs associated with greater site coverage. The 90 percent site coverage typical in tenement fabric was reduced to just over 10 percent. Liberal political rhetoric portrayed the arrangement as a new model of efficiency and security. Although it may have been regarded as efficient to avoid entry duplications in these high-rise towers, the reduction of redundancy in entry was the least efficient arrangement of communication between the tower's residents, one that weakened their resilience.[33] As in any camp or special zone, in this case used to detain or store the urban poor, the reductive organization created a secure position only for those in power, who found the singular control points reassuring as a means of containing a population more subject to poverty. Zygmunt Bauman quotes Loïc Wacquant's term "prisonization" in his description of such secure environments—he calls them sites of "human waste disposal."[34]

After the first subtraction of clearing, the organizational disposition of the building itself initiates a second wave of subtraction. Any user, dealer, criminal, or maintenance problem affected the entire tower through the core, the unavoidable space of circulation. The towers were highly susceptible to contagions. Without multiplication and redundancy of entry, the environment was unable to form alternative networks of association, making it vulnerable to failed maintenance and crime. The towers were so singular, so impossible to partition, so reliant on a central serial core, that they possessed no ability to dissipate disturbance. The reductive organization only escalated the power of these negative influences to create an epidemic or an avalanche. No explosions or bulldozers but, rather, a drop of an addictive drug such as crack could race through the organization, weakening it and radiating reduced real estate value in the surrounding fabric. The high-rises generated more and more abandoned buildings, arson, and demolitions before inducing their final subtraction by implosion.

Like the high-rise housing project, the limited-access highways that were often coupled with them possess active tools of subtraction and attrition within their organization and disposition. Their continuous thirty-foot rights of way produced an unusual network of subtraction, occupying about forty acres of space per mile of roadway. As a mathematical field whose dimensions were a function of traffic volumes at a particular speed, it was a true vacancy, an abyss into which people might furtively drop something as small as a tissue, or abandon something as large as a car. Architects and politicians declared the spaces "ugly," and prepared guidelines that proposed to fill them with shrubs or wildflowers, thus relieving the persistent ailment of what mid-century critics termed "visual monotony." Beyond the thirty feet, the highway broadcast changing real-estate values to form an even more extensive field of influence. While urban land values declined, in exurban areas they increased 200 to 500 percent within one half mile of the roadway, and continued to increase within about a mile of the roadway. Over a longer period of time, however, exurban highways radiated a negative field of real estate value for about 1,000 feet around their surface area.[35] Although it is thinly spread across the entire country, this webbed network of rights of way contacted the largest surface area of any federal landholding, affecting the value of the most diverse properties and ecosystems in the country.[36]

The urban vacancies caused by highways and high-rise housing have often been viewed with sorrow or outrage. Yet while they may be vacant and dormant, they are powerful and potentially active landscapes. Camilo Vergara's successive rephotography of subtractive housing fields in the South Bronx, Detroit, Newark, and Camden illustrates a relatively rapid time-lapse animation of subtraction. Vergara called these subtracted sites "green ghettos," because the vacant lots gradually began to fill with vegetation.[37] In a project called "Erasing Detroit," architect Dan Hoffman marked the areas of recently razed housing stock in the city, as well as areas adjacent to urban highways, noting that "unbuilding has surpassed building as the city's major architectural activity."[38] The demolitions of high-rises perhaps even constitute a significant building project, but not as sites for the next generation of reformed and corrective housing stock, or for a default network of green. Rather, they are sites that reopen a restrictive, often violent environment. They possess a complex ecology of laws, planning decrees, and real estate values any one of which might reactivate the vacancy or recondition the sites it contacts at its edges.

The Omni didn't linger. Its death was quick, loud and dusty.[39]

For the Loizeaux brothers, demolition is not their only job. In their spare time, the brothers play terrorists for the military, in the military's efforts to design terrorist/bomb proof buildings.[40]

6.2 Implosion of Broadway Homes, Baltimore, Maryland. Image courtesy of The Loizeaux Group, LLC, Controlled Demolition, Inc. Photographer: Mr. John Strohsacker, Mystro, Inc., Baltimore, Maryland.

CDI's implosion of the Desert Inn in October 2001 was a bit more somber than some of the previous Las Vegas events, in part because of the startling similarity between these staged implosions and the implosion of the World Trade Center in New York City.[41] Indeed, similar structural failures induced both types of implosions. Both produced the same cloud of fine dust and the same scenes of instantaneous destruction. The implosion technique, unlike demolition, also seemed to inspire, in both cases, sentiments associated with internal destruction, suicide, or death by natural causes.[42]

The World Trade Center was a spectacularly vulnerable adversary when symmetrically aligned with its attackers. Contemporary journalism often focused on the building's "smart" elevator network as just one of its intelligent building systems. But the building's simple volumes had a much less intelligent organizational repertoire. To maximize rentable area, the floors were almost completely segregated, connected only by thin strands of exit stairways. As an organization or a network of spaces, the World Trade Center was, like high-rise housing, a serial rather than a parallel arrangement. In evacuation, the World Trade Center required slow sequential routes of circulation rather than the simultaneous and reciprocal points of contact and exit.[43]

[see *Park*]

Yet the World Trade Center, acting as an adversary or military apparatus of sorts, also demonstrated the agency or disposition that buildings possess. As pawns in a symmetrical warfare between the USA and al-Qaeda, the building was already rendered volatile and friable. If the goal of terrorists is to prompt their enemy's own self-destruction, the weak constitution of the building's organization was part of the fight, an instrument of suicide in a symmetrical standoff between the righteousness of both the USA and al-Qaeda. George W. Bush and Osama bin Laden, two sons of mid-century oil privilege, engaged in a dumb and deadly symmetrical fight in which they cast buildings as major players. Both claimed that their caves or towers were superior in their complexity. Both needed to occupy the other's turf, so as to cleanse it. This competition was staged as a tragic riddle of conflicts and fatal flaws. The characters seemed to carry out involuntarily programmed retaliations and self-protective consolidations. Yet from within this perfect circle of self-reflexivity emerged the most convicted cries of innocence. In these escalations of violence, the World Trade Center both provoked and succumbed to warfare. Its collapse merged the pyrotechnics of warfare from the Defense Department, Hollywood, and the increasingly common urban spectacles of implosion. The USA named its campaign of military retaliation in Afghanistan "Enduring Freedom," and the words "Enduring Spirit of Freedom" are carved into the cornerstone of the retaliating buildings that will replace the World Trade Center.

Pentagon officials have talked about the operation for months: one so concentrated and devastating that it would put the Iraqis in a state of "shock and awe."[44]

US Foreign Policy initiatives are generally the first forum in which the American tax dollar influences relations with other countries. Time is frequently of the essence in the negotiation and implementation of agreements between countries. Controlled Demolition Incorporated (CDI) has, on several occasions, provided negotiation backup and field performance support for US Department of State contracts which are critical to US Government interests. From the design of and modification to missile fabrication facilities in South Africa to the elimination of weapons of mass destruction in Central European countries, Controlled Demolition Incorporated has the technical expertise and international network to assist in budgeting and, subsequently, implementing agreements which make the world a safer place.[45]

Even before September 11, CDI often emphasized the patriotic content of their work, merging with the war heroes, policemen, and emergency workers who attend to these crises. For instance, they imploded what remained of Oklahoma City's Alfred P. Murrah Federal Building after it was the victim of domestic terrorism. The US military has employed CDI to implode Cold War installations like Scud missile launchers or Russian radio towers in Eastern Europe.[46] In America, for instance, the company has worked for the Departments of Housing and Urban Development, State, Defense, Justice, and Energy.[47] CDI currently also offers antiterrorism consulting based on its familiarity with global explosive devices and techniques. Its "anti-terrorist database," as well as its consulting services in "blast-resistant design," will help to shape a new international style. The political "face" or message will replace self-valorizing modernism with innocuous disguise and hidden security features.[48]

Cities are certainly victims of "urbicide"—objectives and remnants in the subtractive fields of warfare. Bucharest, Beirut, Sarajevo, Belgrade, Dili, Kabul, New York City, or Baghdad are only some of the most recent examples of cities that have been deliberately targeted. Yet, like the World Trade Center, cities are also active adversaries, possessing the power to resist, elude, aggress, or stand their ground. The city is a challenging opponent, and to the degree that its strength signals tolerance, diversity, and intelligence, it must be crushed by totalitarian regimes or more conservative factions who are accustomed to seizing power.[49]

However difficult the total destruction of cities in a military theater, the military continues to quantify the value of urbicide as an inducement to surrender. Ryan Bishop and Gregory Clancey recall the episodes of US "target practice" on Japan, Korea, and Vietnam with napalm and nuclear weapons. After Hiroshima and Nagasaki, US generals like Curtis LeMay considered cities in Korea and Vietnam as only smaller targets, some mathematical percentage of which was crucial to the destruction or surrender of an entire nation.[50] The USA had previously contributed to the destruction of so much of Afghanistan that when forces arrived there in late 2001, there was nothing much left to destroy. The bewildered military dispensed with its building targets inside of two weeks, and was unable to stage more spectacular televised destruction until fresh attempts with the "shock and awe" campaigns in Baghdad—a media event in the night sky that was visually very similar to the mock battles that destroyed the Dunes Hotel in Las Vegas. [see *DPRK*]

In the war on terror, buildings and cities become conflicted military apparatuses. Urban warfare requires many different species of soldier, security contractor, and pirate, using various forms of camouflage, as well as lethal and nonlethal weapons. Cities harbor and camouflage their own murders, but can also withstand the destruction of those murders. Their vigilance maintains and sustains a deadly form of urbanism. Urbanness is the multiplication of enemies—so many that war becomes impossible. Yet the city as security compound is reductive organization that eliminates the enemy to create a clean environment of control. In this attempt at absolute control, the compound loses some of its urban camouflage, targets its single enemy, and reinforces its own status as a target.

The Ferris wheel and café on the Prater were owned by Eduard Steiner, a Jew who was murdered at Auschwitz.[51]

Palestinian human and political rights are violated not only by the presence of the settlements, but also by their location, size, form, and internal layout—in short, by their very design. Just like the tank, the gun, and the bulldozer, here building materials and infrastructure are used as weapons to commit crimes. Planning in the West Bank finally shed the last shred of its social pretense of facilitating the welfare of an abstract "public" and ended up as the executive arm of the strategic and geopolitical agenda of the Israeli state.[52]

If bombs and dynamite provide the hardware of subtraction, the software of these deletions is often embedded within special legalities. The failures and false logics of social programs are sanctioned forms of aggression even when they wear the guise of liberal reform, as was the case with American high-rise housing. A battery of legal restrictions may completely disenfranchise a population that threatens the beliefs or sovereignty of those in power. The properties of Jews and Muslims have been seized or Aryanized in European purges for centuries.[53]

Similarly, Israel has for the last three decades implemented a housing policy that restricts Palestinian building in Gaza, East Jerusalem, and the West Bank, while also demolishing Palestinian homes deemed to be illegal. Palestinians are not permitted to build without a permit, but permits are expensive, sometimes as much as $2,500, and only a limited number are issued. Without the ability to establish legal ownership, one may also be denied a permit. Yet in 1968, Israel discontinued land registrations, thus reducing the possibility that a Palestinian could legally own property. Given these difficulties, many Palestinians build illegal structures that are then targeted for demolition. Since the war between Israel and the Palestinians is also fought with population statistics designed to support claims of sovereignty, houses near sites of possible expansion for Israeli settlements are likely targets of demolition. Laws also sanction the demolition of dwellings associated with any firearms or bombs that have been involved in the Palestinian-Israeli conflict.[54] More suicide bombs retaliate for these demolitions, and the selective, piecemeal subtraction becomes a self-perpetuating exchange of destruction.

Demolition is only one form of aggressive subtraction in Israel; development is another. B'Tselem, a human rights organization that has been tracking demolitions of Palestinian homes as well as the buildup of Israeli settlements, joined forces with architect Eyal Weizman to map Israel's techniques of land acquisition in the West Bank. Their special cartography also takes a closer look at what first appear to be North American suburban development patterns—the cul-de-sacs of Radburn, a golf development, or a highway network. But on the West Bank, these banal instruments develop another aggressive repertoire. They are trained to creep, encircle, and cut off nearby Palestinian territory. They favor linear extensions in the land that create walls or fortifications of Israeli territory, but they also gravitate to isolated points, usually on mountaintops. As a consequence of these and other factors, the cartography must also map the vertical axis. Highway overpasses, aqueducts, and sewage infrastructure connect the isolated islands. Occupation of high elevations, sometimes masquerading as an archeological claim to a sacred site, establishes a scenographic command over the land. Moreover, the microwave space of telephony and media broadcasting, is often also Israeli-controlled. Finally, the study compiled graphic evidence of planning as human rights abuse.[55]

Some forms of disenfranchisement are open crusades, too proud of their destruction to hide behind a law. For the Taliban, for instance, subtraction was a highly publicized technique of intimidation, as evidenced by the deletion of the Bamiyan Buddhas. The Hindu protesters' demolition of the Babri mosque in Ayodhya, India, in 1992 was an attempt to eliminate a rival religion, and usurp the site for a new temple. The 500-year-old Moghul mosque was destroyed because the Hindus claim that the god Ram was born in the same spot. This violent form of site preparation and assumption then incited a chain of destructive retaliations. During the most notorious of these, in 2002, Muslims attacked a train filled with Hindu activists traveling from Ayodhya, burning alive many of its passengers.[56] [see *Shining*]

The field of ruin is a mile in width, bounded by the lake on one side and mainly by a branch of the river on the other, and four miles in length, thus being as large as half of New York City from the Battery to the Central Park, or as the whole of the peninsula of Boston. The houses burned set ten feet apart would form a row over a hundred miles in length. I judge that more than a third of the roof-space and fully half of floor space of the city, the population of which was 330,000, was destroyed.

—Frederick Law Olmsted, writing about the aftermath of the Chicago fire[57]

Mr. Gorbachev, tear down this wall.

—President Ronald Reagan, Berlin, June 12, 1987[58]

Build it and we will burn it.

—Earth Liberation Front[59]

CDI also implodes buildings that have already experienced severe damage from a natural disaster, such as those damaged in Mexico City after the earthquake in 1985. Some cataclysmic events of warfare and natural disaster delete so abruptly that sorrow, relief, and restoration rush in to fill the void. The 1995 Kobe earthquake subtracted a space twenty kilometers long and two kilometers wide, leaving 5,500 people dead and 6,400 structures destroyed, but the rapidity and innovation of the rebuilding effort surpassed all expectations.[60]

Catastrophes like Chernobyl or Bhopal, as well as sprawl and environment degradation, inspire activism, even countersubtractions. Some self-appointed pirates of subtraction, like those in the Earth Liberation Front (ELF) counter subtraction with subtraction. As habitats and species disappear, ELF battles in one theater of that environmental war, inflicting hundreds of thousands of dollars' worth of corrective damage on suburbia by burning or defacing suburban McMansions.[61] Frederick Law Olmsted's descriptions of the aftermath of the Chicago fire (1871) are remarkable in the sense that they do not begin with the desire to correct, restore, or usher in new systems of urban parks. Olmsted simply identified a new site by measuring the subtraction, evaluating its constituent parts, and cross-referencing the section it cut through social classes and enterprises in the city.[62]

Whatever the destructive force of architecture, the architect's self-portrayal is often as an innocent healer who appears only in the aftermath of subtraction with a restorative plan. While building may be embedded in volatile or violent urban ecologies, the discipline often does not recognize the warfare or aggression of architecture. Nor is it accustomed to recognizing subtraction as a technique or tool used either deliberately or in collusion. Nevertheless, building is often a subtraction, and subtraction is usually another construction. Subtraction is a primary activity in the ecology of building and making space—an operation of practice or a capacity that all buildings possess, rather than a by-product of destructive forces.

Each species of subtraction presents different techniques, motives, or results. Some subtractions erase information; some release a flood of information and association. Some gradually recondition a space, while others deliver debilitating attrition. Some provide resistance or relief, while others crush resistance, insurgency, or diversity. There are spectacular landscapes of aggressive deletions, as well as *Landschafts* of deletion that cultivate the systemic removal of material over time. The least spectacular deletions, which operate in subterfuge, without dynamite or bombs, may even be the most violent. However gentle the tone of the rhetoric, fundamental to subtraction is the desire to remain innocent, to reduce, preserve, or purify anything that contradicts or threatens the prevailing power.

Offshore

When the U.N. meets to usher in yet another century, will the Maldives and other low-lying island nations be represented here?

—Maumoon Abdul Gaymoom, President of the Maldives, with thirty seconds left to speak at the United Nations Conference on the Millennium, politely reminds all of the other countries about the reality facing his sinking islands[63]

Refugees, the human waste of the global frontier-land, are the "outsiders incarnate," the absolute outsiders, outsiders everywhere and out of place everywhere except in the places that are themselves out of place—the "nowhere places" that appear on no maps used by ordinary humans on their travels. Once outside, indefinitely outside, a secure fence with watching towers is the only contraption needed to make the "indefiniteness" of the out-of-place hold forever.

—Zygmunt Bauman[64]

Nauru, in Oceania just south of the Marshall Islands and north of Australia, achieved independence in 1968, becoming the smallest republic in the world. It was recognized by the United Nations in 1999. With 12,000 people, it is about one-tenth the size of Washington, D.C.[65] The beginning of Nauru's story is typical of the confetti of Empire. A European explorer discovered it in 1798. After guns were sold to the islanders by passing Europeans, the twelve previously peaceful tribes initiated a ten-year war. The Germans conquered the island in 1888. After phosphate was discovered, Australian mining companies paid half a penny per ton to the Nauruians. The island was seized from the Germans and occupied by Australia during World War I. It was captured by the Japanese in 1945, and retaken by Australia that same year. Once a lush tropical island populated with noddy terns and many other bird species, over the past ninety years its phosphate reserves, deriving from the bird guano, have been mined to the point of exhaustion. Brochures typically display the Hotel Mennen, one of Nauru's two hotels. The island's one airplane constitutes "Air Nauru." Electricity is available during specified hours in the day. Broadcasts of Australian-rules football constitute a relaxed cult of sorts on the island. When Nauru's sales of phosphate made it one of the wealthiest countries in the world, the island was lured into questionable investment schemes, including a musical about Leonardo da Vinci's love life. Now nearly bankrupt, it cannot meet its payments on the airplane, and often cannot afford to run its power plant.[66]

Kinza Clodumar, then President of the Republic of Nauru, speaking immediately prior to Vice President Al Gore at the Kyoto Conference in 1997, claimed exploitation by colonial powers in the exhaustion of the phosphate mines and the denuding of the tropical forest. Most of the inhabitants have moved from the balding pate of the island to its fringes along the shore, where they are trapped between the wasted land and a rising sea level. Clodumar admonished the Western world from an island microcosm and ecological bellwether, characterizing the effect of global warming as cultural genocide and "a rising flood of biblical proportions." He went on to say: "Small Island States provide not only a moral compass; we are also a barometer of broader visitations wisely heeded by all."[67]

Journalists from the *New York Times* and *National Geographic* have written about the island's ecological seesaw. A *National Geographic* article in 1921, "Nauru, the Richest Island in the South Seas," told of Nauru's beauty and prosperity; while the *New York Times* article, "A Pacific Island Nation Is Stripped of Everything," emphasized ecological devastation in the wake of globalization. The island has also been characterized as a "crystal ball" or microcosm of the earth in heartfelt stories about global ecological distress and tragedy.[68] Funds permitting, Nauru has developed a plan to vacate the island and buy another atoll, thus becoming an offshore site with its own offshore escape route.

Despite the power of the island's moral compass, the Financial Action Task Force on Money Laundering frequently lists Nauru for its offshore banking misconduct. Russia, The Philippines, Burma, Egypt, Guatemala, Hungary, Indonesia, Nigeria, Bahamas, Cayman Islands, Liechtenstein, and Panama have, at times, appeared on the same list.[69] Inhabitants of Nauru once sheltered 400 offshore banks. The Russian central bank estimated that 70 billion US dollars had been moved through Nauru, but a third of the banks were associated with the Middle East, and over half with the United States.[70] Australia and New Zealand have used Nauru, the Cook Islands, the Marshall Islands, Vanuatu, Western Samoa, and the Marianas as tax havens.[71]

Australia provided Nauru's next money-making scheme when it offered to pay islands—including Nauru, Papua New Guinea, Fiji—millions of dollars to process asylum-seekers from troubled areas around the world. Nauru has accepted boatloads of refugees from Afghanistan, Iran, Iraq, and Pakistan when Australian Prime Minister John Howard turned them away, claiming lack of space and resources.[72]

Nauru's bid for cash in exchange for refugee storage has had some of the same effects as the money-laundering and offshore banking. The attempt to make money from marginality has, again, landed the country in the center of conflict. The Iraqis and Afghani inhabitants seized control of their notoriously grim refugee camp in December 2002.[73] In the spring of 2004, the Iraqis went on a hunger strike.[74] In the interim, the country has been plagued with infrastructure failures, financial difficulties, and shifting leadership. In January 2003 it lost contact with its Intelsat satellite, and thus with the rest of the world.[75] A new president, elected after a no-confidence vote, died of a heart attack, and the presidency has rotated between a few men, mostly previous presidents with health difficulties. Nauru's refusal to permit visas to visitors for the refugees made it a target of Amnesty International.[76] Recently a flotilla of human rights activists attempted to sail to Nauru in protest, only to be turned away by Nauruians.[77]

Seemingly mytho-maniacal dreams of espionage were next. In August 2003, Nauru brought a case against the US government, with whom it had previously had a friendly relationship. The court case was prompted by creditors from the US import-export bank Exim, wishing to repossess the one airplane of Air Nauru. Nauru claimed that the US government had approached the country after the Bali bombings in 2002, and given it assurances that the plane would not be repossessed if it agreed to provide cooperation in the "Korea program," close down its offshore banking, and discontinue illegal passport sales. The "Korea program," according to Nauru, was a plan, under the cooperation of the USA and New Zealand, to build a Nauruian embassy in Beijing that would harbor North Korean defectors.[78] Failure to cooperate, Nauru claimed, would have meant sanctions fatal to the country's economy. In 2003, Nauru launched a counterfantasy by implicating two US officials in an antiterror and defection spy operation. The USA had consistently opposed Nauru's banking and passport operations, in part because of links to terror, and as of mid-July 2003, the country was forced to close its offshore bank. But, Nauru claims, the promised US assistance failed to materialize in return.[79] President Bernard Dowiyogo (elected after the riots and the communication blackout in January 2003) was sent to the USA for medical treatment soon after the election. He received letters from Secretary of State Colin Powell attempting to reinforce the proposed deal, but died in March before being able to confirm an agreement.[80]

The list of insults and injuries continues. Once a country second only to Saudi Arabia in wealth per capita, Nauru has literally been reduced to begging. It imports its water from Australia. It has promised to terminate relations with Taiwan in exchange for millions from the Chinese. It recently defaulted on a last-ditch loan from General Electric, causing it to have to sell off most of its properties, including a hotel in Sydney and Nauru House, its sumptuously furnished quarters in Melbourne's first skyscraper. Nauruians tend to share wealth communally, borrowing or poaching each other's cars or supplies. Yet now, many appear at government offices asking to borrow small sums to buy food.[81]

Former World Bank consultant and Nauru-watcher Helen Hughes—who had previously helped to negotiate the terms of Nauru's phosphate wealth after the island took control of the industry in the 1970s—releases tough soundbites about her subject to the press. "They have blown close to two billion," she has said. "Toes are falling off," Hughes added, in an attempt to characterize the severity of the interrelated epidemics of obesity, diabetes, and alcoholism that are rampant on the island. Even thought it has very few roads, Nauru even has a disproportionately high number of driving accidents.[82]

However tiny it may be, Nauru has the power to attach itself to everything, even the world's superpowers, as a germ or thorn. Yet it is also often a character attracting sympathy given its previous years of exploitation. Nauru always needs to be saved—both from others and from itself. It is both a place of extraction and a dumping ground for the refugees or fugitives that the world considers to be waste. Like a high-maintenance friend, the island is a tiny but infinite black hole for absorbing assistance or attention.

In the dark comedy of missteps, the island's combination of corruption and victimhood is the formula of the superpowers themselves, who also invariably camouflage their violence and cheating with innocence and invisible ink. Nauru already operated from the premise that one lie is bad, but many lies are productive. Its only true dysfunction, when compared with all of its trading partners and lenders, was that it could not proliferate enough lies, enough forms of cheating and piracy, to produce sufficient camouflage. The island did not produce its lawlessness and exception on its own behalf—it merely sold that state of exception as a commodity. Nauru made its trading partners yet more innocent as those partners silently shifted disguises, and moved on to more mobile territories in the slushy sea.

Contemplation: Pirate

Gradually overtaken by slumber, his flaxen head drooped, his whole lamb-like figure relaxed, and, half reclining against the ladder's foot, lay motionless, as some sugar-snow in March.

—Herman Melville[1]

Every generation gets the pirates it deserves.[2]

There is a bit of pirate in global operators of all sorts, on both sides of the law, and in service of Empire or counter-Empire. Pirates are shadow figures—a continuum of characters from the privateer as military entrepreneur to the social bandit as revolutionary and the terrorist as murderer. The pirate maintains a variable proximity to the state as both its secret agent and the criminal agent that disassembles it—as criminal and enforcer. Historically, nonstate actors like pirates, mercenaries, or mercantile companies were the characters exercising aggression between the wars or at the margins of war. Piracy possesses varying degrees of aggression, lawlessness, deception, violence, resistance, and productivity. A proliferation of alternative names for pirate seems to attend the proliferation of political dispositions (condottiere, privateer, corsair, buccaneer, renegade, freebooter, brigand, or sea dog). The pirate is typically considered to be a sailor turned criminal, yet the word is also used to describe contemporary media theft. A precise boundary between pirates and all those who use disguises in any of their various swindles is difficult to draw. Orgmen, diplomats, hackers, confidence men, Rotarians, and resisters share similar repertoires, often even borrowing each other's disguises from time to time. Their masquerades and improvisations with law lend agency to the architecture and urbanism they inhabit.

City councils, sultans, and kings commissioned it; fisherman, knights, and merchant venturers made it their seasonal avocation. Banks backed it; businessmen drew up contracts, crews hired on, and investors realized a healthy return (after taxes) from this high-risk enterprise. So conventionalized and profit-oriented was this medieval activity, that some medieval historians are reluctant to apply terms like pirate or corsair, with their demonic image.[3]

The modern world can provide us today with particularly well developed images of these two directions: worldwide ecumenical machines, but also neoprimitivism. . . . For example, a commercial organization is also a band of pillage, or piracy, for part of its course and in many of its activities; or it is in bands that a religious formation begins to operate. What becomes clear is that bands, no less than worldwide organizations, imply a form irreducible to the State and that this form of exteriority necessarily presents itself as a diffuse and polymorphous war machine.
—Gilles Deleuze and Félix Guattari[4]

Our clients include federal law enforcement agencies, the Department of Defense, Department of State, and Department of Transportation, local and state entities from around the country, multinational corporations, and friendly nations from all over the globe.

We customize and execute solutions for our clients to help keep them at the level of readiness required to meet today's law enforcement, homeland security, and defense challenges.

Any and all defense services supplied to foreign nationals will only be pursuant to proper authorization by the Department of State.
—Blackwater USA, a private security company[5]

State/Nonstate

An ambiguous distinction in piratology concerns the difference between state and nonstate aggression. The pirate is the "war machine," colluding with and resisting the state. While many species of pirate or bandit clearly operate outside the state, and while the aggressions of a standing army are operations of the state, the state also engages, on a temporary basis, outside operatives such as the privateer, mercenary, filibuster, and mercantile company.

For centuries, the Mediterranean incubated almost every species of pirate, from the most bloodthirsty zealot to the most obedient employees of the state. Historian Fernand Braudel describes sixteenth-century mixtures of thieves and profiteers who roamed the waters, sometimes as predatory forces and sometimes as agents of one of the coastal cities or nations. The thriving trade in their plunder of goods or slaves generated regional market hubs in, for instance, North African cities such as Tangiers. The state relied on these special forces, often headquartered in their own independent city-state, to extend its reach and territory. Yet they also generated a kind of extrajurisdictional warfare, a means of absorbing aggressions in between the wars.[6]

One familiar pirate syndrome is often described as the "pirate cycle." Historians speculate that the pirate renegade often exited society as a thief and, after years of plundering, became organized and effective, perhaps during a time of war or trade embargo. His trading and thieving activities softened the field of play, and made him useful to the official state organs that eventually contracted for his services and returned him to a kind of legitimacy. The Dutch, British, Chinese, and Spanish engaged such pirates. In the seventeenth and eighteenth centuries, during the so-called "golden age of piracy," the European countries which were constantly at war issued a letter of marque to pirates that engaged them as privateers.[7]

Thomas W. Gallant suggests the broad term "military entrepreneur" for all of those additional private operators who, for a profit, agreed to be state enforcers. Gallant suggests that while all bandits and pirates could become military entrepreneurs, not all military entrepreneurs became common bandits. The military entrepreneur was a character who belonged to a "class of men at arms who operated in the netherworld between legality and illegality, formal and informal authority, but invariably as non-state entities."[8] From antiquity to the nineteenth century, the state engaged such characters as extensions of their power to open markets, settle territories, enforce a law, collect a tax, break an embargo, or patrol the shores as a kind of coast guard. A mercantile company like the East India Company, while private, was endowed with this special franchise. Similarly, the filibuster was a self-appointed militia that was not sanctioned by the state but, rather, deputized itself as a loyal defender. The mercenary was a military entrepreneur with a slightly different constitution from all of these characters—a "soldier of fortune," who contracted for any state without allegiance.

Reinforced by national and international law, a clear consolidation of state activities in the nineteenth century eliminated a cast of occasionally disobedient peripheral characters, and established a monopoly over markets and aggressions, thus sharpening distinctions between state and nonstate operators. The history prior to that clarifying moment is useful in interrogating the contemporary ambiguities of state boundaries. Many of the previous nonstate affiliations were institutionalized or sanctioned as official roles. Markets were also naturalized as agents of the state and its private internal concerns. Their territory of operation is pervasive, and often exempt from regulation. Like the mercantile company or the soldier of fortune, these markets enjoy state affiliation when it is convenient, but avoid state intrusion.

The evangelical orgman of global commerce is not a military entrepreneur engaged by the state but a political entrepreneur on his own behalf and on behalf of any nation that legislates favorably toward him. He has attributes of both the mercenary and the mercantile company. He conquers territories of desire, time frames, and undermarketed populations. While many orgmen proceed with evangelical enthusiasm, subterfuge, disguise, and camouflage may also accompany their desire for control and expansion of territory. Far from wishing to be identified to potential converts, some orgmen wish to remain undetected, and shelter offshore in any number of special economic zones or enclave formations—the orgman's Salé. Bounded by, for instance, an economic imperative, a natural resource, or a strain of expertise that keeps it segregated, his organization is sometimes more strongly linked to other similar organizations or networks of enclaves than to local conditions, making it easier to get away with a broad low-level violence such as that associated with trade or labor abuse. Occasionally the organization appears to surface for discrete public relations efforts, but it is largely reclusive. Its segregation from other worlds sometimes garners power temporarily, shaping such organizations into distended and dominating territories.

The relationship between state and nonstate actors becomes more complicated when the nation wages war against a war machine. For instance, the

Barbary pirates, a group of Mediterranean pirates whose collective aggressions severely threatened shipping, induced a coalition of nations to declare war against them in the early nineteenth century. The Barbary pirates were clever and well skilled in undoing those European nations from which they had learned so much about warfare, or for whom they may have been special agents. For the coalition, a counterwar was easier than the continual bribery necessary for security. The contemporary war on terrorism is similar in the sense that many of the most forceful enemies associated with the Taliban or al-Qaeda were, at one time, agents of the United States or the Soviet Union. They may have been a band of villains, but they were villains who worked on behalf of these superpowers. Like the Barbary pirates, terrorists do not play by the rules of war that nations have agreed to follow. Yet unlike the Barbary pirates, they have not always occupied a regional territory that concentrates their efforts into a pseudo-nationality of sorts.

In this climate of war against the war machine, the mercenary has returned to warfare. Matching the tactics of the enemy requires an army of special operators and private contractors who are exempt from international law. In addition to CIA or FBI agents, agents are engaged in large numbers to act as soldiers. They constitute a significant fraction of the military, they are paid more than the regular enlisted men, and they may choose the length of their tour of duty. These soldiers of fortune may work for any country, appear as a unit in uniform, or stand guard in plain clothes in urban areas that have literally become battlegrounds.[9] In *The Multitude: War and Democracy in the Age of Empire,* Hardt and Negri have likened the contemporary disconnect between central governmental control and peripheral contractors to that of "Queen Elizabeth and the pirates of the Atlantic in the sixteenth century."[10]

Nations "cheat": they juggle identities and interests. Their ways meander.

—Fouad Ajami[11]

I may without vanity encourage the reader to expect many things wholly new.

—William Dampier[12]

It is possible to discover many TAZ in the activity of pirates. From pirates in the 16th century to radio pirates to data pirates in cyberspace. Though these media sometimes are commercialized and commodified, we could invent and act another style of pirates, because pirates and Capitalism have always been two sides of the same coin.

—Toshiya Ueno[13]

Disposition/Resistance

In warfare, enemies assume a symmetrical posture, mimicking the foe they know so well. There is a symmetrical resemblance between terrorists in a holy war and righteous, innocent adversaries like the United States who are forced to return battle in a "just" war. There is also a resemblance between the righteous state and the righteous insurgent armed with a political theology—a singular resistance to the singular logics of capital that renders all other resistance as trivial and irresponsible collusion.

As they alternate between believing and cheating, most organizations oscillate between a symmetrical and reciprocal stance, between direct warfare and some extra side-game in a larger network. They maintain reciprocal networks of commercial and political associations filled with garden-variety lies and cheating. Yet, given an extra sense of entitlement and innocence, they can descend into a righteous war. Sometimes the extra, reciprocal game only serves as an accessory to the secret agenda of war. Oscillating between symmetrical and reciprocal constitutions, with a masquerade of open flexibility and fluidity, the organization returns to a protective symmetrical stance when it is threatened. It espouses general principles as it runs away from ethical struggles. Patriotism and national sovereignty help to disguise cheating. Although the righteous believer needs the indeterminacy of nonplace, he must often privilege place.[14] When operating on any of the high seas becomes too dangerous or overly regulated, he returns home to its national shelters, seeking military protection and the chance to portray its activities as a way of life, an ethos springing from location-specific roots.

Among the believers and cheaters are also characters of resistance. Some resistance assumes an architecture of rivalry and vengeful warfare. Some Mediterranean pirates, for instance, established North African colonies from which to plot a Holy War to avenge the Spanish expulsion of Jews and Muslims. Another righteous but independent character of resistance is the noble thief, the revolutionary activist who uses all available skills to bring justice to oppressors. He avenges, settles the score, and writes new ethical guidelines for manliness, heroism, and the use of violence. Like Robin Hood, the "social bandit" about whom Eric Hobsbawm wrote is an "avenger" or "expropriator" of the agrarian landscape, and his maritime counterpart is a similarly principled character who steals to deliver justice, or to break embargoes of power abuse.[15] The pirate as social bandit appears all along the great pirate belt of temperate waters from the Mediterranean to the Caribbean to the South China Sea. [see *Seas*]

In *Pirate Utopias,* Peter Lamborn Wilson (a.k.a. Hakim Bey) celebrates pirates and their civilizations. Salé, for instance, on the North African coast, was home to a diverse culture of Africans and Europeans and was, Wilson writes, "neither anarchical or anarchist—but rather, in a strange and unexpected way, democratic," like the sailors in Jacques Rancière's seas.[16] These free spirits turned Turk to escape society and its laws. In Salé, the corsairs spoke "Franco" or "Sabir," a patois mixture of regional languages including Turkish, Spanish, Italian, Arabic, Portuguese, and French. They improvised with the strictures of language, living between vocabularies and rules of syntax with their own lingua franca. Wilson treats this culture "as a pattern of *conversions,* of literal cross-cultural adventure, of *translations.*"

The renegado is another famous pirate of resistance. As the story goes, renegados are noble but disinterested characters, believing in liberty more than in home or principled beliefs. They choose aggression over violent warfare as a means of protecting their freedom or curiosity. The renegado is the dropout with no specific allegiances except to himself and his companions. Like Herman Melville's Nantucket boys, these were citizens of the open ocean. The Caribbean buccaneer, for instance, is often portrayed as a pirate of some leisure. He is known, not only for thieving, but also for hunting and smoking meat. The classic illustration shows him barefoot with his dog, smoking a pipe, surrounded by additional cartoons depicting his smoking activities, which he performs in a semi-recumbent posture.

The celebrated seventeenth-century pirate William Dampier exemplifies this open and uncommitted political disposition. Dampier adopted various roles throughout his life, from sailor to buccaneer to author, all of which were designed to allow him to continue circumnavigating the globe, which he did three times. He pirated so that he could fulfill his passion for bird-watching, climates, botany, and hydrography. As a naturalist, his object was exploration and the description of exotic flora and fauna. He was friendly with some of the intellectuals of his day, and his books later informed Daniel Defoe, Charles Darwin, Jonathan Swift, and Captain James Cook.[17]

Writing about contemporary culture, Peter Lamborn Wilson identifies another kind of pirate enclave, the temporary autonomous zone (TAZ), that can exist in many layers of society, on the street or in the archipelagos of the Internet. Within the web, systems and software hackers deploy the small tactical trick or *perruque,* about which de Certeau writes, as well as the trick that collapses the difference between tactic and strategy.[18] The hacker operates between survival and principled destruction of the powers that be, creating worms that destroy the system by replicating in response to the system's regular functioning.[19]

The supposedly disinterested dropout or renegade raises questions about passivity and its strange resemblance to violence. For instance, Herman Melville's Bartleby is often used as a mascot of this passive stance. His refusal is valorized in standard political scripts of principled objection, because he avoids submitting to authority or assuming an aggressive stance. His blank denials even create a space of intimacy for those around him. Deleuze has portrayed him as a "doctor" to America. He writes in "Bartleby or the Formula" that Bartleby is the "brother of us all."[20] Yet Bartleby's self-destruction is not merely suicidal. It causes the destruction of others through the absolute protection of a domain, through a passivity that in some senses becomes a one-man embodiment of war.[21] Principled stances, in their righteousness and purity, store their own fierceness. Similarly, building, landscape, and urbanism are often regarded as passive, innocent, and static. They are even beloved for this stillness. Yet they too possess a political constitution and disposition that is capable of issuing challenges, generating mobile territories, or commanding a remote network of sites containing their own fierceness and violence.

This retrospective attitude, which deploys instead of unveiling, adds instead of subtracting, fraternizes instead of denouncing, sorts out instead of debunking, I characterize as nonmodern (or amodern). A nonmodern is anyone who takes simultaneously into account the moderns' constitution and the populations of hybrids that that Constitution rejects and allows to proliferate.

—Bruno Latour[22]

In Germany, . . . the merchants of several dozen cities drew together for mutual protection, forming the Hanseatic League in 1358. The German trade with England gave the English the name for their currency: they called the Hanseatic traders "Easterlings," and because of this English currency came to be known as "sterling."[23]

[There were] . . . 857 Germans, 138 Hamburgmen, 300 English, 130 Dutch and Fleming, 160 Danes and Easterlings, 250 Poles Hungarians and Muscovites . . . [living in Algiers under Islam].[24]

Disposition/Masquerade

Herman Melville's *The Confidence Man: His Masquerade* follows the exploits of a charlatan, a satan, who has perfectly fused the techniques of the believer and the cheater. He cheats by propagating a series of lies each of which reinforce the illusion that he is a man of heartfelt beliefs, a pure honest soul who is worthy of the confidence of each person he swindles. Melville's satire of the contemporary transcendental movement counters transcendent monism by multiplying narrative and voice. The story continually exits itself and, through a trap door, enters a new game just as the character's disguises and swindles multiply.

A masquerade intends to fool. Since there are pirates and masquerades on all sides, traditional markers will not reveal the side of the right in these constitutions. The principled stance, the moral imperative, the costumes of good guys and bad guys are finally the worst possible indicators. Aggression can relieve tension and reveal information, while fierce passivity can embody violence. Markets assume many guises, sheltering and occasionally surfacing as whatever bandit or diplomat suits the occasion. Capital can appear disguised in official garb or, for that matter, unofficial garb, and can even appear disguised as its own resistance. Likewise, the mischief of a pirate in collusion with the state is tricky to detect.

c3.1 Hyundai cruise ship used in the Mount Kumgang *I Love Cruise*. Image courtesy of Hyundai-Asan.

In *Laughter,* Henri Bergson wrote that a "man in disguise is comic," theorizing that it was a "masquerade" obscuring nature that was comedic.[25] The comic masquerade is one in which the identity or intention is perhaps partially revealed. The comic hoax inverts and repurposes the world in a way that is both utterly familiar and utterly foreign. The trick being played fools the taker just as they recognize the altered landscape in which they have been fooled. The comedian is constantly propagating masquerades while simultaneously lifting up his mask to expose the trick.

Perhaps the comedian tutors another fabled pirate of resistance who is too smart to be right, too smart to be righteous. This pirate is not principled in the sense that he protects himself behind a fixed set of values or a habituating doctrine. Rather, he operates axiomatically, squarely in the realm of those ethical struggles that accompany colliding worlds. If the world often changes—not because of principled stances, but because of cheating and errors that slip into and degrade regimes—a political imagination might productively entertain fictions and masquerades, as well as the success of errant details or germs. It may not reinforce the fairy tale of resistance as a vast groundswell. It may not serve to topple the Empire of capital with the single, ultimate contradiction of legend. This is an imagination that is opportunistically fascinated with contagions that spawn the most unlikely epidemics of belief. The pirate who is too smart to be right respins the abundant psychological weaknesses, comedies, loopholes, and errors in the market, for partial, perhaps huge, but never totalizing effects. Ideally, the transactions yield more information than they cover up, even if they involve deception or aggression. [see *Error*]

Complex organizations of piracy inhabit and manipulate shared transnational networks, slipping between legal jurisdictions, leveraging advantages in the differential values of labor and currency, brandishing national identity one moment and laundering it the next, translating information between nations and beyond patriotic posturing. Using disguise to neutralize difference, these piratical organizations are the engines of translation and cross-pollination between formats, making and harvesting error. Whatever the claims of dominant logics or optimized procedures, it is this inevitable field of comedy and fallout that presents a huge surface area for manipulation and plunder. These may even become the shores of political negotiation about which Jacques Rancière writes.[26]

As the carrier of improvisations with the state and its laws, the pirate is the protector or blockade-runner determining whether the state will be reclusive or open, information-rich or information-poor. This correlation between pirates and information is itself axiomatic when one is assessing the conundrum of pirate ethics. The pirate presents puzzling moments when the most passive or the most righteous characters are the most dangerous, and when cheating is the most honest thing to do. The pirate may be an instrument of the state's special stupidity, the means by which it gathers only compatible information to consolidate and fortify its self-reflective world. The pirate might also be the instrument of a less violent environment that is rich in information and receptive to contradiction. The pirate who is too smart to be right exploits an error language to unravel beliefs either in his own purity or in the purity of his resistance. Errors, disguises, and jokes substitute mongrel organizational resilience and ingenuity for innocence and the violence of remaining intact.

Notes

Introduction

1. In a chapter entitled "The Orgamerican Phantasy" from *The Tradition of the New* (1959), "Orgman," Harold Rosenberg's nickname for William Whyte's organization man, was the docile mid-twentieth-century individual inhabiting a field of identical tract houses. This book speculates about a new orgman, descended from the fabled character, who has inherited that logistical field and attracted a new set of logistical organizations. See Keller Easterling, "Interchange and Container: The New Orgman," *Perspecta* 30 (1999), 112–121.

2. TEUs, or twenty-foot equivalent units, are cargo container calibrations.

3. Manuel Castells, *The Informational City: Information Technology, Economic Restructuring and the Urban-Regional Process* (Oxford: Blackwell, 1989), 152; Félix Guattari, *The Three Ecologies* (London: Athlone, 2000; Paris: Éditions Galilée, 1989), 48.

4. Giorgio Agamben, *Homo Sacer: Sovereignty, Power and Bare Life* (Stanford: Stanford University Press, 1995), 175.

5. Marc Augé, *An Anthropology for Contemporaneous Worlds* (Stanford: Stanford University Press, 1999), 89–90; Arjun Appadurai, *Modernity at Large: Cultural Dimensions of Globalization* (Minneapolis: University of Minnesota Press, 1996), 33.

6. Scott Lash, "Informational Totemism," *Transurbanism* (Rotterdam: V2_Publishing/Nai Publishers, 2002), 49–63.

7. David Harvey, "Contemporary Globalization" and "Uneven Geographical Developments and Universal Rights," in *Spaces of Hope* (Berkeley: University of California Press, 2000), 53–94; Zygmunt Bauman, *Globalization: The Human Consequences* (New York: Columbia University Press, 1998), 77–102; and Naomi Klein, *Fences and Windows: Dispatches from the Front Lines of the Globalization Debate* (New York: Picador, 2002).

8. Pierre Bourdieu, *The Logic of Practice* (Stanford: Stanford University Press, 1980), 112–121.

9. Scott Lash, *Critique of Information* (London: Sage, 2002), 32.

10. Giorgio Agamben, *Means without End: Notes on Politics* (Minneapolis: University of Minnesota Press, 2000), 90–99.

11. Gilbert Ryle, *The Concept of Mind* (Chicago: University of Chicago Press, 1949), 25–61.

12. Gregory Bateson, "Culture, Content and Schismogenesis," in *Steps to an Ecology of Mind* (Chicago: University of Chicago Press, 1972), 68–69. Predicting intentionality in warfare was, for Norbert Wiener, one of the prompts to the development of cybernetics. Peter Galison, "The Ontology of the Enemy: Norbert Wiener and the Cybernetic Vision," *Critical Inquiry,* no. 21 (Autumn 1994), 228–266. Exceeding the self-reflexive game theories and deadlocked stances of the Cold War era, Bateson offers additional tools and qualifiers for analyzing agency in organizations with complex networks of players.

13. Bruno Latour, *We Have Never Been Modern* (Cambridge, MA: Harvard University Press, 1993), 37.

14. "Even the most complex and flexible theories of global development that have come out of the Marxist tradition (Amin 1980; Mandel 1978; Wallerstein 1974; Wolf 1982) are inadequately quirky and have failed to come to terms with what Scott Lash and John Urry have called disorganized capitalism (1987)." Appadurai, *Modernity at Large,* 33; Michael Hardt and Antonio Negri, *Empire* (Cambridge, MA: Harvard University Press, 2000), 60; Scott Lash and John Urry, *The End of Organized Capitalism* (Madison: University of Wisconsin Press, 1987); Augé, *An Anthropology for Contemporaneous Worlds;* Fouad Ajami, "The Summoning," in Patrick O'Meara, Howard D. Mehlinger, and Matthew Krain, eds. *Globalization and the Challenges of a New Century* (Bloomington: Indiana University Press, 2000), 63–70.

15. Latour, *We Have Never Been Modern,* 128.

16. Lash and Urry, *The End of Organized Capitalism.*

17. Bruno Latour, *Aramis or the Love of Technology* (Cambridge, MA: Harvard University Press, 1996), ix. Latour called his dialogic collection of texts about the fantasies and myths of transportation science "scientification."

18. Agamben, *Homo Sacer,* 175.

19. Latour, *We Have Never Been Modern,* 37.

DPRK

1. *Toronto Star,* July 9, 2000.

2. Among the best press accounts are: *New York Times,* April 23, 2000, 5H; *New York Times,* March 13, 2000, 1E; *New York Times,* March 7, 2000, 1C; *Toronto Star,* June 9, 2000; *New York Times,* January 20, 2002, 10A.

3. Ibid.

4. *BBC News Online Network,* October 13, 1998 <http://bbc.co.uk/1/hi/asia-pacific/192691.stm>; *chaebols* are business conglomerates in South Korea such as Hyundai, Daewoo, and Samsung.

5. Marcus Noland, *Avoiding the Apocalypse: The Future of the Two Koreas* (Washington, DC: Institute for International Economics, 2000), 115, footnote 112.

6. *Toronto Star,* June 9, 2000. Subsequent correspondence with Hyundai confirmed the purchase of the *Island Princess.*

7. DPRK website <http://www.korea.dpr.com>, 2001.

8. *Korea Times,* October 19, 2001.

9. Noland, *Avoiding the Apocalypse,* 139. In note 157, Noland references Cho Seong-kyu, "The Effects of Mt. Kumgang Tour Business on the National and Local Economy," *Economics of Korean Unification* 4, no. 2 (Fall 1999), 154–168.

10. *New York Times,* February 15, 2000, A3; *Lloyd's List International,* June 13, 2001, 22; *Financial Times,* June 21, 2001, 10; *Japan Economic Newswire,* June 8, 2001; *Korea Herald,* June 11, 2001; Noland, *Avoiding the Apocalypse.*

11. *New York Times,* January 20, 2002, 10A; Bruce Cumings, *North Korea: Another Country* (New York: New Press, 2004), 173.

12. Kongdan Oh and Ralph C. Hassig, *North Korea through the Looking Glass* (Washington, DC: Brookings Institution Press, 2000), 33.

13. *The Washington Post,* December 2, 2003, 1C.

14. <http://www.mtkumgang.com>.

15. "Across the DMZ," *Traveltrade,* November 4, 2003.

16. Oh and Hassig, *North Korea through the Looking Glass,* 56.

17. Ibid., 33.

18. *New York Times,* January 20, 2002, 10A.

19. Cumings, *North Korea: Another Country,* 159.

20. Ibid., 161.

21. Dean MacCannell, *The Tourist: A New Theory of the Leisure Class* (Berkeley: University of California Press, 1976), 2.

22. Noland, *Avoiding the Apocalypse,* 62.

23. Cumings, *North Korea: Another Country,* 103–128; Noland, *Avoiding the Apocalypse,* 62.

24. Cumings, *North Korea: Another Country,* 163.

25. *Daily Telegraph,* December 20, 2003, 1.

26. <http://www.asanmuseum.com> (March 26, 2002).

27. *Lloyd's List International,* April 16, 2001, 12; <http://www.ilovecruise.com>. (This site was transferred to Hyundai Merchant Marine and later discontinued. It was last accessed in September 2001.)

28. Noland, *Avoiding the Apocalypse,* 140.

29. *Korea Herald,* December 23, 2000.

30. <http://www.asanmuseum.com>.

31. <http://210.145.168.243/pk/096th_issue/99052602.htm>. A website operating out of Tokyo called "The People's Korea" quotes this old saying as one which was well known to Chung Ju Yung.

32. *New York Times,* August 2, 2001, 4A.

33. Bob Dickinson and Andy Vladimir, *Selling the Sea: An Inside Look at the Cruise Industry* (New York: Wiley, 1997), 28, 152–153, 140–148.

34. Jon Jerde is an architect of themed urbanism in Las Vegas and around the world. John Portman is a developer of atrium hotels and conferencing compounds.

35. Dickinson and Vladimir, *Selling the Sea,* 87, 208.

36. <http://www.freedomship.com/projectupdates/index.htm>.

37. Dickinson and Vladimir, *Selling the Sea,* 217.

38. <http://www.freedomship.com/projectupdates/index.html>.

39. Giorgio Agamben, *Means without End: Notes on Politics* (Minneapolis: University of Minnesota Press, 2000), 84.

40. Guy Debord, *The Society of the Spectacle* (New York: Zone Books, 1995), 32.

41. Ibid., 130, 33.

42. *New York Times,* November 19, 2003, 1W.

43. *Deutsche Presse-Agentur,* May 29, 2001.

44. Oh and Hassig, *North Korea through the Looking Glass,* 127–128.

45. Ibid., 182. Kim Dal Hyon, an "economic reformer" in the DPRK, Rajin-Sonbong is spelled Najin-Sonbong in this Anglicization.

46. *BBC Worldwide Monitoring,* September 16, 2002.

47. *Toronto Star,* June 9, 2000; <http://www.ilovecruise.com>. This site was transferred to Hyundai Merchant Marine and later discontinued. It was last accessed in September 2001.

48. *New York Times,* February 15, 2000, 3A.

49. *Toronto Star,* June 9, 2000; *Japan Economic Newswire,* July 9, 1999.

50. *Lloyd's List International,* June 26, 1999. John Larkin and Shim Jae Hoon, "Big Gamble on a Cruise North," *Far Eastern Economic Review* (February 1, 2001), 21–22. In addition, passenger numbers were shrinking. By April 2001, the North Korean government was unresponsive to Hyundai's proposal to include casinos within the tour. Hyundai Merchant Marine terminated the tour, and began repositioning the cruisers and selling off assets like the floating hotel docked in Chongjon. They transferred the project to Hyundai Asan, another division in the chaebol, and refocused on the shipping business. *Lloyd's List International,* July 24, 2001, 6.

51. *New York Times,* February 19, 2002, 1C.

52. Manuel Castells, *The Rise of the Network Society* (Oxford: Blackwell, 1996), 176–177.

53. Samuel S. Kim, *Korea's Globalization* (New York: Cambridge University Press, 2000), 119–125.

54. *Lloyd's List International,* June 12, 2001, 6; *Financial Times,* June 21, 2001, 10; *Japan Economic Newswire,* June 8, 2001; *Korea Herald,* June 11, 2001; *Japan Economic Newswire,* July 20, 2001.

55. *New York Times,* August 4, 2003, 6A; *Korea Times,* February 12, 2004; *BBC Monitoring International Reports,* May 25, 2004. Although her position as a Hyundai chairwoman is contested as a violation of Confucian tradition, Chung Mong Hun's wife, Hyun Jeong Eun, recently made a visit to the resort to continue its promotion.

56. *Deutsche Presse-Agentur,* May 1, 2001; *Japan Economic Newswire,* November 11, 1999; *Japan Economic Newswire,* September 23, 2000; *Korea Times,* October 17, 2001; *Herald Tribune,* July 1, 2000; *Korea Times,* August 17, 2001.

57. *BBC World,* November 7, 2002.

58. *Japan Economic Newswire,* August 15, 2000.

59. *BBC Worldwide Monitoring,* November 6, 2002; *New York Times,* March 11, 2003, 1C.

60. *BBC Worldwide Monitoring,* October 30, 2002.

61. *New York Times,* November 19, 2003, 1W; *The News Hour with Jim Lehrer,* June 29, 2004.

62. *Daily Record,* Baltimore, January 18, 2000; *The News Hour with Jim Lehrer,* June 29, 2004; *New York Times,* March 11, 2003, 1C; *BBC Monitoring,* April 20; *Korea Times,* November 25, 2002; Noland, *Avoiding the Apocalypse,* 85.

63. *New York Times,* September 25, 2002, 3A; "China's P-Chip Puzzle," *Time Magazine* 160, no. 15 (October 21, 2002); <http://www.time.com/time/asia/magazine/article/0,13673,501021021-364432,00.html>; and <http://www.feer.com/articles/2002/0210_24/p063current.html>.

64. Philip Gurevitch, "Letter from Korea: Alone in the Dark," *New Yorker,* September 8, 2004, 68; Cumings, *North Korea: Another Country,* 97; *Daily Telegraph,* December 20, 2003.

65. *Guardian,* November 29, 2003, 20.

66. Cumings, *North Korea: Another Country,* 31.

67. *New York Times,* August 24, 2003, 14 section 1.

68. *Japan Economic Newswire,* July 20, 2001; *BBC Worldwide Monitoring,* October 6, 2001; *Korea Times,* October 19, 2001.

69. <http://210.104.87.69/n_eng/Jeju_Main/menu/index.as>.

70. <http://210.104.87.69/n_eng/Intro_Jeju/item_07/item_07_01.asp>.

71. Agence France Presse, October 26, 2002; <http://210.104.87.69/h_eng/Jeju_Main/menu/index.asp>.

72. *Economist* 361, no. 8253 (December 12, 2001): 49; *Korea Times,* November 4, 2002; *New York Times,* March 11, 2003, 1C.

73. <http://210.104.87.69/n_eng/Jeju_Main/menu/index.asp>.

74. *Korea Herald,* November 21, 2002; *Korea Herald,* April 1, 2003.

75. Michael T. Klare, "Oil Wars in the South China Sea," in *Resource Wars: The New Landscape of Global Conflict* (New York: Henry Holt, 2001), 109–137; <http://www.un.org/Depts/los/convention_agreements/texts/unclos/closindx.htm>.

76. *Straits Times,* June 17, 2003; "The Snags about Paradise Island," *Economist* 36, no. 8253 (December 22, 2001), 49.

77. <http://210.104.87.69/n_eng/Jeju_Main/menu/index.asp>.

78. Ibid.

79. *Korea Times,* April 20, 2004.

El Ejido

1. *Wall Street Journal,* February 21, 1997, 9AC.

2. Naomi Klein, *Guardian,* January 16, 2003, 23.

3. Merle H. Jensen and Allan J. Malter, *Protected Agriculture: A Global Review* (Washington, DC: The World Bank, 1995), 100; Daniel J. Cantliffe and John J. Vansickle, Florida Agricultural Experiment Station Journal Series no. N-02089, 2001.

4. Data compiled from several sources, including: Daniel J. Cantliffe and John J. Vansickle, "Competitiveness of the Spanish and Dutch Greenhouse Industries with the Florida Fresh Vegetable Industry," Gainesville, Florida Horticultural Sciences Department, Proc. Fla. State Hort. Soc.2001 Paper No. 96; Jensen and Malter, *Protected Agriculture* 100–107; <http://www.canadiangreenhouseconference.com>; <http://www.tropical-seeds.com/tech_forum_/pubs_res/pump_tom_trials.html>; Merle H. Jensen, "Controlled Environment Agriculture in Deserts, Tropics, and Temperate Regions—A World Review," <http://ag.arizona.edu/ceac/research/archive/ceawr_pe.htm>; <http://www.sbceo.k12.ca.us/~uccesb1/sf82001.ht>.

5. <http://www.africana.com/DailyArticles/index_20000216.htm>, sources *Financial Times,* Spanish National Radio, United Press International.

6. <http://www.iacr.bbsrc.ac.uk/enmaria/workshops/almeria98/escobar.html>.

7. Dana G. Dalrymple, *A Global Review of Greenhouse Food Production* (Washington, DC: US Department of Agriculture, 1973), 110.

8. In 1971, there were 2,000 hectares (4,940 acres, 7.72 square miles). In 1990 this number had increased to 25,000 hectares (61,750 acres, 96.5 square miles). In 1999, there were 36,585 hectares (90,365 acres, 141 square miles). And in 2001 there were 46,205 hectares (113,667 acres, 177 square miles). See data sources in note 4 above.

9. *Wall Street Journal,* February 18, 1997.

10. CNN, August 20, 2001, transcript # 082000CN.V05.

11. *Wall Street Journal,* February 27, 1997, 9A.

12. "A Cry of 'Moors Out!' in Andalusia," *Business Week* (May 8, 2000), 20.

13. The vegetable industry has grown, exporting 1.5 million tons annually over its 1980 production of 100,000 tons. *New York Times,* May 8, 2000, 1A; <http://spainforvisitors.com/archive/features/aa081501b.htm>.

14. Visit to C and G seed company, El Ejido, Spain, May 3, 2002.

15. <http://www.africana.com/DailyArticles/index_20000216.htm>.

16. "Riots in Spain's 'Vegetable Patch,'" *Christian Science Monitor,* February 17, 2000, 6.

17. *Independent,* September 30, 2000, 17; "A Cry of 'Moors Out!' in Andalusia."

18. <http://www.iacr.bbsrc.ac.uk/enmaria/workshops/almeria98/escobar.html>.

19. <http://www.humanrights.de/news/el_ejido/1.htm>.

20. *Guardian,* February 14, 2000, 12.

21. Human Rights Watch reported that 500 Moroccans filed complaints, and that of the 46 people arrested, 26 were Moroccan. The organization published accounts accusing the mobs of attempted mass murder. They characterized the situation as one of "systematic" human rights abuse. Most of the workers went on strike, in part to stay out of sight: <http://www.humanrights.de/news/el_ejido/1.htm>.

22. Jacques Rancière, *On the Shores of Politics* (London: Verso, 1995), 105.

23. Giorgio Agamben, *Homo Sacer: Sovereignty, Power and Bare Life* (Stanford: Stanford University Press, 1995), 175.

24. Rancière, *On the Shores of Politics,* 103–107.

25. *New York Times,* May 8, 2000, 1A; *Los Angeles Times,* October 8, 2000, 33A.

26. *New York Times,* July 31, 2003, 3A.

27. Peter Lamborn Wilson, *Pirate Utopias* (Brooklyn: Autonomedia, 1995), 78–79.

28. "A Cry of 'Moors Out!' in Andalusia"; *Guardian,* February 14, 2000, 12.

29. <www.iff.ac.at/sosec/afil/conference99/pdf/bpSanchezForest.pdf-Dec31,2004>: Andrés Sánchez Picón, Juan García Latorre, and Jesús García Latorre, "The Forests of the Desert: About the Environmental History of the Arid South-eastern Spain," 3.

30. Gerald Brenan, *South from Granada: A Sojourn in Southern Spain* (1957; New York: Kodansha International, 1998), 11.

31. Ibid., 53.

32. Ibid., 187–190.

33. Ibid., 137.

34. Wilson, *Pirate Utopias,* 39–49.

35. Andy Higginbottom, "Super-Exploitation of Immigrant Labour in Europe: The Case of Intense Agriculture in Spain," paper to the CSE Conference on Global Capital and Global Struggles: Strategies, Alliances, Alternatives, London, July 1–2, 2000; <http://www.humanrights.de/doc_it/archiv/news/cse_paper_immigrantlabour.htm>.

36. <http://migration.ucdavis.edu/mn/archive_mn/jun_2000–13mn.html>; Associated Press Newswires, October 14, 1997; "Riots in Spain's 'Vegetable Patch,'" 6.

37. Higginbottom, "Super-Exploitation of Immigrant Labour in Europe."

38. "A Cry of 'Moors Out!' in Andalusia."

39. *El País,* July 5, 2001, 22.

40. *El País,* September 14, 2001, 26.

41. Higginbottom, "Super-Exploitation of Immigrant Labour in Europe."

42. Gilles Deleuze and Félix Guattari, "Treatise on Nomadology," in "*A Thousand Plateaus: Capitalism and Schizophrenia* (Minneapolis: University of Minnesota Press, 1987), 351–423.

43. *Wall Street Journal,* February 21, 1997, 9A.

44. Zygmunt Bauman, "Tourists and Vagabonds," in *Globalization: The Human Consequences* (New York: Columbia University Press, 1998), 94–96.

45. Some Spanish shippers produce in Spain, Morocco, and the Canary Islands, and some in the United States move seasonally between locations in North, Central, and South America. Similarly in Mexico, an international assortment of growers contract for field produce all over the country to maintain a supply for supermarkets. By maintaining affiliations in several regions, they can ship on a continuous twelve-month cycle, often to supply supermarket chains. Roberta L. Cook, *International Trends in the Fresh Fruit and Vegetable Sector,* Department of Agriculture and Resource Economics, UC Davis, May 1998, 23; <are.berkeley.edu/library/ERIA97–99/GFMembers/Cook.pdf>.

46. For instance, Sinca Agros is the preeminent producer of greenhouse tomatoes in Mexico, located on a 150-acre site two hours north of Mexico City, specifically chosen because it is a cool mountainous area of Querétaro with the same latitude as North Africa. They use the Dutch type of greenhouse—glass, and entirely computer-controlled. Production is 100 percent for export. The company has five other agricultural projects in Mexico, including citrus production for Coca-Cola. Baron F. Levin, "Fields of Plenty: Agricultural Project Cultivated in the Boardroom," *Business Mexico,* September 1, 1998.

47. <http://www.tropical-seeds.com/tech_forum/pubs_res/pump_tom_trials.html>.

48. Warfare becomes quite confusing, in part because of the contraseasonal trading rhythms. Countries that are ostensibly in competition during some times of the year may also rely on the same nation in the opposing hemisphere for out-of-season fruits and vegetable. Also, some developed countries supply intelligence to developing countries which, performing a little too well, establish a pocket of high-tech industry that competes with the tutor (Jensen and Malter, *Protected Agriculture,* 100).

49. Higginbottom, "Super-Exploitation of Immigrant Labour in Europe."

50. *Manchester Guardian Weekly,* February 7, 2001, 5; "Unwelcome to Iberia," *Economist,* February 8, 2001; <http://www.economist.com/displaystory.cfm?story_id=498699>.

51. Bauman, "Tourists and Vagabonds," 96–97.

52. *Washington Post,* April 24, 1999, 1A.

53. *New York Times,* November 21, 2000, 1F.

54. <www.PSA.es>, visit to Plataforma Solar de Almería, February, 2004; *New York Times,* December 19, 2003, 6A; *New York Times,* January 10, 2004, 4A.

55. <http://www.enviromission.com.au/index1.htm>; <http://www.greenconstruction.co.uk/Archive/RoundUp49.htm>; <http://www.bajandodescargas.com/query/HDD%20Regenerator%201.31.html>. Jorg Schlaich of Schlaich Bergermann and Partner are the designers of the Manzanares project.

56. <http://www.areva.com>.

57. Higginbottom, "Super-Exploitation of Immigrant Labour in Europe."

58. Deutsche Presse-Agentur, July 24, 2002.

59. Gilles Deleuze, "Desert Islands," in *Desert Islands and Other Texts 1953–1974* (New York: Semiotexte, 2004), 9.

60. *Independent,* July 18, 2002, 10.

61. *Independent,* July 18, 2002, 4–5, 10; September 24, 2002, 11; *BBC Monitoring,* August 1 and August 27, 2002.

62. James A. Paul, "Small States and Territories" Global Policy Forum, July 2000; <http://www.globalpolicy.org/nations/micro.htm>.

63. Agence France Presse, August 10, 2002.

64. Peter Gold, "Immigration into the European Union via the Spanish Enclaves of Ceuta and Melilla: A Reflection of Regional Economic Disparities," *Mediterranean Politics* 4, no. 3 (Autumn 1999), 24–35; Mary M. Crain, "New North African Immigration to Spain," *Middle East Report* (Summer 1999), 23–25; Soncia C. Cardenas, "The Contested Territories of Ceuta and Melilla," *Mediterranean Quarterly* 7 (1996), 118.

65. Gold, "Immigration into the European Union," 175; Cardenas, "The Contested Territories of Ceuta and Melilla," 125; Peter Gold, *Europe or Africa? A Contemporary Study of the Spanish North African Enclaves of Ceuta and Melilla* (Liverpool: Liverpool University Press, 2000), 30.

66. *Daily Post,* June 26, 2004; *Guardian,* May 3, 1998, 52; *M2 Presswire,* July 23, 2002. Agriculture has long since yielded to the tourist industry. Lanzarote, designed by Cesar Manrique, is an experiment in low-rise, cosmetically controlled, historicist building. Architect Leon Krier, a proponent of neotraditional architecture and urban design, designed a community for Tenerife named after the fabled island of Atlantis. Commissioned as an ideal community for thinkers and visionaries, Atlantis, although never built, was designed with a church at its center surrounded by a classical cluster of buildings that rolls toward the sea. Partly inspired by the American Academy in Rome, Krier described it as possessing "the humanistic values that transform individuals into citizens."

67. *Sunday Mirror,* May 30, 2004, 6.

Contemplation: Seas

1. Carl Schmitt, *Land and Sea* (Washington, DC: Plutarch Press, 1997), translated from the German by Simona Draghici.

2. *Landskip* is a word with roots in Old English meaning a landscape that appears in pictures as opposed to a *Landschaft,* a working landscape that evolves over time. See James Corner, ed., *Recovering Landscape: Essays in Contemporary Landscape Architecture* (New York: Princeton Architectural Press, 1999), 153–154. Arjun Appadurai uses the suffix (e.g., ethnoscapes, mediascapes) to describe fluid cultural currents and cultural mixtures between globalizing and indigenizing forces. Mark Taylor uses the term skinscapes to describe a field of body fascinations in culture (Arjun Appadurai, *Modernity at Large: Cultural Dimensions of Globalization* [Minneapolis: University of Minnesota Press, 1996], 12; Mark C. Taylor, *Hiding* [Chicago: University of Chicago Press, 1998]).

3. "As for state apparatuses themselves, we relate them to factors like territory, terrain, and deterritorialization: you get a state apparatus when territories are no longer exploited sequentially but compared simultaneously (as land or terrain) and so drawn, from that point on, into a movement of deterritorialization." (Gilles Deleuze, *Negotiations 1972–1990* [New York: Columbia University Press, 1995], 30.)

4. Of so many who use maritime metaphors to discuss territory, perhaps a reverberant open set might include, as a beginning: Ferdinand Braudel, Carl Schmitt, Michel de Certeau, Gilles Deleuze, Manuel De Landa, Michael Hardt and Antonio Negri, and Paul Virilio.

5. Michel de Certeau, *The Practice of Everyday Life* (Berkeley: University of California Press, 1984), 40–41.

6. Michael Hardt, and Antonio Negri, *Empire* (Cambridge, MA: Harvard University Press, 2000), 60, 61.

7. Gilles Deleuze, "The Image of Thought," in *Difference and Repetition* (New York: Columbia University Press, 1994), 304.

8. Fernand Braudel, *The Mediterranean and the Mediterranean World in the Age of Philip II* (London: Harper Collins, 1972), 624–656; Robert I. Burns, "Piracy as an Islamic-Christian Interface in the Thirteenth Century," *Viator: Medieval and Renaissance Studies* 11 (1980), 165.

9. De Certeau, *The Practice of Everyday Life,* 40–41

10. Gilles Deleuze and Félix Guattari, "Treatise on Nomadology," in *A Thousand Plateaus: Capitalism and Schizophrenia* (Minneapolis: University of Minnesota Press, 1987), 387. In Deleuze, *Negotiations,* 30, Braudel is mentioned in an interview question to Deleuze in relation to an implied interest in landscape.

11. Deleuze, "The Image of Thought," 304.

12. Appadurai, *Modernity at Large,* 12; Hardt and Negri, *Empire,* 151.

13. Hardt and Negri, *Empire,* 327, 190.

14. Ibid., 60, 61.

15. Ibid., 60.

16. Michael Hardt and Antonio Negri, *The Multitude: War and Democracy in the Age of Empire* (New York: Penguin Press, 2004), 47–51.

17. Deleuze and Guattari, *A Thousand Plateaus,* 47.

18. Jacques Rancière, *On the Shores of Politics* (London: Verso, 1995), 106.

19. Deleuze and Guattari, "Treatise on Nomadology," 387.

20. Hugo Grotius, *The Freedom of the Seas: or the Right Which Belongs to the Dutch to Take Part in the East Indian Trade* (Kitchener: Batoche Books Limited, 2000; New York: Oxford University Press, 1916, reprinted from 1633 edition), 8.

21. Gilles Deleuze and Félix Guattari, "The Smooth and the Striated," in *A Thousand Plateaus,* 500.

22. Ibid. Deleuze writes: "Of course, smooth spaces are not in themselves liberatory. But the struggle is changed or displaced in them, and life reconstitutes its stakes, confronts new obstacles, invents new paces, switches adversaries. Never believe that a smooth space will suffice to save us."

23. Grotius, *The Freedom of the Seas,* passim; William Langewiesche, *The Outlaw Sea: A World of Freedom, Chaos and Crime* (New York: North Point Press, 2004), 36.

24. Langewiesche, *The Outlaw Sea,* 7.

25. <http://www.un.org/Depts/los/convention_agreements/texts/unclos/closindx.htm>.

26. Joel H. Baer, "'The Complicated Plot of Piracy': Aspects of English Criminal Law and the Image of the Pirate in Defoe," *The Eighteenth Century: Theory and Interpretation* 23, no. 1 (Winter 1982), 13.

27. Rancière, *On the Shores of Politics,* 1–2.

28. Noam Chomsky, *Pirates and Emperors: International Terrorism in the Real World* (New York: Claremont Research and Publications, 1986), 1; Hardt and Negri, *Empire,* 57–58.

29. Rancière, *On the Shores of Politics,* 1–2; Giorgio Agamben, *Homo Sacer: Sovereignty, Power and Bare Life* (Stanford: Stanford University Press, 1995), 172. Agamben quotes Carl Schmitt from "Staat, Bewegung, Volk," in Carl Schmitt, *Die Dreigliederung der politischen Einheit* (Hamburg: Hanseatische Verlaganstalt, 1933) 43–44: "The way forward seems to condemn us to a shoreless sea and to move us ever father from the firm ground of juridical certainty as adherence to the law, which at the same time is still the ground of the judges' independence."

Franchise

1. Maharishi Vedic University, online exhibition booklet, *Building for the Health and Happiness of Everyone: Creating Ideal Housing in Harmony with Natural Law,* 18, 20; <www.sthapatyaveda.com/booklet/index.html>.

2. <http://www.globalcountry.org/Coronation2.html>.

3. *Franchise International,* Spring 1998, 88; *Economist,* April 15, 2004; <www.economist.com/displaystory.cfm?story_id-259881>.

4. Sovereign rights of governance over new territory, historically referred to as *franchise,* was permission granted to a religious organization or mercantile company to develop property or commercial trade in the service of a remote power. In contemporary usage, franchise often refers to repeatable commercial formats sponsored by a brand and made available for individual ownership; Scott Lash, "Informational Totemism," in *Transurbanism* (Rotterdam: V2_Publishing/Nai Publishers, 2002), 49–64.

5. <www.dmca.yale.edu/wildcards>.

6. The Maharishi's organization presides over many affiliated subgroups. Maharishi Global Construction performs some of the activities associated with the Maharishi Global Development Fund, and vice versa.

7. APGM manages over 152 golf courses, some of which it has designed. Assuming 2,000 acres per golf course, the total land area under the company's management equals approximately 300,000 acres (468 square miles; 1,212 square kilometers). The area of Hong Kong is 1,075 square kilometers. <http://www.palmergolf.com>; <http://www.palmerdesign.com>.

8. *Financial Times,* December 31, 2002, 9; <http://www.palmerdesign.com>.

9. <http://www.tm.nl/zeeland/LarryKing_MMY_CNN.htm>.

10. <http://www.agpf.de/TM-Immobilien.htm>; <http://www.tm.nl/zeeland/LarryKing_MMY_CNN.htm>.

11. <http://www.tm.nl/zeeland/LarryKing_MMY_CNN.htm>.

12. <http://www.tm.org/main_pages/maharishi.html>; <http://www.maharishitm.org/en/maharishen.htm>; <http://www.afbis.com/analysis/mozambiq.htm>.

13. Ken Roseboro, "Reconstructing the World: Maharishi Global Construction uses designs that mirror laws of nature," <http://fairfield.freehosting.net/97March/global.html>.

14. According to the TM organization, "Scientific research on this assembly" validated the "Maharishi's prediction that when the square root of one percent of the world's population practices the TM-Sidhi program, including Yogic Flying, together in one place, positive trends increase and negative tendencies decrease throughout the whole world." Since that time, the published number of yogic flyers necessary for "the effect" has been increased to 8,000. <http://www.tm.org/main_pages/maharishi.htm>; <http://www.maharishitm.org/en/maharishen.htm>; <http://www.worldpeaceendowment.org/invincibility/invincibility13b.html>; *Guardian,* September 22, 2001, 19.

15. Conversation and tour with Jon Lipman, architect of Sthapatya Veda buildings in Fairfield, Iowa, July 2001.

16. *New York Times,* January 18, 2004, 9 section 1.

17. Ibid.; <http://www.tm.org/main_pages/maharishi.html>; <http://www.maharishitm.org/en/maharishen.htm>.

18. *Boston Globe,* June 1, 2003, 1B. To facilitate this urban enterprise, among the various affiliated TM organizations are for-profit and nonprofit development and construction companies like the Maharishi Global Development Fund or the Maharishi Global Construction Company, the World Government of the Age of Enlightenment, and the Global Country of World Peace.

19. <http://www.tm.org/main pages/maharishi html>; <http://www.globalcountry.org/EasyWeb.asp?pcpid=60>.

20. Reports of the tower's height and cost varied, as did reports of the total number of towers to be built. Some releases from the organization referred to the possibility of 1,000 such towers. Some sources include: *Calgary Herald,* May 14, 1999, 12E; *Christchurch Press,* May 29, 1999, 24; *Financial Times,* May 13,1999, 27 <http://www.enlightenment-magazine.org/06/6tallest.htm.>

21. *Calgary Herald,* May 14, 1999, 12E; *Financial Times,* May 13, 1999, 27; <http://www.rickross.com/reference/tm/tm13.html>, May 8, 2000.

22. *Guardian,* October 25, 2000, 2; *CNN.com,* October 24, 2000.

23. *Time Colonist,* October 26, 2000, 12A.

24. *Enlightenment Online,* June 1998, <http://www.enmag.org/01/1nanews.htm>; <http://www.geocities.com/bbrigante/big.html>; New York City telephone book, 2001.

25. <http://www.palmergolf.com>.

26. Ibid.

27. R. E. Somol, "Golf Space: Join the Club," *Wired,* June 2003, <http://www.wired.com/wired/archive/11.06>.

28. Advertisement, *Urban Land,* August 1997, back cover.

29. <http://cbs.sportsline.com/u/palmer/courses/pcd.htm>.

30. <http://www.golftoday.co.uk/news/yeartodate/news99/palmer7.html>.

31. <http://www.palmergolf.com>; <http://www.palmerdesign.com>.

32. Desmond Muirhead and Guy L. Rando, "Variations in Golf Course Design," *Urban Land,* August 1997, 44; Rees L. Jones and Guy L. Rando, *Golf Course Developments,* ULI—the Urban Land Institute Technical Booklet 70 (Washington, DC, 1974), 22, 30.

33. <http://www.apgm.com/management/brand.htm>.

34. *Business Line,* March 8, 2000; Liquidgolf.com.

35. Howard Schultz and Dori Jones Young, *Pour Your Heart into It* (New York: Hyperion, 1997), 252–253.

36. "Dressed for Success? Or Failure?" *Barron's,* March 29, 1999, 13G–15B.

37. <http://www.thegolfchannel.com/>.

38. <http://www.mou.org/mou/overview/raja_nader_ram/>.

39. <http://www.globalcountry.org/Coronation2.html>.

40. <http://www.mov.org/mov/overview/raja_nader_ram/>; *Calgary Sun,* February 5, 2003, 36.

41. <http://www.nicklaus.com>.

42. "Dressed for Success? Or Failure?"

43. Karl Marx, "Commodity Fetishism," in *Capital* (London: Penguin, 1990), 1: 163–177.

44. Pierre Bourdieu, *The Logic of Practice* (Stanford: Stanford University Press, 1980), 120. For a discussion of symbolic capital, see 112–120.

45. Barna Update, June 23, 2003, <www.barna.org>.

46. Schultz and Young, *Pour Your Heart into It,* 244.

47. <http://www.vedaland.com>.

48. Barna Updates, May, 19, 2003, March 18, 2003, April 3, 2003, <www.barna.org>.

49. John Heinerman and Anson Shupe, *The Mormon Corporate Empire: The Eye-Opening Report on the Church and Its Political Agenda* (Boston: Beacon Press, 1988); David Van Bieme, "Kingdom Come," *Time* 150, no. 5 (August 4, 1997).

50. *Life Magazine,* October 23, 1990, 4A.

51. <http://www.watchman.org/na/vedaland.htm>.

52. <http://www.vedaland.com/>.

53. <http://artoflivinguk.org/biography.htm>.

54. *Economist,* December 18, 2003, <http://www.economist.com/displaystory.cfm?story_id=2281664>.

55. <http://artoflivinguk.org/biography.htm>.

56. *New York Times,* July 25, 2001, 1A.

57. *New York Times,* February 10, 2003, 1A, 18A.

58. <http://hirr.hartsem.edu/org/faith_megachurches.html>; *New York Times,* May 9, 2002, 1F, 6F, "Megachurches, Megabusinesses," *Forbes,* September 17, 2003; <http://www.forbes.com>.

59. <http://www.palmergolf.com/partner.aspx>.

60. <www.arnoldpalmer.com>.

61. <http://www.nicklaus.com>.

62. Sandra S. Vance and Roy V. Scott, *Wal-Mart: A History of Sam Walton's Retail Phenomenon* (New York, Simon & Schuster, 1997), 68.

63. *Economist,* December 6, 2001, <http://www.economist.com/displaystory.cfm?story_id=895888>.

64. Bob L. Martin, president and CEO of Wal-Mart International, Wal-Mart Annual Report, 1999, 40, 11.

65. *New York Times,* April 5, 2004, 14A; April 11, 2004, 10 Section 4.

66. Schultz and Jones Young, *Pour Your Heart into It,* 244–280, 5.

67. <http://www.maharishi.no/miki/nyheter/int/CelebrNewWorldOrderofpeace.html>.

68. *TM Bulletin* 2, no. 11 (July 2002), <http://www.tmbulletin.net/TMBulletinV2I11.htm#New%20Nation>.

69. <http://www.globalcountry.org/Coronation2.html>.

70. Lists of countries in question vary in the TM reports. <http://www.mum.edu/m_effect/32_int_relations/> and <http://www.worldpeaceendowment.org/invincibility/invincibilityl3b.html>.

71. <http://www.worldpeaceendowment.org/invincibility/invincibility13b.html>, published on the web in 1999.

72. *Journal of Conflict Resolution, Social Indicators Research, International Journal of Neuroscience, Journal of Crime and Justice,* and *Journal of Mind and Behavior* are among the journals that have published articles about TM, and Dr. Lee Leffler, who has a PhD in consciousness-based military defense, believes that one percent of the population meditating can produce the Maharishi effect. He believes that this principle was demonstrated in Mozambique when a segment of its military tried the technique. Dr. David and Mrs. Lee Leffler, "Mozambique's Prevention Wing of the Military: End Civil War, Improve the Economy," *African Economic Analysis,* 2000, <http://www.afbis.com/analysis/mozambiq.htm>.

73. *Guardian,* September 22, 2001, 19; <http://www.tm.org/main_pages/maharishi.html>.

74. <http://www.agpf.de/TM-Immobilien.htm>.

75. *CNN News,* June 5, 2001, <http://www.globalcountry.org/Coronation2.html>; <http://www.geocities.com/bbrigante/>; <http://www.newsindia-times.com/2002/07/12/dias32-rika.html>; <http://www.agpf.de/TM-CostaRica.htm>.

76. <http://www.globalcountry.org/mayors_1–2.html>.

77. *Time Colonist,* May 5, 2003 8D; *Boston Globe,* June 1, 2003, 1B; *Hobart Mercury,* May 2, 2002; *Townsville Bulletin,* May 20, 2005, *The Gazette,* May 2, 2003, 6A; *Canadian Press Newswire,* May 1, 2003; *Canada Newswire,* September 10, 2002.

78. *Press Trust of India,* June 13, 2000.

79. <http://www.palmergolf.com>.

80. Arthur Yeo, general manager of a Chinese golf development, *Business Times Singapore,* June 4, 2004, 10.

81. *Business Times Singapore,* June 4, 2004, 10.

82. *South China Morning Post,* June 25, 2004, 4; *Straits Times,* June 19, 2004.

83. *China Daily,* March 16, 2004. *China Daily* reported that only 10 of the 176 courses had been approved.

84. *Business Times Singapore,* June 4, 2004, 10.

85. *Christian Science Monitor,* March 10, 2003, 9.

86. David Plotz, "Greens Peace," *New York Times Magazine,* June 4, 2000, 32.

87. *New York Times,* June 10, 2004, 14A; Deutsche Press Agentur, April 18, 2004.

88. <www.wgv.com>.

89. *Toronto Star,* January 14, 2002, 1A.

90. <http://www.nettime.org>, The Political Sociology of Golf in Southeast Asia.

91. <http://www.globalcountry.org>, *Maharishi* 2, no. 7 (March 2002).

92. Religious leader speaking about Hossein Sabat, hotel owner in Kish. *New York Times,* April 15, 2002, 4A.

93. <http://www.spacedaily.com/news/020328041702.ixj7exir.htm>. 1; *Sydney Morning Herald,* December 15, 2001, 33.

94. <http://www.globalcountry.org>; <http://the.honoluluadvertiser.com/article/2002/Apr/13/op/op02a.html>.

95. *New York Times,* April 15, 2002, 4A.

96. <http://www.kfzo.com>.

97. <http://www.palmisland.co.ae/swf/main.html>.

98. <http://www.thewold.dubai-city.de/>.

Park

1. <http://www.kca.or.kr/eng/KCTA/index.html>.

2. Allan Sekula, *Fish Story* (Düsseldorf: Richter Verlag, 1995), 50.

3. *Washington Times,* October 3, 2002.

4. <www.world-ports.com>.

5. Xiangming Chen, "The Evolution of Free Economic Zones and the Recent Development of Cross-National Growth Zones," *International Journal of Urban and Regional Research* 19, no. 4 (1995), 593–621.

6. <http://www.psa.com.sg>. P & O operate 21 ports in 15 countries. PSA operate a network of ports in Belgium, Brunei, China, India, Italy, Korea, Portugal, and Yemen.

7. <http://www.sysconn.com/harbor/SEG/Commrpts/EWG/Design%20vessel%20selection%20process.htm>; <http://www.tpl.com.sg/timesnet/data/cna/docs/cna6638.html>.

8. <http://www.hkcsi.org.hk/papers/submit/9912ecomm.htm>; <http://www.taiwanheadlines.gov.tw/20010402/20010402b1.html>; <http://www.fujitaresearch.com/industrypark/tsugashima.html>; <http://www.jtc.gov.sg/Products/industry+clusters/logistics.asp>; <www.connekt.com>.

9. <http://www.alliancetexas.com>.

10. <http://www.ncgtp.com>.

11. Stephen Graham and Simon Marvin, *Splintering Urbanism: Networked Infrastructures, Technological Mobilities and the Urban Condition* (London: Routledge, 2001), passim.

12. "Hong Kong as the World's Leading Port," a concept paper on e-commerce and logistics, December 1999, submitted to the Hong Kong Coalition of Service Industries, a think tank of Hong Kong's Chamber of Commerce, <http://www.hkcsi.org.hk/papers/submit/9912ecomm.htm>.

13. Barry Lopez, *About This Life: Journeys on the Threshold of Memory* (New York: Knopf, 1998), 81.

14. A good discussion of commodity chains can be found in Gary Geretti and Miguel Korzenwicz, eds., *Commodity Chains and Global Capitalism* (Westport, CT: Praeger, 1994).

15. <http://www.frog.nl/eng/cargo/situation/index.html>.

16. <http://www.eaglehawksc.vic.edu.au/kla/technology/robots/autodock/article.htm>.

17. Les Gould, "Free-ranging AGVs Cover 100,000-sq-ft Assembly Area," *Modern Materials Handling* 49, no. 14 (December 1994), 46–48. FROG stands for free ranging on grid.

18. Kevin Kelly, *New Rules for the New Economy* (New York: Penguin, 1998), 76.

19. <www.SoftAcademia.com>.

20. Huan Li, John Sweeney, Krithi Ramamritham, Roderic Grupen, and Prashant Shenoy, "Real-time Support for Mobile Robots," Department of Computer Science, University of Massachusetts, <www-robotics.cs.umass.edu/Papers/rtas03_li_huan.pdf>.

21. Manuel Castells, *The Rise of the Network Society* (Oxford: Blackwell, 1996), 158.

22. *Economist,* June 24, 2004, <http://www.economist.com/displaystory.cfm?story_id=2794472>.

23. Kelly, *New Rules for the New Economy,* frontipiece. A review of Kelly's book *Out of Control* in *Forbes* called it "required reading."

24. Kelly, *New Rules for the New Economy,* 14–15, 39–49.

25. *To New Horizons,* General Motors, 1939, <http://barbra-puclic.alexa.com:8080/ramgen/net/movie1/0/pub/movies/reallb/07906.rm>.

26. <http://www.moma.org/expansion/charette/architects/koolhaas>.

27. <http://www.translogic-corp.com/jcpenney_apps.htm>.

28. Bruno Latour, *Aramis, or the Love of Technology* (Cambridge, MA: Harvard University Press, 1996), 1–50; Keller Easterling, *Organization Space: Landscapes, Houses, and Highways in America* (Cambridge, MA: MIT Press, 1999).

29. <http://www.otis.com/aboutotis/companyinfo/0,1360,CLI1_RES1,00.html>.

30. <http://www.containershipping.nl/containerhistoryOK.html>; "AGVs: A Bigger Hit in Other Places—By Far," *Modern Materials Handling* 51 (April 1996), 4, 13; <http://www.frog.nl/eng/industry/situation/index.html>.

31. <http://www.frog.nl/eng/peoplemovers/solution/solution.html>. One experiment is the Park Shuttle, a set of AGVs that transport from Schiphol airport to the long-term parking lot. A similar project in nearby Rivium links a public transport hub and a business park.

32. <http://faculty.washington.edu/jbs/itrans/parkshut.htm>.

33. Alexander Verbraeck and Comé Versteegt, "Logistical Control for Fully Automated Large-scale Freight Transport Systems," Delft University of Technology, 2000. A proposed underground logistics system at Schiphol (OLS) would connect air cargo to the Flower Auction at Aalsmeer, to logistics centers in the surrounding area, and to a rail terminal planned for the Schiphol area. <http://216.239.51.100/search?q=cache:APTZzOxExK0C:cttrailf.ct.tudelft.nl/ftam/papers/verbraeck_versteegt_ieee.pdf+automated+logistics+tunnel&hl=en&ie=UTF-8>; Ir. C. Versteegt and Professor dr. H. G. Sol, "The Design of Logistic Control for Intermodal Transport Chains of the 21st Century," TRAIL Research School, Delft, December, 1999, 14.

34. Miriam Lacob, "Elevators on the Move," *Scientific American* (October 1997). Otis marketed the Odyssey system to skyscrapers planned in China, Indonesia, Hong Kong, Korea, and Singapore, but has since discontinued the project.

35. <http://www.schindler.com/man/webnews2.nsf/Web/Corporate-010116e>.

36. Translogic merged a company producing global supply chain mechanisms and a company that previously designed pneumatic tube systems in Detroit. <http://www.translogic-corp.com/jcpenney_apps.htm>.

37. Lacob, "Elevators on the Move."

38. <http://www.singaporepsa.com/html/terminals/keppel_distri.html>.

39. <http://www.coreconagvs.com/DSPMDAT1.htm>.

40. Connekt Annual Conference 2000, <www.connekt.nl>.

41. Xiangming Chen, "The Geoeconomic Reconfiguration of the Semiperiphery: The Asian-Pacific Transborder Subregions in the World-System," in Georgi M. Derluguian and Scott L. Greer, eds., *Questioning Geopolitics: Political Projects in a Changing World-System* (New York: Praeger, 2000), 192.

42. Kenichi Ohmae, "The Rise of the Region State," in Patrick O'Meara, Howard Mehlinger, and Matthew Krain, eds., *Globalization and the Challenges of a New Century* (Bloomington: Indiana University Press, 2000), 93–94.

43. Ibid., 100.

44. Chen, "The Evolution of Free Economic Zones and the Recent Development of Cross-National Growth Zones," 593–621.

45. Leslie Sklair, "Free Zones Development and New International Division of Labour," review of *Investing in Free Export Processing Zones* by Antoine Basile and Dimitri Germidis, *Journal of Development Studies,* London School of Economics, 2002, 754; <http://www.ilo.org>.

46. Andrew Shrank, "Export Processing Zones: Free Market Islands or Bridges to Structural Transformation?," *Developmental Policy Review* 19, no. 2 (2001), 223–242.

47. Chen, "The Evolution of Free Economic Zones and the Recent Development of Cross-National Growth Zones," 593–621; Xiangming Chen, "Regional Integration, Networked Production, and Technological Competition: The Greater China Economic Circle Through and Beyond 1997," in Pedro Conceição, David Gibson, Manuel Heitor, and Syed Shariq, eds., *Science Technology and Innovation Policy,* International Series of Technology Policy and Innovation (Westport: Quorum Books, 2000), 459–471.

48. *New York Times,* February 28, 2004, 1A.

49. *The Edge Singapore,* May 3, 2004.

50. John S. Burnett, *Dangerous Waters* (New York: Dutton, 2002), 117.

51. Michael T. Klare, "Oil Wars in the South China Sea," in *Resource Wars: The New Landscape of Global Conflict* (New York: Henry Holt, 2001), 112.

52. Chen, "The Evolution of Free Economic Zones and the Recent Development of Cross-National Growth Zones," 593–621.

53. Chen, "The Geoeconomic Reconfiguration of the Semiperiphery," 189.

54. Manuel De Landa, "The Nonlinear Development of Cities" in *Eco-tec: Architecture of the In-Between* (New York: Princeton Architectural Press, 1999), 23–31.

55. *Associated Press Online,* June 23, 2004.

56. *Economist,* June 10, 2004, <http://www.economist.com/displaystory.cfm?story_id=2752802>; *Business Times Singapore,* June 17, 2004. The most recent agreement is the International Ship and Port Security Code (ISPS), 2004.

57. Klare, *Resource Wars,* 109.

58. Roberta E. Weisbrod, "Ports of the Twentieth Century: The Age of Aquarius," in Richard Hanley, ed., *Moving People, Goods and Information in the 21st Century* (London: Routledge, 2004), 47–61; *New York Times,* July 27, 2004, 12A.

59. <http://www.hillwood.com>.

60. *BBC News,* June 27, 2001, "Fact and Fiction at Piracy Conference," <http://news.bbc.co.uk/1/hi/world/asia-pacific/1410413.stm>.

61. John S. Burnett, *Dangerous Waters* (New York: Dutton, 2002), 106.

62. Ibid., 226.

63. Ibid., 204.

64. The best contemporary bibliography of piracy is maintained by Mark Bruyneel, <http://home.wanadoo.nl/m.bruyneel/archive/bblgrphy.htm>.

65. *Economist,* July 19, 2001, <http://www.economist.com/displaystory.cfm?story_id=702508>.

66. Burnett, *Dangerous Waters,* 21.

67. Peter Chalk, "Low Intensity Conflict in Southeast Asia: Piracy, Drug Trafficking and Political Terrorism" (Research Institute for the Study of Conflict and Terrorism, January/February 1998), 2.

68. Burnett, *Dangerous Waters,* 204.

69. Ibid., 117.

70. Ken Cottril, "Modern Marauders," <popularmechanics.com/science/law_enforcement/1997/12/south_seas_pirates>.

71. <www.crg.com>.

Contemplation: Error

1. Paul Virilio, "Surfing the Accident," in *The Art of the Accident: Art Architecture and Media Technology* (Rotterdam: NIA Publishers, 1998), 30.

2. Gilles Deleuze, "The Image of Thought," in *Difference and Repetition* (New York: Columbia University Press, 1994), 148.

3. Avital Ronell, *Stupidity* (Urbana: University of Illinois Press, 2002), 20.

4. Virilio, "Surfing the Accident."

5. Deleuze, "The Image of Thought," 148.

6. Ronell, *Stupidity,* 3–28.

7. James Reason, *Human Error* (Cambridge: Cambridge University Press, 1990), 10.

8. Guy Benveniste, *The Twenty-First Century Organization* (San Francisco: Jossey-Bass, 1994), 60.

9. Manuel Castells, *The Rise of the Network Society* (Oxford: Blackwell, 1996), 158.

10. Reason, *Human Error,* 2–4.

11. Benveniste, *The Twenty-First Century Organization,* 57–90.

12. H. Allen Smith, *Don't Get Perconal with a Chicken* (Boston: Little, Brown, 1957), 39.

13. Gilbert Ryle, *The Concept of Mind* (Chicago: University of Chicago Press, 1984), 40.

14. Morton D. Davis, *Game Theory: A Nontechnical Introduction* (Mineola, NY: Dover Publications, 1983), 9.

15. Gregory Bateson, *Mind and Nature: A Necessary Unity* (New York: Dutton, 1979), 102.

16. Steve Joshua Heims, *The Cybernetics Group* (Cambridge, MA: MIT Press, 1991), 109. Heims quotes from *Transactions* of the ninth meeting of the Cybernetics group.

17. Henri Bergson, *Laughter* (Garden City, NY: Anchor Books, 1956), 61–290.

18. John Rajchman, *Deleuze Connections* (Cambridge, MA: MIT Press, 2000), 17, 43.

19. Ryle, *The Concept of Mind,* 16–17.

20. Ibid., 20, 22, 27–32.

21. Sandra Blakeslee, "Paradox in Game Theory: Losing Strategy That Wins," *New York Times,* January 25, 2000, 5F.

22. Davis, *Game Theory,* 9.

23. The Macy Conferences (1946–53) theorized about automatic or self-balancing systems in biological and technological ecologies. Warren McCullough, Norbert Wiener, John von Neumann, Margaret Mead, and Bateson were among those invited, and their discussions mixed methodologies and evidence from a broad range of disciplines including anthropology, neurophysiology, mathematics, logic, and computational networks. Their research into circuits, languages, and behaviors naturally often returned to questions about the mind's structure, and to the tantalizing possibility of some similarity between neurophysiology and electronic circuitry. Heims, *The Cybernetics Group,* passim.

24. Heims, *The Cybernetics Group,* 109. Heims quotes *Transactions* of the ninth meeting of the Cybernetics group.

25. Ibid., 108–109.

26. Gregory Bateson, "Toward a Theory of Schizophrenia," in *Steps to an Ecology of Mind* (1972; Chicago: University of Chicago Press, 2000), 222.

27. Heims, *The Cybernetics Group,* 157.

28. Bateson, *Steps to an Ecology of Mind,* 1–58.

29. Bateson, "Metalogue: Why Do Things Have Outlines?," in ibid., 31.

30. Slavoj Žižek, *Organs without Bodies: On Deleuze and Consequences* (New York: Routledge, 2004), 213.

31. Jacques Rancière, *On the Shores of Politics* (London: Verso, 1995), 103–107.

Shining

1. *Siliconindia* 5, no. 3 (March 2001), 30.

2. <http://www.satnewsasia.com/Monthly_Summary/oct2002.htm>.

3. Lisa Parks, "Satellite and Cyber Visualities," in Nicholas Mirzoeff, ed., *Visual Culture Reader* (London: Routledge, 2002), 288.

4. <http://www.lyngsat.com/headlines.shtml>.

5. <http://www.hq.nasa.gov/office/pao/History/satcomhistory.html>.

6. Dan Schiller, *Digital Capitalism: Networking the Global Market System* (Cambridge, MA: MIT Press, 1999), 67.

7. <http://www.indosat.com/iframes_page.asp?konten=About_Corp_Brief.htm&kanan=about>; M. Richharia, *Satellite Communications Systems: Design Principles* (New York: McGraw-Hill, 1999), 3. Asiasat (1988) was Asia's first privately owned regional fleet <http://www.asiasat.com>; private consortia such as SES Global, the largest satellite company in the world, own stakes in many regional and global companies: <http://www.ses-global.com/corporate/index.htm>.

8. <http://www.sealaunch.com>.

9. *New York Times,* February 18, 2003, 1F.

10. <http://www.e-sax.com>.

11. Alvin Toffler, "Gandhi with Satellites," in *The Third Wave* (New York: William Morrow, 1980), 362. Toffler writes, quoting Jagdish Kapur in *India 2000 A.D.,* "A new balance has now to be struck between" the most advanced science and technology available to the human race and "the Gandhian vision of the idyllic green pastures, the village republics." Such a practical combination, Kapur declares, requires a "total transformation of the society, its symbols and values, its system of education, its incentives, the flow of it energy resources, its scientific and industrial research and a whole lot of other institutions."

12. *Business Today,* March 14, 2004, 52.

13. Stephen Graham and Simon Marvin, *Splintering Urbanism: Networked Infrastructures, Technological Mobilities and the Urban Condition* (London: Routledge, 2001), 385.

14. Benjamin Barber, "Jihad vs. McWorld," in Patrick O'Meara, Howard D. Mehlinger, and Matthew Krain, eds., *Globalization and the Challenges of a New Century: A Reader* (Bloomington: Indiana University Press, 2000), 25–26, 27.

15. *Gulf News,* June 24, 2002.

16. <http://www.dubaiinternetcity.com>.

17. <http://www.mdc.com.my/>.

18. The CIS is a coalition of 12 former Soviet states including Azerbaijan, Armenia, Belarus, Georgia, Kazakhstan, Kyrgyzstan, Moldova, the Russian Federation, Tajikistan, Turkmenistan, Ukraine, and Uzbekistan.

19. *Gulf News,* October 22, 2003.

20. <http://www.mdc.com.my/>.

21. *The Times* (London), February 7, 2003, 36; David Page and William Crawley, *Satellites over South Asia: Broadcasting Culture and the Public Interest* (New Delhi: Sage, 2001), 76–77.

22. *Asiaweek,* October 27, 2000, 18; <http://www.cyberport.com.hk.>.

23. <http://www.dubaiinternetcity.com>.

24. <http://www.isro.org/about_isro.htm>.

25. "A Survey of India's Economy," *Economist,* May 31, 2001, <http://www.economist.com/displaystory.cfm?story_id=637873>.

26. <http://www.isro.org/about_isro.htm>.

27. <http://www.geo-orbit.org/sizepgs/geodef.html#anchor1302357>.

28. Page and Crawley, *Satellites over South Asia,* 65.

29. <http://www.isro.org/old_sat.htm#site>.

30. Ibid. Insat-1A in 1982 and Insat-1B in 1983. Insat-1A lasted only six months, but subsequent satellites Insat-1C, launched by the European Ariane vehicle, lasted one and a half years. The Insat-1D, launched by the United States, is still in service. Insat now has Insat-2A-E and Insat-3A-E.

31. <http://www.isro.org/sat.htm#insat>.

32. John Stremlau, "Dateline Bangalore: Third World Technopolis," *Foreign Policy* 102 (Spring 1996), 152–169. Srinagar, Moahli Shimia, Delhi, Noida, Jaipu, Indore, Ganhinagar, Calcutta, Bhubaneswar, Navi Mumbai, Aurangabad, Pune, Hyderabad, Bisag, Manipal, Bangalore, Chennai, Coimbatore, Mysore, and Thiruvananthapuram are among India's earth stations.

33. STPI Powerpoint presentation, <http://www/stpi.soft.net>.

34. Stremlau, "Dateline Bangalore." Bangalore is headquarters to many global companies, many of them related to IT. Citibank, American Express, General Electric, IBM, Reebok, Texas Instruments, Hewlett-Packard, and Compaq all rely on software tailored for them in India. The complexion of the IT industry in Hyderabad in Andhra Pradesh is very different from that of Bangalore. The Nizam rulers of Andhra Pradesh governed independently of the British, from their palaces, ancient and recent, in the capital of Hyderabad until independence in 1948.

35. Visit to Bangalore, January 2002.

36. <http://www.business-standard.com/special/billion/year2000/prof5.htm>.

37. Arvind Rajagopal, *Politics after Television: Hindu Nationalism and the Reshaping of the Public in India* (Cambridge: Cambridge University Press, 2001), 176.

38. Gurcharan Das, *India Unbound: The Social and Economic Revolution from Independence to the Global Information Age* (New York: Anchor Books, 2000), 255–258; *Asiaweek* (January 21, 2000), <http://www.asiaweek.com/asiaweek/magazine/2010/0121/is.chandra.html>.

39. *Asiaweek,* January 21, 2000; Page and Crawley, *Satellites over South Asia,* 76–83.

40. Rajagopal, *Politics after Television,* 12–20; Page and Crawley, *Satellites over South Asia,* 79.

41. <http://views.narendramodi.org/>.

42. *BBC News,* May 22, 2004.

43. *Christian Science Monitor,* September 22, 1998, 1C.

44. Pimm Fox, "Bill the Role Model," *Computerworld* 34, no. 44 (October 30, 2000), 48.

45. *Hindu,* January 20, 2000.

46. *National Press Trust of India,* February 21, 2004.

47. *New York Times,* March 21, 2001, 1A.

48. *Christian Science Monitor,* September 22, 1998, 1C.

49. Chandrababu Naidu with Sevanti Ninan, *Plain Speaking* (New Delhi: Viking, 2000), 7–9.

50. Subhash Bhatnagar and Robert Schware, eds., *Information and Communication Technology in Development: Cases from India* (New Delhi: Sage, 2000).

51. <http://www.chandrababunaidufanclub.com/profile.htm>.

52. Naidu, *Plain Speaking.*

53. *National Press Trust of India,* February 21, 2004; *India Today,* February 16, 2004.

54. *Hindu,* March 24, 2000.

55. *Siliconindia* 4, no. 5 (May 2000), 62.

56. Raghav S. Nandyal, "The Banes and Boons of India's IT Industry," *Siliconindia* 4, no. 10 (October 2000), 52. The entire project should take ten years to complete, and cost US $375 million.

57. Hyderabad Urban Development Authority (HUDA) originally proposed the development of a string of parks and villages around Hyderabad funded with money from the World Bank and USAID. Hyderabad has a growth rate close to that of Bombay, and was

included in the World Bank's Megacities project in India. USAID is funding the promotion of green businesses. <http://www.hudahyd.org>.

58. *Hindu,* July 23, 2000, December 26, 2000, January 20, 2000; *Business Line,* January 30, 2001.

59. Chris Winters, "Dome Sweet Dome for India Techies: Microsoft Alums Plan $100 Million Village of Future," *Journal Business Reporter,* June 28, 2000; *Wired,* July 2001; *New York Times,* March 18, 2002, 3C; <http://www.catalytic.com>.

60. The technology of inflatable formwork was actually developed earlier, without contributions from Buckminster Fuller. One example is the prefabricated Neff Air Form house designed by Wallace Neff. Burnham Kelly, *The Prefabrication of Houses* (Cambridge, MA: MIT Press, 1951), 242.

61. <www.catalytic.com>; *Wall Street Journal,* January 7, 2002.

62. Arjun Appadurai, *Modernity at Large: Cultural Dimensions of Globalization* (Minneapolis: University of Minnesota Press, 1996). Appadurai distinguishes between fantasy and the agency of cultural imagination.

63. *Times of India,* October 2, 2003, December 28, 2003.

64. <http://www.chandrababunaidufanclub.com/polls.htm>.

65. Bhatnagar and Schware, eds., *Information and Communication Technology in Development,* 140. India's software exports increased 700 times between 1991 and 2000. One supposed development formula is that a 1 percent investment in telecommunications results in a 3 percent increase in GDP (*Siliconindia* 4, no. 5 [October 2000], 62). Andhra Pradesh's percentage of poor people dropped in 1993–99 from 22 to 16; its percentage of literate people rose in 1991–2001 from 44 to 61.

66. *New York Times,* May 12, 2004, 3A, 1W.

67. <http://www.greaternoida.com>.

68. *India Business Insight,* January 26, 2003.

69. <http://www.cidcoindia.com/schemes_iip.html>; "How EZ is it to build and own your own city?," *Cities* 20, no. 1 (2003), 1–2; <www.elsevier.com/locate/cities>.

70. 40,000 hectares = 98,400 acres or 153 square miles.

71. *Business India,* May 13, 2002, September 2, 2002. Malls are developing by the hundreds in India. Beginning with only two malls in 2000, KSA Technopak will have developed 150 malls between 2000 and 2004. *New York Times,* October 20, 2003, 1A, 7A.

72. <http://www.cidcoindia.com/schemes_iip.html>.

73. *Business Line, The Hindu,* August 10, 2003; Indian Express, May 5, 2004.

74. *Economist,* May 10, 2003, 55–56; <http://www.isro.org/commercial.htm>.

75. <http://www.satnewsasia.com/Monthly_Summary/oct2002.htm>.

76. *Economist,* January 23, 2003 <http://www.economist.com/displaystory.cfm?story-id= 15525445>. A number of companies—some of which have long histories in India, including Bharti, Hutchison, Reliance Infocomm, and IDEA (a joint venture of Tatas, AT&T, and Birlas)—are among those involved; *Economist,* May 29, 2003, <http://www.economist.com/ displaystory.cfm?story_id=1812344>. Three groups applied for DTH television licenses and were denied: Agrani and Essel Shyam (promoted by Zee group's Subhash Chandra), and Space TV (backed by STAR); *Financial Express,* May 5, 2003.

77. *Economist,* July 24, 2004, <http://www.economist.com/displaystory.cfm?story_id= 2951325>.

78. *Times of India,* January 6, 2004.

79. *Economist,* November 20, 2003, <http://www.economist.com/displaystory.cfm?story_ id=2227568>.

80. *New York Times,* July 24, 2004, 1A.

81. *Television Asia* 9, no. 9 (November 2002), 18; <http://www.business-leaders.com/ 2002nov/feat06.htm>.

82. *BBC Monitoring International,* June 27, 2002; *Asiaweek,* January 21, 2000. France's Arianespace will launch the satellite (*Television Asia,* December 2002, 10). After months of bureaucratic denials, Chandra launched his DHT network, a network best suited to "colonies" or clusters of new residential building. *Business Today,* March 14, 2002, 52.

83. Ravi Sundaram, "Recycling Modernity: Pirate Electronic Cultures in India," *Sarai Reader: 2001;* or <http://www.nettime.org/Lists-Archives/nettime-1–9809/msg00040.html>.

84. Gaurab Raj Upadhaya, "Digital Delusions in the South," <http://www.himalmag.com/ 2002/august/essay.htm>.

85. Sundaram, "Recycling Modernity."

86. Stan Mathis, "Four Scripts of Rural Tele-densification in India," May 8, 2003 (in mimeo); J. L. Singh, K. D. Gaur, and Ravi Kumar Pandey, *Communication and Social Transformation: Indian Experience* (New Delhi: Manak, 2000, 122); and Thaha Vijayadharan, *IT Landscape in India Focus: Agriculture and Rural Development* (Hyderabad: Centre for Rural and Urban Studies and Training, 2001), 58, 60, 62. In 1994, there were 10.7 telephones per thousand people. As of 2000/01 there were 22 wired telephones per thousand people, 1 mobile phone per thousand, and 3 personal computers per thousand. In China, a country in a

similar position developmentally, with 1.4 times as many people, registered 70 wired phones, 19 mobile phones, and 9 personal computers per thousand.

87. Gaurab Raj Upadhaya, "Digital Delusions in the South," <http://www.himalmag.com/2002/august/essay.htm>.

88. Sundaram, "Recycling Modernity."

89. *South China Morning Post,* July 22, 2003, 2.

90. *South China Morning Post,* March 18, 2003, 2.

91. <http://www.comminit.com/trends/ctrends2003/trends-85.html>; *Economist,* May 29, 2003.

92. *Business Line, The Hindu,* October 8, 2002, <http://www.blonnet.com/2002/10/08/stories/2002100800470700.htm>.

93. *Business Line,* October 8, 2002, June 16, 2003; *Business Insight,* October 8, 2002; September 27, 2002; *Economic Times,* September 11, 2002.

94. <http://www.comminit.com/Commentary/sld-5606.html>.

95. Rosabelle Laville, "In the Politics of the Rainbow: Creoles and Civil Society in Mauritius," *Journal of Contemporary African Studies* 18, no. 2 (2000).

96. Thomas Meisenhelder, "The Developmental State in Mauritius," *Journal of Modern African Studies* 35, no. 2 (1997), 279–297.

97. Claire Anderson, *Convicts in the Indian Ocean: Transportation from South Asia to Mauritius, 1815–53* (New York: St. Martin's Press, 2000).

98. Henry Srebrnik, "'Full of Sound and Fury': Three Decades of Parliamentary Politics in Mauritius," *Journal of Southern African Studies* 28, no. 2 (June 2002), 277–289.

99. Presidential remarks on US-Mauritian relations, US Government Printing Office, 1991.

100. <http://www.indiantelevision.com/headlines/y2k2/jan/jan103.htm>.

101. *Southscan,* April 2, 2002; Suzanne Chazan-Gillig, "Ethnicity and Free Exchange in Mauritian Society," *Social Anthropology* 8, no. 1 (2000), 33–44.

102. Chazan-Gillig, "Ethnicity and Free Exchange in Mauritian Society."

103. *Southscan,* April 2, 2002.

104. Jan Rogozinski, *Pirates! Brigands, Buccaneers, and Privateers in Fact, Fiction, and Legend* (New York: Facts on File, 1995), 40–41. Tales of the Welsh pirate John Bowen and his travels in the Indian Ocean, Red Sea, and Persian Gulf often include Mauritius.

Subtraction

1. <http://www.reviewjournal.com/hotels/desertinn/>, October 23, 2001. Last viewed 2002.

2. Bruno Latour, *We Have Never Been Modern* (Cambridge, MA: Harvard University Press, 1993), 38.

3. Rem Koolhaas, "Urban Operations," *Documents* 3 (1993), 25–57. Koolhaas's project for La Défense inverted the customary habits for producing a tabula rasa by subtracting not the oldest but the most recent fabric of the city in sequence by decade. This iterative technique used subtraction as a space-making tool, yet it also maintained a continuous dialogue with ancestral heroes about the tabula rasa as a means of conquest, a means to seize the floor with the next in a succession of spatial aesthetics.

4. Stephen Graham notes that the term "urbicide" was "coined, more or less simultaneously in the early nineties, by Marshall Berman and a group of Bosnian architects: 'urbicide,' of the deliberate wrecking or killing of the city." Stephen Graham, "Lessons in Urbicide," *New Left Review* 19 (January/February 2003), 1–2. Graham cites Marshall Berman, "Falling Towers: City Life after Urbicide," in Dennis Crow, ed., *Geography and Identity* (Washington, DC: Maisonneuve Press, 1996), 172–196; Martin Coward, "Community as Heterogeneous Ensemble: Mostar and Multiculturalism," *Alternatives* 27 (2002), 29–66.

5. In most active organization (e.g., biological, financial) gains and losses, additions and subtractions, are considered to be part of the normal constitution of any network or system of exchange. Geology or psychiatry, disciplines that previously organized information according to physical artifacts and visual records, gradually developed vocabulary for both visible and invisible processes that might be described with infinitive expressions rather than artifacts.

6. *Los Angeles Times,* March 23, 1998, 1B.

7. *Tampa Tribune,* April 12, 1999, 4.

8. <http://www.casinoplayer.com/archive9809ep/html/1993.html>.

9. Peter Hall, *Cities of Tomorrow* (Cambridge, MA: Basil Blackwell, 1988), 235.

10. Helene Liss, *Demolition: The Art of Demolishing, Dismantling, Imploding, Toppling and Razing* (New York: Black Dog, 2000). Implosion brought down the six-hundred-room Traymore Hotel in Atlantic City, New Jersey, in 1972, the same year that Pruitt-Igoe fell.

11. <http://www.controlled-demolition.co.uk/index1.html>.

12. <www.cdi-uk.com/implosion.htm>.

13. <http://www.controlled-demolition.com>.

14. Ibid.; CDI has demolished several resorts in the Bahamas, including the Pirates Cove Holiday Inn, the Fort Montague Beach Hotel, the Emeralds Beach Hotel, and the Atlantic Beach Resort. The Barbados Hilton, the Royal Palm Resort in Guam, and the Beirut Beach Hotel are among the company's other implosions. CDI also imploded the Chicago Beach Hotel in Dubai, a 1,000-foot-tall futuristic structure: <www.cdi-uk.com/implosion.htm>; <www.controlled-demolition.com>.

15. The Bellagio, a megaresort costing 1.6 billion dollars, replaced the Dunes. A convention center costing two billion dollars replaced the Landmark Hotel, which was imploded in 1995. The two-billion-dollar Venetian Resort replaced the Sands, razed in 1996. The Mandalay Bay megaresort replaced the Hacienda. Two hotel casinos with a shipping complex called Desert Passages replaced the Aladdin, imploded in 1998. In October 2000, El Rancho was imploded (not by CDI) to make way for condominiums. In October 2001, the Desert Inn was imploded to make way for the Le Rêve, a 2,455-room hotel, to be completed in 2004 at a cost of 1.6 billion dollars. John Villani, "On a Roll: In Las Vegas, the Casino-Resort Concept Is Reaching New Heights," *Urban Land* 59, no. 3 (March 2000), 42–45, 91.

16. Rem Koolhaas, Stefano Boeri, Sanford Kwinter, Nadia Tazi, and Hans Ulrich Obrist, *Mutations* (Barcelona and Bordeaux: Actar and Arc en rêve centre d'architecture, 2000), 165.

17. Houston's Astrodome, Denver's McNichols Sports Arena, Tampa's Houlihan Stadium, Toronto's Exhibition Stadium, and Pittsburgh's Three Rivers Stadium are among those abandoned or deleted. Houston's Astrodome, opened in 1965, is being abandoned. Denver's McNichols Sports Arena was torn down in 2000: *Los Angeles Times,* March 26, 2000 10A. The 32-year-old Houlihan Stadium in Tampa was torn down in 1999: *Tampa Tribune,* April 12, 1999. Exhibition Stadium in Toronto was also demolished in 1999: *Toronto Sun,* February 19, 1999. The Three Rivers Stadium, home of the Steelers and the Pirates, was 30 years old and cost $36 million to build. It was demolished in February 2001, after a new $284 million stadium for the Steelers was built just 80 feet from it, *Pittsburgh Post-Gazette,* February 16, 2001, 1A; *New York Times,* January 28, 2001, 3A; February 12, 2001, 9D.

18. The "dome" was composed of 20 double-ribbed arches pressing against each other, all supported on a grid of columns. *Baltimore Sun,* March 20, 2000, 1C.

19. *Los Angeles Times,* March 26, 2000, 10A.

20. Pittsburgh has imploded many things, including its 131,000 square-foot, twenty year-old convention center to be replaced by a 1.6 million-square-foot facility costing $324 million. The design was incompatible with the new convention center designed by Rafael Vinoly. *Pittsburgh Post-Gazette,* June 12, 2001, 3B; July 2, 2001, 1A. The 25-year-old Omni Coliseum was demolished in Atlanta in 1997. *Atlanta Journal and Constitution,* July 27, 1997, 8G.

21. *Los Angeles Times,* May 19, 2000, 3B.

22. *New York Times,* December 24, 2003, 10A.

23. *Los Angeles Times,* March 26, 2000, 10A.

24. "Downtowns Get a Sporting Chance," *Urban Land* 58, no. 5 (May 1999). Some architects, among them Peter Eisenman, have teamed up with these firms on projects for sports arenas.

25. *New York Times,* July 7, 2002, 10A.

26. Michel de Certeau, *The Practice of Everyday Life* (Berkeley: University of California Press, 1984), 200–201.

27. <http://www.controlled-demolition.com/default.asp?regLocId=10>.

28. *Chicago Sun-Times,* May 31, 1996 51; <http://www.implosionworld.com/>; <http://www.library.njit.edu/archlib/exhibits/highrise/>; <http://www.controlled-demolition.com/wrecking.html>; Liss, *Demolition; New York Times,* December 24, 2000, 10A; *Philadelphia Inquirer,* October 18, 1999, 1B; *Chicago Sun-Times,* April 11, 1999, 4; *Chicago Sun-Times,* December 13, 1998, 33; *Star Tribune,* September 22, 1997, 1A; *Baltimore Sun,* July 28, 1996, 1B; *Baltimore Sun,* July 9, 2000, 1B; *Chicago Sun-Times,* December 12, 1998, 8; *Baltimore Sun,* October 27, 1998, 1A; *Star Tribune,* December 1, 1996, 1B; *Chicago Sun-Times,* May 31, 1996, 51.

29. <http://www.pbs.org/newshour/bb/entertainment/july-dec02/hwl_10–2.html>; and <http://www.phila.gov/mayor/jfs/mayorsnti/news/releases/releases_9.html>.

30. *New York Times,* July 7, 2002, 10. "Philadelphia has issued $160 million in bonds to demolish 10,000 structures in five years in the hopes of assembling larger, developable parcels. Baltimore is trying to obtain titles to 5,000 properties, and plans to give or sell the lots to residents to use as yards or gardens. In West Palm Beach, Florida, 50 abandoned buildings were leveled and a commercial and residential development called City Place constructed, raising property values to $85 per square foot from $7."

31. *The Straits Times,* January 29, 2003.

32. Marshall Berman, *All That Is Solid Melts into Air* (London: Verso, 1982).

33. Richard Plunz, *A History of Housing in New York City: Dwelling Type and Social Change in the American Metropolis* (New York: Columbia University Press, 1990), 265–272. Plunz discusses in particular, Bunshaft's Sedgwick Houses of 1950.

34. Zygmunt Bauman, *Wasted Lives: Modernity and Its Outcasts* (Cambridge: Polity, 2004), 82, 84–85.

35. Peter Wolf, *Land in America: Its Value, Use, and Control* (New York: Pantheon, 1981), 224, 232–234.

36. The over two million acres of networked land that constitutes the highway system is nothing like the size of the 25 million acres controlled by the United States Park Service, and is perhaps more comparable to the one million acres of the Tennessee Valley Authority. Still, it contacts the largest surface area. Ibid., 448.

37. Camilo José Vergara, *The New American Ghetto* (New Brunswick, NJ: Rutgers University Press, 1997).

38. Dan Hoffman, ed., "Erasing Detroit," in *Architecture Studio: Cranbrook Academy of Art, 1986–1993* (New York: Rizzoli, 1994), 28.

39. *Atlanta Journal and Constitution,* July 27, 1997, 8G. The Omni was a convention center in Atlanta.

40. <http://www.physics.nwu.edu/classes/2001Spring/135–1/Projects/7/dpgsite3.htm>.

41. Villani, "On a Roll."

42. *Atlanta Journal and Constitution,* July 27, 1997, 8G.

43. Builders of more recent supertowers, working within similar limits, would make the elevator core the means of fire-safety egress, and dedicate a separate bank of elevators for firefighting, thus extending the intelligent redundancies of the infrastructure to safety issues, and facilitating better communication between floors.

44. *New York Times,* March 22, 2003, 1A.

45. <http://www.controlled-demolition.com/>.

46. CDI imploded a SS-25 foundation pad in Belarus for the Nuclear Defense Agency, and destroyed a Scud missile system in Warsaw, another in Bucharest, and a Rocket Facility in Cape Town, South Africa. For the Department of Defense and the Army Corp of Engineers, the company imploded a Russian radar facility in Skrunda, Latvia, for which they brought down a 19-story, 300-foot-tall receiver building, and an eight-story, 800,000-square-foot transmitter building. <www.timberline.com/products/stories/cdi.htm>; <http://www.controlled-demolition.com/wrecking.html>; and correspondence with Stacey Loizeaux on November 2, 2001.

47. <http://www.controlled-demolition.com/default.asp?reqLocId=10>.

48. Ibid.

49. Stephen Graham, ed., *Cities, War and Terrorism: Towards an Urban Geopolitics* (Oxford: Blackwell, 2004).

50. Ryan Bishop and Gregory Clancey, "The City-as-Target, or Perpetuation and Death," in Graham, *Cities, War, and Terrorism,* 54–74.

51. *New York Times,* March 7, 2002, 1A: a book review of *Our Vienna* by Tina Waltzer and Stephan Templ.

52. Eyal Weizman, "The Politics of Verticality: The West Bank as an Architectural Construction," in Anselm Franke and Eyal Weizman, eds., *Territories: Islands, Camps and Other States of Utopia* (Cologne: Verlag der Buchhandlung König, 2003), 98.

53. *New York Times,* March 7, 2002, 1A. All over Europe, during the Second World War, Jewish property was redesignated as a technique of profiteering, and as just one means of erasing a profile of legal documentation for an individual. In Nazi Vienna, for instance, housing stock, offices, even tourist attractions like the Ferris Wheel at the Prater were seized from the Jews and "Aryanized."

54. <http://www.btselem.org/English/House_Demolitions/Statistics.asp>; <http://www.salam.org/palestine/housing.html>. Various human rights groups attempt to collect data about the numbers of demolitions of illegal homes and other structures, and although the numbers may vary, one tally for East Jerusalem from 1987 to 2002 is 662 structures. The tally for the West Bank and Gaza is 1,939 structures. Regulation 119, dating back from 1945, also allows for the demolition of any building from which "any firearm has been illegally discharged, or any bomb, grenade or explosive or incendiary article illegally thrown. . . ." The human rights group B'Tselem estimates that between 1987 and 1997, 449 houses were demolished, 62 partially demolished, 296 completely sealed, and 118 partially sealed as punishments for aggression. One estimate of the number of people rendered homeless by these demolitions is approximately 10,000.

55. Franke and Weizman, *Territories.*

56. CNN, February 28, 2002; *Christian Science Monitor,* February 28, 2002, 7. The demolition was led by Hindu activists in the BJP and VHP parties (nationalist Bharatiya Janata Party and World Hindu Council). My thanks to Vyjayanthi Rao for first suggesting the inclusion of some of these examples.

57. Frederick Law Olmsted, "Chicago in Distress," *Nation* (November 8, 1871), 302–305.

58. *New York Times,* June 13, 1987, 3 section 1.

59. <http://www.emagazine.com/view/?698>.

60. George Horwich, "Economic Lessons of the Kobe Earthquake," *Economic Development and Cultural Change* (Chicago: University of Chicago Press, 2000), 521–542.

61. <http://www.emagazine.com/view/?698>.

62. Olmsted, "Chicago in Distress."

63. *New York Times,* September 7, 2000, 16A.

64. Bauman, *Wasted Lives,* 80.

65. *Economist,* September 6, 2001, <http://www.economist.com/displaystory.cfm?story_id =771076>.

66. <http://www.cia.gov/cia/publications/factbook/geos/nr.html>; *Economist,* March 6, 2003, <http://economist.com/displaystory.cfm?story_id=1623170>; <http://www.pacificislandtravel.com/nauru>, *Independent,* September 3, 2001; Carl M. Daniel and John M. Gowdy, *Paradise for Sale: A Parable of Nature* (Berkeley: University of California Press, 2000), 29–51.

67. Statement to the Press, His Excellency Kinza Clodumar, December 8, 1997, <http://www.forumsec.org.fj/news/1997/dec04.htm>; *Australian,* March 4, 2002, 2; *Sydney Morning Herald,* December 15, 2001, 33; *New York Times,* March 2, 1997, 1 section 1. Nauru was one of those island nations that lobbied against global warming in Bonn in 1997.

68. Daniel and Gowdy, *Paradise for Sale,* 6, 7, 44–47; Rosamond Dobson Rhone, "Nauru, the Richest Island in the South Seas," *National Geographic* 40 (1921), 549–589; *New York Times,* December 10, 1995, 3 section 1.

69. *New York Times,* June 23, 2001, 6A.

70. *Weekend Australian,* June 14, 2003, 15.

71. <http://www.offshorecorpservices.com/trends.html>.

72. *New York Times,* October 5, 2001, 8A; *New York Times,* November 24, 2001, 3A. In one celebrated incident, Richard Branson and a Norwegian ship captain, who rescued a shipwrecked group and tried to deliver them to Australia's Christmas Island, both became advocates for the rights of refugees. *Independent,* September 3, 2001, 3.

73. *Economist,* March 8–14, 2003 <http://www.economist.com/displaystory.cfm?story_id =1632873>.

74. *BBC Monitoring,* June 15, 2004; *Newsday,* August 27, 2004, 86A.

75. *Economist,* March 6, 2003, <http://www.economist.com/displaystory.cfm?story_id=1623170>.

76. *BBC Worldwide Monitoring,* August 15, 2003; *AAP Information Services,* July 30, 2003.

77. *BBC Monitoring,* May 15, 2004.

78. *New Zealand Herald,* August 2, 2003; *Weekend Australian,* August 16, 2003, 8.

79. Ibid.; *Weekend Australian,* June 14, 2003, 15.

80. *Weekend Australian,* June 14, 2003, 15; *Age* (Melbourne), March 11, 2003, 9.

81. "A Sad Tale of Riches to Rags: Nauru in Pacific: GE Calls in Receiver," *National Post's Financial Post & FP Investing,* June 2, 2004.

82. "Island unto Themselves," *Newsday,* August 27, 2004; Quest Economics Database World of Information Country Report, June 23, 2004; "Nauru Learning to Live without Wealth," *Financial Times,* August 18, 2004.

Contemplation: Pirate

1. Herman Melville, *The Confidence Man: His Masquerade* (New York: Norton, 1971), 4.

2. Robert I. Burns, "Piracy as an Islamic-Christian Interface in the Thirteenth Century," in *Viator: Medieval and Renaissance Studies* 11 (1980), 166.

3. Ibid., 165.

4. Gilles Deleuze and Félix Guattari, "Treatise on Nomadology," in *A Thousand Plateaus: Capitalism and Schizophrenia* (Minneapolis: University of Minnesota Press, 1987), 360.

5. <www.blackwaterusa.com>.

6. Fernand Braudel, *The Mediterranean and the Mediterranean World in the Age of Philip II* (London: HarperCollins, 1972), 624–656.

7. J. L. Anderson, "Piracy and World History: An Economic Perspective on Maritime Predation," *Journal of World History* 6, no. 2 (1995), 184; Marcus Rediker, *Villains of All Nations: Atlantic Pirates in the Golden Age* (Boston: Beacon Press, 2004).

8. Thomas W. Gallant, "Brigandage, Piracy, Capitalism, and State-formation: Transnational Crime from a Historical World-Systems Perspective," in *States and Illegal Practices* (Oxford: Berg, 1999), 45.

9. <www.blackwaterusa.com>; <www.crg.com>.

10. Michael Hardt and Antonio Negri, *The Multitude: War and Democracy in the Age of Empire* (New York: Penguin, 2004), 47–51, 48.

11. Fouad Ajami, "The Summoning," in Patrick O'Meara, Howard D. Mehlinger, and Matthew Krain, *Globalization and the Challenges of a New Century* (Bloomington: Indiana University Press, 2000), 66.

12. Diana and Michael Preston, *A Pirate of Exquisite Mind—Explorer, Naturalist, and Buccaneer: The Life of William Dampier* (New York: Walker & Company, 2004). Diana and Michael Preston use this quote of Dampier's on the inside cover of their book.

13. Toshiya Ueno, "Pirates and Capitalism 1 and 2," <http://amsterdam.nettime.org/Lists-Archives/nettime-1–9705/msg00048.html>.

14. Marc Augé, "New Worlds," in *An Anthropology for Contemporaneous Worlds* (Stanford: Stanford University Press, 1999) 89–126.

15. Eric Hobsbawm, *Bandits* (New York: New York Press, 2000), 19–33, 63–76, 120–138.

16. Peter Lamborn Wilson, *Pirate Utopias* (Brooklyn: Autonomedia, 1995), 30.

17. Diana and Michael Preston, *A Pirate of Exquisite Mind,* passim.

18. Hakim Bey, *T.A.Z.: The Temporary Autonomous Zone* (New York: Autonomedia, 2003); Michel de Certeau, *The Practice of Everyday Life* (Berkeley: University of California Press, 1984), 24–28.

19. Malcolm Gadwell, *The Tipping Point: How Little Things Can Make a Big Difference* (Boston: Back Bay Books, 2002); Seth Godin, *Unleashing the Idea Virus* (New York: Do You Zoom, 2001); Emanuel Rosen, *The Anatomy of Buzz* (New York: Doubleday, 2000). Popular books about viral marketing identity cultural contagions and hubs of connection—the so-called "sneezers" or "connectors" from which persuasions will replicate and spread like an epidemic through a population.

20. Gilles Deleuze, *Essays Critical and Clinical* (Minneapolis: University of Minnesota Press, 1997), 68–90.

21. Hardt and Negri, *Empire,* 203–204. Hardt and Negri look at Bartleby, and add Michael K. (J. M. Coetzee, *The Life and Times of Michael K.*) together in a brief contemplation of passivity and resistance to authority. Michael K. is a simple-minded gardener who, like a traveling growth of vines, stumbles unscathed across every dangerous political and social barrier, because he remains oblivious to those barriers. They assess the importance of a refusal of in both cases, but they also caution against the fragility of its purity.

22. Bruno Latour, *We Have Never Been Modern* (Cambridge, MA: Harvard University Press, 1993), 47.

23. <http://www.killeeroos.com/2/crusrus.htm>.

24. Wilson, *Pirate Utopias,* 40.

25. Henri Bergson, *Laughter* (Garden City, NY: Anchor Books, 1956), 88; <http://www.stanford.edu/dept/HPS/Haraway/CyborgManifesto.html>.

26. Jacques Rancière, *On the Shores of Politics* (London: Verso, 1995).

Index